THE
LENT BOOK

An ML Book
Edited by
Lonni Collins Pratt

 Resource Publications, Inc.
San Jose, California

Reprint Department
Resource Publications, Inc.
160 E. Virginia Street #290
San Jose, CA 95112-5876
1-408-286-8505 (voice)
1-408-287-8748 (fax)

Library of Congress Cataloging-in-Publication Data

   The Lent book / edited by Lonni Collins Pratt.
      p.   cm.
    ISBN 0-89390-446-5 (pbk.)
    1. Lent. 2. Catholic Church — Liturgy — Texts.
  I. Pratt, Lonni Collins, 1953– .
  BX2170.L4L46   1999
  263'.92—dc21

Printed in the United States of America

03 02 01 00 99 | 5 4 3 2 1

Editorial director: Nick Wagner
Prepress manager: Elizabeth J. Asborno
Production coordinator: Mike Sagara

Acknowledgments

Original sources are cited at the end of each reprinted
article.

Contents

Introduction

PART 1

Ash Wednesday

PART 2

Sundays of Lent

PART 3

Stories and Dramas

PART 4

Reconciliation

APPENDIX

Lenten Music

Introduction

ALIVE! … in Lent?

Walter Burghardt, SJ

For all too many Christians, Lent is b-o-r-i-n-g. It is still chilly outside; the February crocuses were a scam; meatless Fridays don't threaten you with sin anymore; Lauderdale and Appalachia are student memories; you give up something that would make Lent livable: cigar with your coffee, Chevas Regal or Bud Lite, sex? Forty days dead. Even Jesus ends up dead. Is that what Lent is all about — death?

In point of fact, Lent is *life*. Ezekiel, Paul, Lazarus — each reading stresses life, what it means to be actually alive. Let me explain in three stages. (1) What does it mean to you to be alive? When do you feel most alive? (2) What does God's Word add to that? For Ezekiel and Paul and Jesus, what does it mean to be alive? (3) How does, or should, all this affect the last two weeks of your Lenten living — better still, the rest of your life?

What Does It Mean to Be Alive?

Obviously, to be alive means different things to different people, different things at different times. Michael Jordan is incredibly alive soaring to the basket from the foul line, Rostropovich when he is attacking his cello. Mother Teresa was never more alive than when she was rescuing infants from the rubble of Lebanon or plucking the starving aged from the excrement of Calcutta. Dorothy Day lived most intensely in the Houses of Hospitality where she shared room and board with the homeless. Martin Luther King Jr. was vividly alive on the march from Selma and in his D.C. dream for an America rid of racism.

It's endless in its variety. Shelley shaping his ode "To a Skylark" and Michelangelo commanding his "Moses" to "Speak!" A husband and wife each giving self totally to the other, a mother looking on her first infant, a child discovering his first star. John Milton creating his *Paradise Lost*, Jonas Salk discovering his vaccine against polio. Pavarotti rising to a high C, Hammer in the throes of his "dance." Ignatius Loyola in ecstasy over the sky at night, Teresa of Avila ravished by a rose.

If you can credit the commercials, you're never more alive than when you gargle with Scope, when you guzzle that Pepsi on a beauty-bathed beach, when you race the latest dreamboat with a built-in sexual overdrive.

I must confess that, on a natural level, I myself feel most alive when I give birth to a fresh idea, when I create a homily that is a work of art, when I see hope come to life in another's eyes, when my eyes meet another's in affection or love — even when I preach to a congregation that responds to my strange brand of humor.

From your experience, what is it that makes *you* come alive, feel alive, shout at the stars in sheer joy?

What Does God's Word Add to That?

What can it possibly add? A gift of life far more profound, far more intense, than a Jordan dunk, a life that does not negate your natural experience but gives it incomparable depth and meaning.

Take Ezekiel. Dramatically, he contrasts dry, dead bones and the wind, the breath, the spirit of

God. The bones of his vision, "bleached, scattered on the ground and very, very dry, represent the total destruction of Israel by an attacking army … Babylon" (Lawrence Boadt, CSP). His is a mission to Israel in near despair. Thousands have been deported to Babylon, to live amid false gods, their public worship emasculated, their sacrifice a thing of the past. Israel is dead. Ezekiel's mission? By preaching the Word of God, to bring new life to a dead people. What sort of life? God declares it: "I will put my spirit within you, and you shall live, and I will place you on your own soil; then you shall know that I, the Lord, have spoken, and will act" (37:14).

Take Paul. He spells out in a Christian context what the life is that Christ bought by his death. Not only are you "in the Spirit"; the Spirit of God, the Spirit of Christ, Christ himself, "dwells, lives, in you" (Rom 8:9. Here I am indebted to Joseph A. Fitzmyer, SJ). You share God's own life; "*your* spirit is alive" (v. 10). For the Spirit of God, of Christ, is for Paul an energizing force, a Spirit of power; the Spirit is dynamite. How come? God's Spirit in you makes it possible for you to believe what you cannot see, to hope when all else invites despair, to love as Jesus loved — to be crucified with Christ. More than that: Because God's Spirit lived in you, the Father "who raised Christ from the dead will give life" to your dead body (v. 11).

That last promise was anticipated in Lazarus. In healing the blind man, Jesus showed that he was the "light" of the world (Jn 9:5). In raising his dear friend, Jesus shows that he is the world's "life" as well. If, gifted by the Spirit, you believe in Jesus — the evangelist John means if you accept him and what he claims to be, if you dedicate your life to him, if you are willing to do what he demands of you — you will not only rise up on the last day; you will never die totally. Your body may rot, but the Spirit of Jesus will never leave you.

During Lent's last two weeks, read the Gospel of John. It is the Gospel of life. "Eternal life" for John is the life by which God lives. It is the supreme gift God's Son took flesh to give us, the gift he died to give us: a sharing in God's own life. It is not a life that begins after death; it was given each of you in your baptism. Its real enemy is not death but sin. Death cannot destroy it; only sin can. You are alive with God's life as long as you remain a branch on the vine that is Jesus, as long as you feed on the Bread that means life now and life for ever. A powerful, breath-taking promise of Jesus to Martha grieving over her dead brother: "Those who believe in me, even though they die [physically], will live, and everyone who lives [in me] and believes in me will never die" (Jn 11:25–26).

Little wonder that St. Paul calls you "a new creation, a new creature" (2 Cor 5:17; Gal 6:15).

"We are," he exclaims, "God's work of art, created in Christ Jesus for good works" (Eph 2:10).

What Does This Mean to You?

Which brings me to my third question: How does, or should, all this affect the last two weeks of your Lenten living — better still, the rest of your life? Two suggestions. One has to do with joy — joy in Jesus; the other, with dying — dying with Jesus.

First, joy in Jesus. I suspect that, on the law of averages, any number of Christians resembles Ezekiel's "dry bones." Like the Israelites in exile, they are not physically dead. They breathe in and out; they eat and drink, work hard and play handicap golf, sweat and pray; they talk and laugh, marry and bear children, may covet but do not take their neighbor's spouse or goods. They are good people, and an internal-medicine man might well pronounce them good insurance risks. But the joy Jesus promised is not there — the joy he promised "no one will take from you" (Jn 16:22). God's Spirit, the Spirit of Jesus, may actually be within them, but that Spirit does not come alive.

My question: Acknowledging as I do that the Son of God "came that [we] may have life, and have it abundantly" (Jn 10:10), how aware am I of God's life within me? Not abstractly, as in "I accept everything God has revealed." Is the Spirit-within-me as real, as vibrant, as dynamic as the dynamite that drives Michael Jordan to a basket, Jodie Foster to an Oscar? Am I as dynamized by divine presence as Mozart was by the musical notes in his head? Am I ever so inundated by my Spirit-God that I can hardly breathe, that I can only exclaim "Wow"? Is it only water-in-the-shower that stimulates me to sing, or is there ceaselessly a song in my heart because the Spirit is there?

This is not pious sentimentality. We have been dreadfully conditioned by an Anglo-Saxon "cool it" mentality, an American "religion is a private affair." Rave about Jesus at a cocktail party? You must be out of your cotton-pickin' mind! We can excuse African-American Soul-singing; it's in black blood. We share so much of our feelings with one another: high fives over a Redskin touchdown, boisterous laughter over Jay Leno or David Letterman, tears of joy over someone's baby, out of control over rock 'n' roll. But don't ask the "developed" world to "praise the Lord" in public.

Second suggestion: dying with Jesus. You see, in its profound religious sense, living comes from dying — not only on my final cross, not only in Lent, but every day of my life. I can feel God's life within me only to the extent that I die to sin — another way of saying, die to self. For some reason, it reminds me of basketball. Though ceaselessly amazed by high-scoring forward Michael Jordan, I am even more intrigued by point guards — he or she makes the team move. How? By giving, by passing off, by being utterly selfless. The point guard who lives only to shoot, you sell off fast.

I am a Christian. I follow Christ to the extent that I move out of my narrow self, to the extent that I give, give of myself, give myself, die to sin and self. I did that first in my baptism, without my being able to appreciate it. Recall Paul's striking sentence: "Through baptism we have been buried with [Christ] in death, so that just as Christ was raised from the dead through the Father's glory, so we too might live a new life. For if we have grown into a union with him by undergoing a death like his, so we shall [grow into union with him] by being raised to life like him" (Rom 6:4–5). In dying to sin, we live a new life — now — Christ's life, flowing through us like another bloodstream. In dying to myself, I rise to life in Christ.

But I am likely to feel that life, tremble with it, get goose pimples, only if I share it with others. In some measure, you already do. Husband or wife, father or mother, you die to self, else home is a zoo where all the animals have visiting privileges. Bank or university president, CEO or senior partner, politician or priest, teacher or administrator, you give — your time, your talent, your self, else your operation is another failed Savings and Loan. But an even more difficult dying to self happens when you have to turn your whole life around because God is clearly asking it of you. An Eastern Orthodox Christian lady pictured it vividly:

> One of my favorite icons of the Annunciation shows Mary sitting quietly while the angel Gabriel comes bounding in like an acrobat, arms held aloft, announcing the Incarnation. Suddenly Mary was being asked to redirect her whole life — to risk public disapproval (unmarried and pregnant) and to live in the shadow of her own child. Her response was

the perfect one — perfect because she made it without batting an eye. The Christian life is just like that. In the middle of all our carefully made plans an angel comes bounding in and says, 'How about giving it all up?' Who's ready to make the perfect response? (Nancy Forest-Flier, "Why Catholics Should Hold Fast to Fasting," *U.S. Catholic* [March 1992].)

Move from yourself to others — to the child abused and the elderly left to die; to the jobless and the loveless, the homeless and the hopeless; to the untold thousands in D.C. hungering for food or a kind word, thirsting for drink or the milk of human kindness. Share your Christlife with such as these and the Christian paradox will come into play: The more you give, the more you have; the more life you share with another, the more of God's life God shares with you.

It is the time to discover, or rediscover, what it means to be alive — how to come alive by dying — now. That paradox I can discover only by joining Mary and John on Calvary, sweating drops of blood as I struggle to understand that basic Gospel declaration, "God so loved [us] that God gave" not some thing, not an angel, but God's "only Son," gave him not only to Bethlehem but to Calvary, to a crucifying death, "that whoever believes in him ... may have [God's] life" ... right now and for ever (Jn 3:16).

Let that revelation grab you and you'll start flipping Frisbees on Good Friday in the sheer joy of being alive — alive in Christ. Let these next 12 days echo for you the prayer of the Psalmist:

> Let me hear joy and gladness;
> let the bones that you have crushed rejoice.
> Create in me a clean heart, O God,
> and put a new and steadfast spirit within me.
> Restore to me the joy of your salvation
> (Ps 51:8, 10, 12).

The *joy* of your salvation.

"ALIVE! ... in Lent?" originally appeared in MODERN LITURGY magazine (Resource Publications, Inc.).

An Introduction to the Spirituality of Lent

Liturgy Plus *Planning Software*

Because Lent in its history and earliest development may be said to have its beginning and derivation from the feast of Easter, the whole character of its spirituality is shaped and inspired by the Easter celebration.

Easter preceded Lent in its liturgical history. These historical facts about the origins of Lent yield a theological principle that is critical in the attempt to capture the true sense of the Lenten experience. The principle: Lent is defined by Easter. Lent gets all its meaning from Easter, for which it is the preparation. Lent is the lived experience for six weeks in which the community enters stage by stage into the fullness of the Easter feast. Lent is the community's journey together in which its members prepare for Easter by living the paschal experience of dying and rising with Jesus Christ with a new focus of intensity.

The most important truth to grasp about the Lenten journey, then, is that, like Easter itself, from which Lent derives its whole reality, Lent is the community living and celebrating the mystery of dying and rising with Christ. Lent is not about only suffering and dying, with the postponement of thoughts about resurrection till after one's physical death, as had mistakenly been thought for many centuries. The thrust of Lent, faithful to the gospel message, is more immediate and more abundant and more complete.

The gospel announces that Jesus Christ has already suffered and died and been raised up by his Abba, who reached into the tragedy and wretched misery of death to transform all that desolation into new life, new creation. This transformation of death into life is resurrection.

Lent celebrates this paschal mystery through the course of its six weeks. The opening prayer of its first Sunday sets the theme:

> Father,
> through our observance of Lent,
> help us to understand the meaning
> of your Son's death and resurrection,
> and teach us to reflect it in our lives.

There is no dividing death from resurrection, Lent from Easter. Both Lent and Easter celebrate both the death and rising and our immersion in this holy mystery. As the Lenten journey unfolds week by week, people's hearts in our assembly burn with a new fire of love and hope, and are turned more and more fully toward the climax of these weeks in the Easter Triduum. There is no doubt about the classical characteristics of the Lenten experience, even if they have been muted or blurred or ignored for some centuries: Lent celebrates the mystery of our dying and rising with Christ.

Beginning the Journey

The first days of the Lenten liturgy (from Ash Wednesday to the following Saturday) give us the means to assess our priorities and realign ourselves along the way that leads to salvation — prayer, fasting, giving alms. Lent is not a time of self-deprivation in order to train self-will. It is rather a time to take concrete steps to recommit ourselves to God in Christ, to grow in the likeness of Christ, and to share our bread with the hungry. Fasting, prayer, and giving alms are important means, not ends. Their purpose is to enable us to put the things of this earth into proper perspective, and to empty ourselves so that Christ may fill us with his mercy, love, and peace. The liturgy is a central means for allowing Christ to act among us to lead us on the journey that leads to him alone.

The liturgy of the first Sunday asks us to identify with Jesus as he was tempted in the desert. Just as Israel wandered in the wilderness for forty years and was tempted to apostasy, so Jesus wandered through a desert for forty days and was tempted to apostasy, to elusive power, and to food that sustains the body but not the soul.

We ourselves enter and move through a spiritual desert each year in Lent. It is a place of no protections, no places to hide. It is a place where, like Jesus, we engage in battle with Satan.

Christ's temptations recounted in the gospels are paradigmatic. They invite us to examine the ways in which we are tempted, and to discover the things that prevent us from conforming ourselves fully to Christ. The gospel account of the things that plague Jesus, exemplified in human hunger, earthly power, and worship of false gods, invites us to examine the depths of our being and to discover there what tempts us to hunger after false power, self-delusion, and things that will not lead us to God. The liturgy this Sunday is an invitation to welcome the desert of Lent.

The second Lenten Sunday invites us to ascend the mountain of the transfiguration. It invites us to identify with Peter, James, and John to experience in a privileged way through the liturgy the glory of Christ. We are asked to see all things in life, particularly all religious things, in relation to the glory of God revealed through Christ's paschal mystery. We are to look beyond Moses and Elijah, beyond the law and the prophets, to Christ's new law of love, and to him as the fulfillment of all that the prophets had assured would come to be in Christ. This second Sunday offers a glimpse of what will be revealed fully at Easter — the glory of the risen Christ.

Scrutiny Sundays

Each year on the third, fourth, and fifth Sundays of Lent we engage in the scrutinies for the elect who will be initiated at Easter. We pray over them and with them. Along with them we hear the gospels (in the "A" Lectionary cycle) of the Samaritan woman, the man born blind, and the raising of Lazarus.

On the third Sunday we examine ourselves to see what really slakes our thirst, and whether we thirst for the living God alone. On the fourth Sunday we examine the ways in which we are blinded to the needs of others or are blind to the ways in which God reveals himself to us in our daily lives. On the fifth Sunday we identify with Mary and Martha in professing our faith once again in Christ as Messiah, the son of God. Each year in Lent we journey with catechumens and sponsors, and renew our conversion to the Lord whose very life is given to us in baptism. These Sundays prepare us for the Easter Vigil. On that night of baptism, the elect and the whole Christian community are plunged (literally and figuratively) into live-giving waters that remove our blindness and confirm our act of faith in Christ.

Ash Wednesday

The assembly's prayer with ashes today, most particularly in light of the scriptural readings and the Eucharistic celebration of Christ's death and rising, is not intended to speak only of death and frailty. If the ashes describe our finiteness and our involvement with the force of death, they are even more emphatically a proclamation of hope, a cry for rescue. Ashes give symbolic expression to humanity's trusting dependence on the Lord. We look for the Savior to liberate us and set us free.

So the prophecy of Joel today calls out with a loving invitation to rescue: "Come back to me!" This is no threat, no harsh demand for submission, no condemnation to punishment. It is, rather, the gracious and even passionate offer of reconciliation and peace. Paul makes astonishingly concrete the dimensions of Joel's call to reconciliation. Paul explains that the community is the place where reconciliation is to be found. The assembly is the living Christ, head and members of the mystical body, and this community of believers is the sacrament of the Christ who is Savior of the world: "we are ambassadors of reconciliation."

When we hear today the call, "come back to me, "the "me" is to be translated as "community," which is the living Christ.

First Sunday of Lent

The desert experience has two aspects to it. The desert, first, is the place of thirst and hunger, wandering and confusion, where one is beset by demons and crowded by the terror that goes with vulnerability to wild animals and other potentially hostile forces. At the same time, the desert is the place of encounter with the Lord. It is the place where God has brought the scattered and broken peoples to make them the beloved of the Lord, to strike with them a covenant of love. Those who were "no people" become the people of God. "I shall lead her into the desert," proclaims Hosea, "and speak to her words of love." The desert is a place of intimacy and discovery of faithful love.

Jesus experienced both these aspects of desert: there was hostility and danger in the temptations, and rescue when God's angels came to minister to him. Rescue for all humanity, crippled in the sin of Adam and Eve, becomes possible because the new Adam makes a new world and creation that shines in the glory of resurrection.

So our desert experience, apt image for the human journey which we all take, includes elements of both death and rising. This beginning of Lent points our attention toward a more intense experience of life in the midst of death. Rescue in the desert means, concretely, rescue offered by the community alive in Christ and continuing his saving mission in the world and its history.

Second Sunday of Lent

The transfiguration of all humanity and the human journey finds its image in today's liturgy in the transfiguration of Jesus Christ: "His face became as dazzling as the sun, his clothes as radiant as light," Matthew's gospel tells us. The event of transfiguration comes for Jesus as he makes his way up to Jerusalem, where he will embrace the agony of suffering and death, and in its midst discover the glory of resurrection. The road to Jerusalem is the death march.

By giving himself to this journey of death, Jesus turns himself over to the malevolent forces of destruction. Yet the power of life is more vigorous than the power of death. The radiant glory of light overcomes the darkness of death's blow. So Jesus is "dazzling as the sun." In him, all humanity is dazzling!

We are called to the same journey, as Paul tells us today: "Bear your share of the hardship which the gospel entails." But there is more than death for us. Just as there was transfiguration for Jesus, the gift of God's life is made to us as well, to transfigure us: "God has saved us and called us to a holy life. He has robbed death of its power and has brought life and immortality with clear light through the gospel." When Abram responded to

God's call to leave his kinsfolk for a foreign land, he went with the Lord's promise that this deathly journey would yield new life: "I will make of you a great nation, and I will bless you." For Abram, for Jesus, and for us and all humanity, the human journey is transfigured by the bursting forth of splendor and light that is the divine presence. This Lenten message is repeated today and is intensified by the repeating.

Third Sunday of Lent

The Samaritan woman of today's liturgy is the image of us all. Her thirst and her emptiness describe the human agony that is characteristic of loneliness, and the sense of incompleteness and unfulfillment that goes with repeated experience of false starts, looking in the wrong places for life, making foolish demands on personal relationships.

This woman, an outsider to the Jews because she is Samaritan, has a history of spoiled relationships and broken commitments. Perhaps she is no more alone now, in the melancholy scene painted by the gospel story, than she had been, but the pain of her aloneness is more intense, its fire more searing, and so, in this awful thirst, she makes her way to the well. Like the people who wandered in the desert of the Exodus reading today, who "in their thirst for water" were full of grumbling and restless discontent, the Samaritan woman is upset and disconnected. When she finally encounters Jesus at the well, her own preoccupations so entirely control her perceptions that she does not recognize him, and engages in a ghoulish and pointless discussion with him. Finally Jesus speaks to her with a directness she cannot elude, and her life changes. The water she begins to see is the water of real life, water that will never fail her or ever fail to slake her thirst, for the water is the divine life she encounters in Jesus.

Once again the Lenten message is sounded: water is discovered in the most awful thirst; that is, life is discovered in death. Today's scrutinies with the elect bring added emphasis to the liturgy's power: "Grant that these catechumens, who, like the woman of Samaria, thirst for living water, may turn to the Lord as they hear his word, and acknowledge the sins and weaknesses that weight them down." This prayer of exorcism speaks the desires of all our hearts!

Fourth Sunday of Lent

The man born blind is presented today as an example of what may be called a hopeless case, because he had been born blind. It was not that he had sight and then lost it. He never had it! All he has ever known is darkness. There has never been light. It all seems hopeless.

But in this all-inclusive darkness, Jesus appears as the person of light who drives the darkness away. We begin in our imagination to leap forward to the night of the Vigil, when the light of the paschal candle will proclaim the presence of Christ in the world's darkness: "May the light of Christ, rising in glory, dispel the darkness of our hearts and minds" is the prayer we will make on Easter night. Today the exorcism prayer in the scrutiny develops the same theme: "Lord God, source of unfailing light, by the death and resurrection of Christ you have cast out the darkness of hatred and lies, and poured forth the light of truth and love upon the human family."

The eyes of the blind man are opened by the presence of Christ, and so are our own eyes blessed with a new vision in the encounter with Christ the light. Paul makes the message clear: "There was a time when you were darkness, but now you are light in the Lord." Nothing is hopeless, even our most complete blindness and darkness, because vision breaks through and the light erupts with the arrival of Jesus the light. We hear again the Lenten message: light is discovered in the midst of darkness.

Fifth Sunday of Lent

Today the image of rising from death completely dominates the proclamation of holy scripture. Paul makes all the connections for us: "If the Spirit of him who raised Jesus from the dead dwells in you, then he who raised Christ from the dead will bring your mortal bodies to life also through his Spirit dwelling in you."

In this context we hear the prophecy of Ezekiel come to its fullest possible sense: "Thus says the Lord God: O my people, I will open your graves and have you rise from them." Every kind of grave is opened, every prison is broken open, every bond of oppression and chain of slavery is loosed, for Jesus Christ breaks into our lives to rescue us from death and prison and slavery. The prayer of exorcism explicitly includes the entire assembly: "Father of life and God not of the dead but of the living, you sent your Son to proclaim

life, to snatch us from the realm of death, and to lead us to the resurrection." Jesus Christ is life in the midst of death.

Lazarus is in a case that cannot get any worse. He is dead! He is trapped in a prison of death with a great stone rolled up to its opening. There is no escape. Everything is finished. It has been four days since he has been put in this place, and the fear is that, if it is opened, "surely there will be a stench!" Everywhere, in every part of this scene, there is a sense of finality.

This Lazarus is likewise an image of ourselves, put to death by all the wounds that afflict our fragile persons, betrayed by all the sin of our own doing and that visited upon us by others, pitifully undone by the fury of merciless tragedy that falls upon humanity in its journey. But Jesus, the person of life, strides into the place of death and, full of compassion and care and covered by tears of love, calls out to Lazarus and to ourselves the words of life: "Lazarus, come forth!" Jesus is the life that erupts in the midst of death, for Lazarus and for us. The second exorcism prayer expresses it well: "Lord Jesus, by raising Lazarus from the dead you showed that you came that we might have life and have it more abundantly." With Lazarus and with Jesus, we rise from the dead. Now.

Passion Sunday

Jerusalem is the city of our destiny, because it is there that we may discover most completely who we are and from what source our fulfillment will come. But first it was the city of destiny for Jesus, because it was there that his holy mission came to its fullness. Thus the old city of Jerusalem, the place of betrayal and suffering, tragedy and weakness, intrigue and deception, becomes transformed by Jesus as he takes hold of it in his arms of love and brings it to his Abba for transformation.

Transformation of this sad city makes it the New Jerusalem, the place of the new creation, for Jesus and for all humanity who rise with him to new life. Faced with the suffering and brokenness of our world, Jesus does not put it to one side, but enters the city of our madness and foolish ways, to bring it rescue.

So the cries of "Hosanna" in this beautiful celebration are not pieces of irony inserted, as it were, into the text to make us reflect on the flighty instability of the human heart that moves so quickly from the song of "Praise him" to a savage "crucify him" in a few short hours. No. The cry of praise is genuine, and meant to be a response to the gesture of Jesus the Savior as he rides into the city to bring it rescue. It is in Jerusalem where Jesus embraces the cross of death, and it is transformed into the cross of glory.

In Jerusalem, all the paradox of the paschal mystery erupts! Life is achieved by embracing death. The paschal journey of Jesus now comes to its climax, and we hear the summons to follow him along this way of the cross that leads to glory.

The opening prayer gathers our sentiments into focus: "Today we joyfully acclaim Jesus our Messiah and King. May we reach one day the happiness of the new and everlasting Jerusalem by faithfully following him." With Jesus we cry: "My face I did not shield from buffets and spitting." Paul encourages us: "Your attitude must be Christ's," that is, as we go this way of humility, being empty and in the form of a slave, we are filled with God's life as Jesus was and is, and find exaltation with him. "Let us go forth in peace, praising Jesus our Messiah, as did the crowds who welcomed him to Jerusalem." Today's feast explains our journey.

"An Introduction to the Spirituality of Lent" originally appeared in Liturgy Plus *Planning Software (Resource Publications, Inc.).*

A Parish Lenten Spirituality

Paul Holland, SJ, and Ray Guertin

The problem and possibility of Lenten liturgy is not to "create" religious experience or spiritual growth, but to discover how and where God is and has been already present, and to bring that presence to ritual expression celebrating and allowing the Lord to transform us. If the Lord is often absent or silent, his presence ambiguous or minimal, what experiences of God have we to bring to expression? Precisely that silence and ambiguity.

Walter Burghardt reminds us that "Christian worship is an anamnesis: it is an actualizing memory, an active representation (quoting Yves Congar) 'of the acts by which God intervened to make a covenant with us and to save us.'" This worship is our response to God's self-revelation, which is grace. Grace never supplants nor destroys human experience, but emerges within it to transform it. Thus, the beginning of Christian anamnesis must be human remembering, and Lent offers us a time for healing of memories. Painful memories and present sufferings obscure the Lord's nearness. To uncover God's presence, we must first recover those memories and address our brokenness.

Weekly prayer services, prepared in the previous Sunday liturgy and supplemented by personal journals, are an aide to heal memories. Such services require sensitive presiders, careful selection of music, slides and texts, and ample time for silence. Most of all, they require a willingness to trust that the congregation and the Lord know better than the liturgical planners what "ought to happen" in such healing services. However, since "good things don't just happen,"

here is an outline for the six weeks of Lent, plus a model Ash Wednesday liturgy.

The Sunday before Ash Wednesday can anticipate our communal journey "down memory lane" if we reflect by the gifts of memory and imagination — our tools of prayer. This may mean noting how photographs, feasts, reunions, holidays and storytelling all serve as reminders of the special moments of our lives. Similarly, the Christian community gathers to remember those moments of our lives with God, and we respond by giving thanks.

The sample Ash Wednesday service focuses on our amnesia and our struggle to remember with thanks; the congregation will explore those human moments which have brought joy and hope. We are then invited to discover God's love in the midst of our human loves.

During the second week, our remembrance unearths many painful, even terrifying memories: alcoholic parents, ridicule by schoolmates, the death of a close relative, and the terrible guilt of an abiding sense of worthlessness. We begin to reclaim our lives by letting the Lord bring to the surface our childhood and adolescence. We then invite Christ into our most painful experiences, and ask His Spirit to empower us, not only to accept, but to choose our parents. For in choosing them, we choose ourselves, as God has created us.

In the third week we focus on our adult lives: our families and responsibilities. Here we uncover relationships with our spouse, our children, our supervisors and co-workers. Again we ask the Lord to reveal those times of resentment and lack of forgiveness, and to empower us to seek healing.

11

During the fourth week we face our anger at God and the Church. We can admit the deep resentment so often felt at God, perhaps for letting a friend suffer a painful death, or for saddling us with a handicapped child. (*May I Hate God*, by Pierre Wolf [Deus, 1979] contains very helpful reflections.) We can explore our frustration with the Church and the local parish: for example, our dissatisfaction with the pastor, the alienation we have felt over divorce or contraception, and our rage at racism, sexism or clericalism in the Church.

While the presider must always tread carefully, this might well be the most difficult yet most liberating and healing service; admitting anger at God can be very threatening, yet the communal prayer setting allows a release of that deeply felt but often denied anguish.

The service for the fifth week of Lent brings us to healing our guilt and self-hatred. We trace out our self-inflicted wounds, the patterns of self-deception which enslave us in destructive behavior and alienation. Although each week's service will move from painful memory to prayer for healing, this final one culminates in the service of reconciliation during Holy Week. (See MODERN LITURGY 2, no. 1 [January 1975], for several models.)

Ash Wednesday Service For the Healing of Memories

The church is dimly lit as the community gathers. One of the ministers of the Word greets the congregation, inviting it to a communal healing of memories. The minister notes that our lives are ambiguous — full, yet difficult — and that choosing them as our own renders them a gift. The community is then called to silent recollection.

Procession: "We Thank You Father" (Weston Priory, *Locusts and Wild Honey*, 1971)

Opening Greeting and Prayer:

> **Presider:**
> God, grant us wisdom, discernment, and courage that we all might let you lead us to retrace our lives' journeys, to discover your paths as you lead us forward. We ask this through Christ our Lord.

Two lectors and the presider lead the congregation in a triptych of readings and responses:

I.

Lector 1:
Isaiah 41:8–14 ("Do not be afraid; I am with you.")

Lector 2:
"But I am afraid. I read your words, yet so often they seem empty. Where were you when I needed you, when I prayed so hard, wanted so much to believe? I remember those times, God. Do you?"

Presider:
We ask the Lord to take us back to one memory of our brokenness, and to be with us in it now.

(Brief Silent Reflection)

Presider:
God, lead us back to our wounds so we may find you where you seemed absent. Lord, have mercy!

All:
Lord, have mercy!

II.

Lector 1:
Sirach 28:2–7 ("Forgive others if you wish to be forgiven.")

Lector 2:
"Never will I forgive. If I lay down my hate, I lose the only weapon of survival I have. How can I forgive that one after what happened?"

Presider:
Lord, reveal to us one broken relationship which you wish to heal in our lives.

(Silent Reflection)

Presider:
God, give us the living memory of your forgiveness, that we might forgive the person we now pray for.

All:
Lord, have mercy!

Song: "Lay Your Hands," by Carey Landry

III.

Lector 1:
Revelation 21:1–8 ("He will wipe away all tears from their eyes.")

Lector 2:

"Can you really wipe away my tears? And my fears? With death stalking us daily, with our struggles just to make ends meet, with all we've seen, how can we really find any hope in your promises?"

Presider:

Let us ask the Lord to uncover our unnamed fear.

(Silent Reflection)

Presider:

Lord, help each of us face the fear and anxiety we have called to mind, so you might heal our past, present and future.

All:

Lord, have mercy.

Song: "Yahweh the Faithful One," by Dan Schutte, SJ

Blessing of the Ashes

Presider:

Loving God, these ashes are all that remain of the palm branches we waved last year to hail your son Jesus on his entrance into the holy city. Then, the branches were green and supple; but cut off from the source of life they grew dry and died, and we have cast them into the fire. Father, this is true of ourselves as well. The times of brokenness and rejection, of hatred and hurt and fears, cut us off from your life, and we grow dry and brittle. Help us, with these ashes, to place our wounds in the fire of your healing love, that we might become a holocaust of praise to your fidelity.

Distribution of Ashes

Song: "Son of David," by John Foley (This can be used during or after the distribution of ashes, as a meditation piece.)

Closing Prayer

Presider:

Loving Father, Jesus is our alpha and omega, our source and destiny. Lead us during Lent to those moments in our lives which you wish to heal for us, so that, finding you in our past, we might also find you revealed in our present and in our future. We ask this through Christ, our Lord.

Recessional

How to Make a Lenten Journal

1. Compose some questions appropriate for each week's meditations. For example: describe for yourself in detail the circumstances surrounding your birth; what are your happiest remembrances of high school; recall a time in childhood when you were reduced to tears.

2. Reproduce these questions on two pieces of 8½" x 4" (or 8½" x 11") paper. By folding the two sheets together you produce an eight-page booklet:
   Page 1   Cover
   Page 2   Ash Wednesday
   Page 3   Second Week
   Page 4   Third Week
   Page 5   Fourth Week
   Page 6   Fifth Week
   Page 7   Sixth Week
   Page 8   Holy Week

3. Once folded and stapled in the center, the booklets can be distributed on the Sunday after Ash Wednesday.

This Lenten healing of memories will color the tone of the Triduum services: Holy Thursday can concentrate on incarnating memories in sacraments; Good Friday will recapitulate our wounds, as well as the hope we have experienced in the unity of Jesus in our suffering; the Vigil will make use of the time of waiting and watching, and of recounting the saving deeds of God in our real lives. We ourselves will have passed through flood and desert and death, and perhaps even have found something of healing and liberation.

In planning these services, consider those individuals who will want preparation before coming to the communal service. Good preparation in the Sunday liturgy, plus a simple journal distributed by the parish containing some provocative questions, will help people pray and remember.

Lest this become "psychological scab-picking," the healing of memories should always be done in the context of prayer, with the Lord guiding us to those experiences to be healed. The communal setting should make us aware that others are suffering as we are; reaching out to them is a way of tending our own wounds. Members of the parish team, including priests, should always be available afterwards for those who may need to talk individually.

"A Parish Lenten Spirituality" originally appeared in MODERN LITURGY magazine (Resource Publications Inc.).

Lent: Springtime Renewal of Christian Life

Gerald T. Cobb, SJ

What do carnivals and quarantines, pretzels and fasts, yellow roses and ashes all have in common? In one way or another they have been incorporated into the Church's observance of the Lenten season down through the centuries. The panoply of Lenten customs defies thorough description, but we can note some general trends and some specific adaptations of the season.

The early Church saw Easter as the key liturgical event and therefore stressed its observance by a vigil of waiting and preparation. This vigil was soon extended by various communities to a period of two days, seven days, or even fourteen days.

The arithmetic of Lenten calendars thus became quite complicated. The Council of Nicea first mentions a forty-day season in 325, but in 329 St. Athanasius was still urging the Alexandrian church to observe only a week's fast prior to Easter. Several years later he adopted the forty day season. To complicate matters further, in some places Sundays were exempt from fasting, so the ordinary six weeks of Lent yielded but 36 fast days; therefore in the sixth century four extra days were added to the season, thus making Wednesday before the first Sunday of Lent the "Beginning of the Feast." The actual name "Ash Wednesday" did not come into use until 1099 under Pope Urban II.

In the second century, Irenaeus described the diverse ways Christians prepared for Easter: "The difference of opinion is not about the day alone, but about the manner of fasting; for some think they are to fast one day, some two, some more."

People even argued about what constituted a Lenten day — some suggesting it was not a 24-hour period but rather the 40-hour period which was the approximate time between Jesus' death and his resurrection.

Lenten Catechumens

Everyone in the early church did agree that Lent had something especially to do with the catechumens, the men and women preparing for baptismal entrance into full church membership. Although the catechumens' period of preparation actually extended over one or more years, Lent was the final, more intense period of preparation. A church pastoral directive from the year 90 urges, "Before the baptism let the baptizer and him who is to be baptized fast, and all others who are able." In this way the whole community entered into the spirit of the baptismal preparation of the catechumens. Already, then, the season was assuming an importance for the entire community's renewal of its Christian life.

Quarantines: Forty Days of Penance

As the whole church began more and more to "go on retreat" during Lent and to spend time in self-examination, it is not surprising that the season began to be associated with penitential practices. The Roman church developed a liturgy for imposing public penance on Ash Wednesday. The 40-day period of Lenten penance for public sinners was called a "quarantine," which suggests the way many of the penitents were kept specially segregated for their own private prayer, fasting, and penance. In some places they were not allowed even to bathe or to cut their hair. But by Holy Thursday they had been reconciled and had received communion as a sign of their restoration to community fellowship.

Just as the baptismal preparation of the catechumens had gradually involved the whole church, so too the experience of the public penitents during Lent led the whole church to focus on its need for conversion and reconciliation. By the fourth century not only public sinners, but all Christians received ashes on Ash Wednesday and did penance during Lent. Long after the original Lenten baptismal emphasis diminished, this penitential emphasis persisted.

Later in the Middle Ages, the English wore black clothing during Lent and banned many forms of entertainment. The custom of Easter confession and communion became fixed; and in Russia during the week before the Easter confession all the people in a household would ask each other's mutual forgiveness for sins committed during the past year.

"Farewell, Meat; Hello, Pretzels"

Yet the spirit of joyfulness and the movement to fuller life that had been present in the anticipation of the catechumens' baptism could not be completely eliminated by the penitential tendencies; it now surfaced in other ways. The days immediately preceding Lent became a joyful feasting time known as "carnival" or literally, "farewell to the meat." During the carnival period, people consumed in a great festival all the provisions that they would not be allowed to eat during the upcoming penitential season.

Since forbidden foods by the Middle Ages also included milk products, people had a wonderful time just before Lent making cakes, consuming cheese, and in general celebrating fullness of life prior to the serious business of Lent. The pre-Lenten period culminated in some places with the Mardi Gras, or Fat Tuesday, celebration.

Thus one could say that Lent, as a joyful vigil leading up to the Easter celebration of humankind's redemption, became a more penitential season with time, but in that very process generated its own vigil which included rituals and customs preserving the flavor of joyful community and fullness of life in Christ. We even owe the invention of pretzels to Lent, because Roman Christians marked their Lenten fasts by preparing little breads in the shape of crossed and praying arms.

Boy Mates Girl: Lenten Love

In addition to the raucous period just prior to Lent, people also found other ways to introduce joy and to relax momentarily their Lenten regimen. Laetare Sunday is the most notable example of this. In England during the Middle Ages this was called Mothering Sunday because children would flock home both to their "mother parishes" and also to their own mothers, whom they would regale with stories, gifts, and helpful chores.

Some other countries spent Laetare Sunday reenacting the triumph of springtime over winter, by adorning wells and fountains with flowers to show they were no longer subject to paralyzing ice. The word "Lent" itself comes from an Anglo-Saxon word meaning "spring."

And although the Council of Laodicea in 363 forbade any marriage ceremonies during Lent, in Austria and Germany Laetare Sunday became the special time for young men and women to publicly announce and declare their engagement to each other. In the midst of an otherwise serious and penitential season, then, Laetare Sunday was truly what its name suggested — a joyful day.

The German name for Laetare Sunday was "Rosensonntag," or Sunday of the Rose. This name derived from the custom (dating from at least as early as the eleventh century) of the Pope sending a golden rose to some person or shrine that singularly expressed the beauty of Christian living. This rose originally was a real flower but in time became a bejeweled piece of artwork made from gold.

Passiontide: Lent Within Lent

Since originally Lent was a concentrated period of vigil that became a longer and longer season, it is not surprising that the Church's observance of the season grew more intense as one drew closer to Easter itself. The final two weeks of the Lenten period came to be known as Passiontide, and generated its own set of customs in different churches. In Jerusalem the gospel stories of Jesus' last days were collated and presented to the people chronologically over several days to correspond more or less to the actual times that the events would have occurred in Christ's life. In Rome, by contrast, the passion of Jesus was considered a single unity and therefore was read all at once on Palm Sunday.

During Passiontide the Roman Church also covered all the images in the church with purple cloth as a sign of sorrow and of Jesus' departure from the Temple. Some churches also hung a "Lenten Veil" or cloth between the altar and the congregation. The stations of the cross also developed as a devotional way for the faithful to retrace Jesus' path to Calvary. And in Germany on the Friday after Passion Sunday, the feast of Mary's Seven Sorrows was gastronomically observed by serving a dinner soup that combined seven bitter tasting herbs.

Growth in Daily Liturgies

The growth of the Lenten period also shaped the practice of daily Eucharist in the Church as an intensification of Christian life and Devotion. Originally Christians celebrated Eucharist only on Sundays, but this was soon extended to include Wednesdays and Fridays which were already fast days anyway. Monday Eucharists were added in the fifth century, and then Tuesdays and Saturdays; finally in the eighth century, Thursdays were added to complete the weekly cycle. Yet even in the ninth century, Pope Nicholas I told a group of converts that daily reception of the Eucharist should normally be confined to the Lenten season.

The Buried Alleluia

Thus the Church came to feel herself inherently called by the Lenten season into a renewal of the mystery of her own life as most radically illuminated by the Easter event. To enter properly into the Easter Alleluia as a full-throated cry and song, it was necessary, as some churches actually did, to "bury the Alleluia" symbolically for a time, by a period of self-renewal.

This was seen as a conscious identification with the catechumens' preparation for baptism, and the public penitents' preparation for reconciliation. In other words, all were to be incorporated or restored, and therefore all regarded this as a specially graced "season of honesty." The nature of the Easter event itself suggested that no one could remain a bystander to the wondrous events taking place by God's initiative on the behalf of humankind.

So Lent developed in different ways to become the annual retreat of the Church; it was a collective spring cleaning and the message of renewal was proclaimed even by the earth itself in the movement from winter into spring and summer. In this seasonal change the Church noted how winter's cold death did in fact blend into and give birth to a fuller season. The earth itself seemed to be going through a process that, in sympathy with the human spirit and the redemptive act of Christ, proclaimed the possibility of a new kind of life. Whether fasting or feasting, draped in black or the joyful pink of Laetare Sunday, wearing ashes or roses, the Church moved in grace and beauty through Lent toward her Easter Lord.

"Lent: Springtime Renewal of Christian Life" originally appeared in MODERN LITURGY magazine (Resource Publications, Inc.).

The Origins of Lent

Adapted from Liturgy Plus *Planning Software*

The name "Lent" is derived from the Old English word for "Spring." According to the findings of contemporary research into the history of the liturgy, Lent as we know it has a double origin. In the first place it consisted of a fast in preparation for the celebration of the paschal vigil. According to the early Christian writer Irenaeus of Lyons this fast lasted one or two days. It resembled the fast of the Jews in preparation for the Passover.

Before the Council of Nicea (325) this period of fasting was extended in different Christian centers to a week (Alexandria, Syria) or even to three weeks (Rome). The extension of the fast was related to the practice of initiating catechumens into the Church at the paschal vigil, a practice originating in the early third century.

That Lent was comprised of a forty-day period may, however, have its origins in a fast celebrated in Egypt which followed directly upon Epiphany and concluded with the rites of initiation celebrated at a time independent of Easter (at least, this is the recent theory proposed by Thomas Talley, a theory which has not yet gained wide acceptance).

By the middle of the fourth century Lent consisted everywhere of a forty-day period of fasting and preparation for the Easter Triduum. How the forty days of fasting were assigned differed from place to place. In the Christian East, Saturdays and Sundays did not figure as fast days; so Lent was counted as a period that extended forty days over seven weeks. In Rome the forty-day period was originally counted continuously from the First Sunday of Lent for a six-week period ending on Holy Thursday.

Lent was observed not only by fasting but by an intensified period of prayer and good works. The whole community engaged in this preparation for Easter, but the focus was on the "elect," that is, those who were preparing for baptism at the Easter Vigil.

Development of Lent in the East

Lent developed in various ways in Eastern Christianity. Just a few points will be made here as to the character of Lent in the Byzantine Church (that is, the church that derives its liturgy from the great capital, Constantinople). This is only one (albeit the most influential) among the Christian churches of the East, which included Antioch and Alexandria.

The Byzantine Church added two weeks of preparation for Lent, a kind of pre-Lenten fast to the forty days. These weeks are called Meat-fare and Cheese-fare weeks, respectively, for during them the people abstained first from meat and then from milk products. The Byzantine fast was most rigorous and consisted of Monday through Friday, Saturdays and Sundays not being considered fast days.

Another peculiarity of the Byzantine celebration of Lent consists in a practice known as the Liturgy of the Presanctified, a vespers service combined with the reception of Holy Communion. Since the Byzantines made a strict distinction (unlike the West) between fast days and days on which the Eucharist was celebrated, they did not celebrate the Eucharist on Lenten weekdays, but only on Saturdays and Sundays. The other days of the week were marked by the

Liturgy of the Presanctified (as is still the practice today).

Several of the days during Lent took on a distinctive character in the course of the medieval period. First, Mid-Lent was celebrated on the Wednesday of the fourth week. (The Byzantines count their liturgical weeks from Monday on instead of from Sunday as in the West.) This day had the character of a special celebration of the Cross. Later the commemoration was shifted to the following Sunday (the Fourth Sunday of Lent), which is to this day the Sunday of the Holy Cross in the Byzantine tradition.

Another development was the special commemoration of the raising of Lazarus on the sixth Saturday of Lent (the day before Palm Sunday). The fact that tenth-century Byzantine service books still refer to baptisms on this day may be a holdover from the original Egyptian practice of baptizing forty days after Epiphany — a practice which seems to have been amalgamated with a pre-Easter Lent already in fourth-century Jerusalem.

A third day which was marked with special commemoration in the Byzantine Lent was March 25, the Feast of the Annunciation. Because this important feast often fell within Holy Week, the Byzantines devised a complicated system for figuring out how a particular Lenten day was to be celebrated when the Annunciation coincided with it. Finally, at the end of the ninth century, the First Sunday of Lent received the name "Sunday of Orthodoxy," for it also commemorated the decisive victory of icon-venerators over iconoclasts in 845.

Development of Lent in the West

The development of Lent in the West was heavily dependent on the liturgy of the city of Rome, a model which gradually spread throughout the West, especially after the eighth century. The system of "stational churches" (that is, churches where the Bishop of Rome presided at the Eucharist on any given day) persisted in the Roman Missal up to 1969, even though the practice itself died out at the beginning of the fourteenth century, except for a brief revival under Pope John XXIII in 1960.

The first major development in Lent was the addition of four extra days. As we have seen, the Roman Lent (of the fourth and early fifth centuries) consisted of forty continuous days leading up to the beginning of the Easter Triduum on Holy Thursday.

At some point in the fifth century, however, the idea of forty fast days predominated. Since the original Lent contained six Sundays, on which Western Christians did not fast (they did fast on Saturdays, unlike in the East), it was necessary to add six days to Lent.

First, Holy Thursday and Good Friday were considered to be part of Lent, as Holy Week rather than a distinct Triduum took on more importance. The four days were added to the Lenten observance. Counting four days back from the first Sunday puts us on Wednesday of the seventh week before Easter. This Wednesday became the day on which the fast was solemnly begun. Eventually the Northern European custom of sprinkling ashes over the heads of those who were to do public penance during Lent spread both to other areas of Europe and to the Christian populace as a whole, as the penitential mood of Christianity grew during the Middle Ages.

The notion of Lent as the communal penitential period for Christians coincided with a decrease in the number of candidates for adult initiation in the church at Easter from the fifth century on. As infant baptism came to be the almost exclusive practice of a Christianized Europe, the rites that had been associated with Lent as a period of preparation of the elect began to disappear or be radically transformed.

A major result of this shift away from adult initiation at Easter consisted in a shift in the lectionary readings assigned to the Sundays of Lent. At the end of the fifth century we know that the scrutinies for the elect were held on the Third, Fourth, and Fifth Sundays of Lent. The Gospel readings on those days were almost certainly the encounter of Jesus with the Samaritan woman (John 4), the story of the man born blind (John 9), and the raising of Lazarus (John 11). As adult initiation declined, these rich readings were moved to weekdays, along with the scrutinies, which by the end of the sixth century numbered seven and also took place on weekdays.

As we have noted above, the Eucharist was celebrated by the Pope at a different church in the city of Rome on each weekday during Lent. At least, this was the situation in the eighth century.

In the fifth century it seems that special liturgical services (not the Eucharist) were held on Wednesdays and Fridays in Lent, since these were fast days for Christians throughout the year. By the beginning of the sixth century, both Wednesday and Friday, as well as Monday, Tuesday, and Saturday, were marked with the celebration of the Eucharist. Thursdays were added only in the early eighth century (under Pope Gregory II). In the same period, the fourth week of Lent received the name "Mediana" (middle), probably because it had originally been the middle week of the earliest form of Lent that Rome knew: a three-week period.

Later this same Fourth Sunday received the name "Laetare" (Rejoice), from the first Latin word of the entrance antiphon for the Mass. This denoted no particular reference to joy. Rather, the entrance antiphon corresponded to the stational liturgy — the Basilica of the Holy Cross in Jerusalem, and thus the psalm verse "Rejoice, Jerusalem!" The use of rose-colored vestments on this day sprang from the custom of the Pope giving a golden rose to certain civil authorities on this day as he processed from the Lateran Palace to the stational church. The color rose was substituted for the golden rose, and the custom caught on.

Another major celebration in Lent is Palm Sunday. Originally known as Passion Sunday at Rome itself, the name Palm Sunday corresponded to the Jerusalem custom of having a procession down the Mount of Olives to Jerusalem on this Sunday afternoon. This practice stems from the fourth century. The liturgical customs of Jerusalem enjoyed great popularity in the countries of the western Mediterranean, and so a number of churches adapted this procession.

Rome, however, was notoriously slow in adopting new customs, and the Pope did not participate in a procession with palms on this day until the twelfth century. Northern European countries such as England, on the other hand, created elaborate rituals for the procession which preceded the Eucharist on this day, which came to be thought of as the beginning of Holy Week. The strong attraction of the notion of Holy Week as the preparation for Easter prevailed over the early distinction between Lent and the Triduum, a distinction which has not been emphasized until our own day.

Other Lenten Developments

Three further comments are relevant to the historical development of Lent. First, by the late sixth century a three-week preparatory season preceded the First Sunday of Lent. The season began with Septuagesima ("seventieth day") Sunday, and was followed by Sexagesima ("sixtieth") and Quinquagesima ("fiftieth") Sundays. Thus history notes a tendency to expand the penitential season. Actually, these three weeks were added in the course of the troubled times of the sixth century, when Rome experienced siege, plague, and famine. This preparatory season was eliminated from the Roman Calendar after Vatican II.

Second, the old Roman custom of Ember Days was joined to Lent in such a way that the Spring Ember Days coincided with the first week of Lent. The origin of the Ember Days is obscure, but they seem to have been related to the turning of the seasons. Perhaps they were holdovers from the ancient practice of fasting on Wednesdays and Fridays. Ember weeks were observed with fasting and religious services on Wednesday and Friday, with a special day of fast and prayer and an all-night vigil on Saturday. Thus in the earliest Roman sources, no formula was given for the papal Mass on the Second Sunday of Lent. The pope had presided the night before at the Eucharist, which concluded the long vigil at St. Peter's Basilica.

Finally, Lent was concluded by two ceremonies that have a long and complex history. The first was the solemn reconciliation of public penitents by the bishop. This took place on the morning of Holy Thursday. This ceremony long outlasted the practice of public penance.

The second ceremony was the consecration of the chrism (for the post-baptismal anointing at the Easter Vigil). In Rome this blessing originally took place at the Mass of the Lord's Supper. North of the Alps, however, a special Mass was celebrated on Holy Thursday morning, combining the consecration of chrism with the blessing of the oil of the catechumens and the oil of the sick. The Roman Rite officially adopted a special Chrism Mass only after Vatican II.

Questions

Review and discuss the following questions with the entire parish liturgy team:

I. How did Lenten celebrations start?

- Where?
- When?
- Why?

II. What new insights did we gain from the origins of the celebrations? from their historical development?

III. How did the celebrations develop? Why?

IV. What surprised us? Why?

V. How can contemporary communities be made more aware of the history of these celebrations? What are some practical ideas for our own community?

"The Origins of Lent" originally appeared in Liturgy Plus *Planning Software (Resource Publications, Inc.).*

Questions About Lent

Nick Wagner and Paul Niemann

Where does the tradition of wearing ashes on Ash Wednesday come from?

In the early centuries of the church, people who had committed serious sin and wished to be forgiven would perform public penances. This sometimes included the penitents sprinkling ashes on their heads, which derived from the practice of public repentance in the Old Testament.

By the Middle Ages, public penance had died out. However, in the tenth and eleventh centuries Christians began to take on a modified form of public penance at the beginning of the lenten season. They would come to church on the Wednesday before Lent to receive ashes. Men would be sprinkled over their heads with ashes and women would receive a cross of ashes on their foreheads. The ashes were made from the burnt palms from the previous Palm Sunday.

This ritual used to be done before Mass but is now done after the homily. A Mass is not required, however, and the ashes may be given in the context of the Liturgy of the Word.

May lay ministers assist in the distribution of ashes?

Yes. While the blessing is reserved to a priest or deacon, lay ministers such as communion ministers may help distribute the ashes to the people so that the Mass is not unduly prolonged.

It should also be noted that the burning of palms is not part of the liturgy of Ash Wednesday and should be done in advance.

Why don't we give up meat on Friday anymore?

Some Catholics still do. When the requirement to abstain from meat was lifted, it was done so Catholics might make their own choices about how to fast and abstain. But abstaining from meat was still recommended as a spiritual benefit. Then, in their statement on peace and justice, the U.S. bishops recommended that all American Catholics abstain from meat on Friday as a reminder to work for lasting peace in the world and to pray for God's help.

Catholics are still required to abstain from meat on Ash Wednesday, the Fridays of Lent, and Good Friday. In addition, Catholics are strongly urged to abstain from meat on Holy Saturday as part of the paschal feast.

Is it allowable to veil statues and images?

The April 1995 issue of the *BCL Newsletter* addressed this question and reminds us that the practice of veiling statues was abrogated in the United States with the publication of the 1970 sacramentary and that "individual parishes are not free to reinstate the practice."

Is it okay to celebrate confirmation in Lent?

This question comes up more and more because of the restoration of the catechumenate.

Parishes put much effort into helping the catechumens understand Lent as a time of preparation for the initiation sacraments, which will be celebrated at the Easter Vigil. Then, right in the middle of their preparation, the parish celebrates a big initiation moment with the teenagers of the community. The bishop comes, the church is full, there is much planning and partying. All this contradictory to what the catechumens have been learning about Lent as an ascetical season of fasting and preparation.

The practical reason some parishes celebrate confirmation in Lent is that confirmation preparation programs are often run on a school-year model. Children begin their preparation in September and have completed their preparation in the spring. The culmination of their preparation is focused on celebrating confirmation near the date of the completion of that preparation. For some parishes in the diocese, it works out that they are able to have this celebration in the Easter season or the early summer. The bishops of most dioceses, however, cannot get to every parish in the diocese in that time frame. Given the choice of delaying confirmation into the later summer months or celebrating the sacrament in the earlier spring, most parishes choose to celebrate confirmation during Lent.

However, as more parishes are experiencing the dissonance this practice causes with their catechumenate initiation process, they are choosing to delay confirmation until the fall of the following year. In a few dioceses, bishops are authorizing pastors or other designated priests to serve as ministers of confirmation so more parishes can celebrate the sacrament in the Easter season.

Is it okay to celebrate infant baptisms during Lent?

The only justifiable reason—if there is one—for celebrating confirmation during Lent is the schedule of the bishop demands it. That is not so with baptisms. Parish priests and deacons have the flexibility to arrange their schedules so that baptisms can be celebrated in the Easter season and other seasons outside Lent.

It may be idealistic to hope for, but, at least in smaller parishes, it is not unthinkable to schedule almost all baptisms—infant, child or adult—for the Easter Vigil. The Vigil is the premier time for baptism, and families may begin to long to have their babies baptized at that great feast. Even in large parishes, the usual "Lenten" baptisms might be celebrated at the Easter Vigil and the bulk of the infant baptisms celebrated throughout the year.

If Lent ends with the Mass of the Lord's Supper, the days of Lent do not add up to forty. Why not?

In the Roman Rite, Lent originally began on the sixth Sunday before Easter. That made for a forty-day season, which ended on Holy Thursday evening. However, Sundays were not considered fast days so Lent only had thirty-four days. In the fifth century, Good Friday and Holy Saturday became separated from the paschal Triduum and included Lent. This increased the number of fast days to thirty-six. In the sixth century, Lent was beginning on the Wednesday before the sixth Sunday before Easter—what we now call Ash Wednesday—and Lent had its forty fast days.

In the twentieth century, with the reform of Holy Week and the liturgical reforms of the Second Vatican Council, Good Friday and Holy Saturday were restored to their place in the Triduum. However, the church leaders did not think it would be pastorally wise to eliminate Ash Wednesday in order to begin Lent on the sixth Sunday before Easter. So in our current reckoning, Lent has thirty-eight days if you do not count the Sundays and forty-four days if you do.

These questions originally appeared in Modern Liturgy Answers the 101 Most-Asked Questions about Liturgy *by Nick Wagner (Resource Publications, Inc., 1996), and in the article "Questions on Lent and Triduum Practices" by Paul Niemann in* MODERN LITURGY *magazine (Resource Publications, Inc.).*

Celebrating the Beginning of Lent

Eileen E. Freeman

As a young girl, I looked forward each year to Ash Wednesday. There was a certain fascination in getting up very early in the cold dark and going off to receive ashes on my forehead before I went to school. All day long I watched over the dark smudge as if it were a medal, or perhaps the mark of admission to a secret society. Those of us who had been to early services greeted each other as members of an in-crowd and discussed important topics like what we were giving up for Lent
that year.

Like most children and many adults, I am impressed by what the Church used to call sacramentals. By a sacramental I mean all those things we touch, feel, smell, hear, etc., which remind us of the reality of God.

Nowadays, when I go to church on Ash Wednesday, I hope my attitudes have matured. I no longer compare my ashy smudge with others' or discuss my Lenten regime. But, I am still impressed by the drama of going up to the altar to receive the ashes and renew my commitment to "repent and believe the Good News." I have to choose whether or not to step forward each year and be counted publicly by my whole parish community as a sinner, and that is not always an easy thing to do.

We can and should make the first Sunday of Lent a celebration for the whole community. Ash Wednesday, for all its awesomeness and solemnity, is still a weekday on which many Catholics cannot get to Mass. Furthermore, the liturgy for Ash Wednesday has a distinctly private quality to it. It is as though each individual is wrapped up in his or her own feelings of sinfulness and inadequacy.

The first Sunday of Lent is also the first time the whole parish community comes together as a body to celebrate the Lenten mysteries. It is when we center on the fact that even though we are stubborn, sinful and willful, we are also a holy people redeemed already by Jesus. We celebrate the fact that repentance, that is, turning away from all that cannot lead us to God, is a communal thing as well as an individual one.

There are a number of ways in which a parish can focus, in community, on a change of life and attitudes. This often involves more than just prayers, and may include processions, gestures, special music, anything which points up the communal aspect of repentance. For example, most parishes are accustomed to beginning Mass with an entrance procession accompanied by a hymn.

On the first Sunday of Lent, try changing this: have a silent procession or an instrumental one. Sing a solemn and more lengthy version of the second penitential rite during the procession itself. Have everyone, celebrant included, kneel for the penitential rite. All these things are extraordinary and can wake up a congregation.

During the liturgy for the first Sunday of Lent, a growing number of parishes take time to enroll parishioners in a sort of "order of penitents." This is a modern analog to the ancient practice of the Church, when those who had committed grave sins of a public nature were required to do public penance during Lent. Large baskets are filled with small squares of burlap and/or purple felt.

At an appropriate time, for example, after the homily, they are blessed with holy water and incense (symbols of purity of heart and total self-giving) in these or similar words: "Father of mercy, bless these badges of cloth which your people will wear this Lent as a sign of their desire to give their lives to You completely. Grant us your help at every moment, so that what we promise with our hearts we may live out in our lives. We pray through Jesus Christ our Lord."

After receiving communion, those who wish to declare publicly their intention to reform their lives take a piece from one of the baskets and pin it on their lapel or coat. They wear these badges during all of Lent; after the liturgy on Good Friday they leave them in baskets at the rear of the church.

Our choice of music should reflect the communal nature of liturgical penitence. The first Sunday of Lent is a particularly bad time to choose hymns that emphasize a "me-and-Jesus" relationship to the exclusion of all else.

To celebrate the first Sunday of Lent a parish might undertake some community venture. Use the Sunday liturgy to commit itself to sponsoring a poorer parish or an organization like the St. Vincent dePaul Society. An offering of groceries can also serve to unite a parish in fruitful repentance. Another type of offering could be: each parishioner who wants to writes on a card some service that he or she is willing to donate to another parishioner, such as babysitting, snow shoveling, window washing, fixing leaky facets, baking a cake, etc. These cards are taken up as a special collection and tabulated by a volunteer. Parishioners in need of a particular kind of help or service then call the person in charge of the list, who tries to pair that person up with a particular volunteer.

These ideas for celebrating the first Sunday of Lent require a little prior catechesis. The week before Lent, begin by putting a notice in the bulletin about what is going to happen. Have the school and CCD children participate by decorating boxes for groceries. Have the parish Liturgical Commission discuss what they might do by way of processions or banners or whatever to help emphasize the project. On the first Sunday of Lent the project should be explained, possibly as part of the homily, and put into operation.

The beginning of Lent is a time for each parish to grow closer in love and giving. There is no room for the type of penance that turns so in on itself that it leaves no room for or interest in the needs and hungers of the human family.

Jesus made it quite clear that even in our personal self-denial, we are not to let the world

know. It seems to me that the days between Ash Wednesday and the first Sunday of Lent give us time to consider specifically in what ways we still need to turn to the Lord and our sisters and brothers. Then on Sunday we come together as a community, painfully aware of our own personal failings, but confident in our hope of growth.

"Celebrating the Beginning of Lent" originally appeared in MODERN LITURGY magazine (Resource Publications, Inc.).

Shaping the Ritual: A Sensuous Lent

Samuel Torvend

"Most of the time I feel like a cheerleader, a very energetic cheerleader who rehearses, coordinates, and counsels dozens of people every weekend!"

We should not assume that the parish liturgy planner who made this remark was complaining. If anything, she was accurately describing the various aspects of her work and the amount of energy expended in the preparation and celebration of multiple weekend liturgies. At the same time, she was pointing to another matter that deserves our attention: the feeling we may have that we are removed from the very people whom we serve.

While much of our rhetoric may focus on the assembly and its needs, the greater part of our time is spent with those who help the assembly worship: musicians, cantors, readers, ushers, servers, presiders and artists. Don't get me wrong; I am not suggesting that parish team members should stop rehearsing, coordinating or counseling the many people who enrich the liturgy with their gifts. Rather, I am asking if you ever sit in the middle of the assembly to listen and to watch what goes on. If you do, can you hear and see what enables and instructs the assembly in its work?

Consider the season of Lent from this perspective. The restoration of the 40 days as a communal preparation for the renewal and celebration of baptism and the Easter Vigil ought to serve as the framework for seasonal planning. Music selection, homily preparation, changes in the visual environment, ritual gestures, additional liturgies—all of these are the practical means through which the assembly enters into this season of baptismal preparation, a return to the

place of our birth. Yet we need to ask if our preparation and doing of the liturgy actually communicate the baptismal orientation of the paschal season.

How can we answer the question? Take a poll among many parishioners during the weeks before Lent by asking this question: "When you hear the word 'Lent,' what two or three short phrases come to mind?" Before you ask the question, let the people know that there is no right or wrong answer; you are simply looking for impressions.

Have each person write his or her response on a note card (this is an activity best done in the context of parish meetings rather than at Mass). Unscientific as it is, this exercise gives some indication of what people remember of Lent. As you read through the cards, ask yourself if you see any general thematic trends in the responses. Do the communal, baptismal and paschal dimensions of the season appear? If they are absent, then the pastoral question becomes clear: How do we graciously uncover the baptismal and paschal aspects of what can be a privatized focus on personal sin, "doing better," or the Lord's death? How do we do this together?

In addition to noting what they associate with Lent, parishioners will give clues as to how they remember Lent. Look for words or phrases that trigger memory: color, images of the environment (purple, barren); songs, instruments or musical styles (chant, minimal accompaniment); gestures or bodily movement (kneeling, stations of the cross); smells (wet wool, incense); sensations or feelings (somber, cool, introspective). The "how" responses suggest the ways in which we experience a season or feast day sensually, and how we associate color, scent, gesture, movement and sound with images and concepts.

Such a poll is clearly limited. It isn't intended as an evaluation of previous seasons nor is it prescriptive for effectual liturgy planning. The responses simply offer hints of what people may associate with Lent and how they remember the 40 days. They give the pastoral liturgy planner some indication of what is primary in people's minds and the manner in which we are shaped by the liturgy. And such responses do more; they remind us or teach anew that our entrance into a season (or any liturgy, for that matter) is shaped more comprehensively by our senses than by a reliance on words spoken and sung.

The Trajectory of the 40 Days

The framework for preparation of the 40 days is set forth in the movement of the readings and rites specific to the season. The Gospel readings are not so much individual glimpses into the life of Jesus as a movement forward toward his, and our, destiny.

- The temptation in the wilderness leads to the transfiguration on the mountain and its hint as to what "he was about to accomplish in Jerusalem" (First and Second Sundays of Lent).

- In catechumenal parishes, the temptation-transfiguration imagery set forth in the first two Sundays is intensified ritually in the scrutinies celebrated on the next three Sundays. Paschal-baptismal imagery emerges in these three Sundays; drinking water, receiving the light, smearing with oil, rising from the darkness (Third and Fourth Sundays of Lent, Second Scrutiny, Fifth Sunday of Lent, Third Scrutiny).

- The Passion Sunday Gospel focuses on what will be celebrated in the paschal Triduum—our passage with the Lord from death to resurrection.

Thus, the readings (in particular, the Gospels) lead us from the solemn beginning on Ash Wednesday (ashes from fire) to the paschal Triduum, and within the Triduum to the Easter Vigil (fire to paschal light). There is a passage or journey-toward-a-goal motif in this season, an image that is favored by Luke, who uses the journey as the underlying structure of his Gospel.

Let us consider, then, the ways in which ritual welcomes the assembly into this passage.

A Procession Through This World

A student recently asked me why the Hebrews took 40 years to get through the wilderness. A number of responses came to mind, ranging from the symbolic to the historical-critical, but I turned the question back to the student: "What do you think?"

"Well, maybe they had to go as slow as the slowest person, you know, so no one would be left behind."

My immediate thought? Is this why change comes so slowly in the church — because we need to make sure that no one is left behind?

His question does point to a primary and recent image of the church as a pilgrim people, present in this world more as a movement than a self-enclosed enclave. Such an image complements the journey or passage theme of Lent and invites the assembly to join in procession on the First Sunday of Lent at the principle Mass of the day. In some parishes there is a reluctance to celebrate processions; they demand more planning and can be messy and slow.

"Oh God," grumped one man behind me on the First Sunday of Lent. "We'll get lousy seats if we join the procession." Yet, two years later, after celebrating processions consistently, the people look forward to the ritual actions of these special events. They have come to enjoy carrying things (branches, palms, candles, streamers), singing acclamations and moving together as a body.

We don't "sit" during Lent; we "move" during Lent. And, like the Hebrew people in the wilderness we may need to move slowly so that no one is left behind.

Three other processions invite careful planning: the procession of the Gospel Book from the altar to the ambo with candles and incense; the procession of the eucharistic gifts of bread and wine; and the procession of the people for communion. If the parish uses a common lenten psalm, the communion procession would serve as an obvious occasion to have cantors/choir sing it while the people sing the refrain.

The Color Purple

To speak of a sensuous Lent that begins with movement also conjures up the first visual signal that something has changed: the shift in color. From the green of winter ordinary time, the church moves into Lent's purple and the altered environment of this season. First, consider the plain and austere decoration of various spaces during Lent:

- the exterior portals or doors leading into the building (practical and symbolic passages)

- the walls or beams that surround the assembly, the font, and the altar.

Avoid gaudy purples and banners that are busy with symbols and words. Consider blending deep purple with shades of gray or another earthy color. To express the culminating movement toward the Triduum you might layer colors, beginning with gray, adding purple, and then adding hints of scarlet/deep red on the Fifth Sunday of Lent in preparation for Passion Sunday.

Large drapings of cloth over the altar are best reserved for the Triduum, but a simple gray or purple cross of cloth placed over the drained and cleaned font points toward the Vigil. Remember, less is more during Lent.

In the midst of an austere environment we hear the resounding call of the lenten eucharistic preface: "Each year you give this joyful season when we prepare to celebrate the paschal mystery with mind and heart renewed."

"Shaping the Ritual: A Sensuous Lent" originally appeared in MODERN LITURGY magazine (Resource Publications, Inc.).

Praying the Psalms for Peace and Unity

Robert Hale, OSB Cam, and Roy Parker, OHC

To what extent can praying the psalms nourish a community? To what extent can the psalms unite Christians of various denominations? In the past two years, our ecumenical Priory has been praying a special form of Divine Office which has remarkably strengthened and united us.

At Incarnation Priory in Berkeley, California, monks of the (Anglican) Order of the Holy Cross and the (Roman Catholic) Camaldolese Benedictines have been celebrating the Office by using the breviary of each community in an alternate pattern, maintaining the integrity of both traditions in terms of texts and music. An analogous approach is used at the Priory of Chevetogne in Belgium, which maintains the integrity of both the Roman Catholic Benedictine and the Eastern Orthodox liturgical heritages.

A primary objective of ecumenism today is not only reunion but also diversity — we want to safeguard the rich pluralism of liturgical, theological, and spiritual traditions. Pope Paul VI, greeting the Archbishop of Canterbury, Dr. Donald Coggan in 1977, affirmed, "These words of hope, 'The Anglican Church united not absorbed,' are no longer a mere dream." And in 1970 the Pope spoke of "the Anglican Church ... ever beloved sister." Sisters are rarely identical twins, and as we move away from the we-are-the-only true-Church model to the biblical (see 2 John 13) and patristic notion of sister churches, we open the door again to a wealth of liturgical and spiritual diversity, with all the pastoral resources that implies.

Thus Incarnation Priory, instead of artificially composing a new single liturgy, a kind of amalgam of our two heritages, has chosen to follow both heritages in creative confrontation. The brethren themselves seek to be the living point of encounter of these two traditions.

In its urban, academic situation at the Graduate Theological Union in Berkeley, the monks of Incarnation gather for Morning Prayer before the day's work and study, and again for Evening Prayer at 6 p.m., and finally for Compline before bed. Structurally the Holy Cross and Camaldolese Offices progress through an introductory canticle or hymn, psalter, readings, responsorial canticle and intercession, with each Office taking about twenty-five minutes. The readings consist of a selection from the Old Testament, another from the New, in narrative sequence except for feasts, when special biblical readings are used. The intercessory portion consists of free intercession, the Our Father (in the ecumenical form), and a collect. The Office of Compline provides another opportunity for dialogue between the two traditions, including a regular reading of the Rule of St. Benedict and that of the Order of the Holy Cross according to a monthly cycle.

While Church discipline does not yet permit eucharistic sharing, we find that what we experience in the celebration of the Office is, in fact, a eucharistic liturgy in one of its essential biblical dimensions — the sacrifice of praise and thanksgiving, the "opus Dei" or "work of God" which uniquely serves to bring one's whole being, and the community as such, into the presence of God. Certainly the praying of the psalms and the proclaiming of the Word constitute a most ideal ecumenical worship, for they recall our deepest roots in the prayer of Israel and in Christ, himself the fulfillment of the psalms, who prayed them with his own disciples; such worship also characterized the patristic period and the monastic and medieval heritage. But such worship causes us not only to look backward in anamnesis, remembrance of God's mighty works in salvation history — our common heritage — but also enables us to discover Christ now as our common center, as the primary liturgist who carries us in his prayer to our one Father, through our one Spirit. The psalms and Word are also prophetic of the future, of that communion of the kingdom which we shall forever celebrate. Thus, praying the Office draws us into a unique liturgical time which opens up the horizons of beginning and end.

This common prayer also impels us to return to our daily life, work, and ministry outside the "sanctuary" of sacred liturgy; and, our ecumenical commitment requires the shared experience of meals, tasks, house meetings, communal discernment, and inevitably, tensions. To discover how the Lord works in and through two liturgical heritages, and also in and through the events and tasks of daily life is, of course, to learn something of the meaning of "unity in diversity." We are enabled to do this through participation in the mystery of the Trinitarian life which our Lord proposes in the prayer: "Father, may they be one in us, as you are in me and I in you" (John 17:21). Christ's paschal mystery of going to the Father in the Spirit and drawing us all with him constitutes the living context of ecumenism, liturgy and work.

This Priory's example of ecumenical worship and life may be useful for other communities — parish, religious, lay — in that it proposes a liturgically profound manner of worshiping which, while not the Eucharist, is complementary to it, and is also ecumenically permitted. It moves beyond overly individualistic forms of piety as well as excessively improvised and modish forms of community prayer. In fact, it could be argued that the cumulative, transforming effects of praying the psalms and proclaiming the Word in an ecumenically open form represent an ideal preparation for the Eucharist and for deep personal prayer.

Although the singing of the psalms adds a particular depth to the worship experience, we have found that when numbers are so reduced as to render singing difficult, a slow, meditative, quiet recitation of the psalms antiphonally also opens up a contemplative dimension.

A priest from a large, urban parish in Italy who has brought a group of his parishioners to the Camaldolese mother house for many summers has instituted the community office of Morning Prayer and Evening Prayer in his own parish. A large group of the laity have committed themselves to participating, even if sometimes this is only possible on a rotating basis; and, the parish has found that prayer experience has been decisive in forming a group of lay catechists who enable the parish priest to carry on the parish ministry to the thousands of faithful in that area.

Laity from other parishes also come to participate in the Morning and Evening Prayer service. Although there is not an ecumenical dimension to the experience, this is simply because of the overwhelming predominance of Catholics in the city; there is nothing preventing such an experience in America from taking on an ecumenical character.

Certainly the tradition of Morning Prayer and Evening Prayer in the Episcopal Church renders the praying of the psalms a particularly accessible form of liturgical worship for Episcopalians. The "Malta Report," issued by the Anglican/Roman Catholic Joint Preparatory Commission in 1968, affirmed that "our similar liturgical and spiritual traditions make extensive sharing possible and desirable" (n. 11) and "since our liturgies are closely related by reason of their common source, the ferment of liturgical renewal and reform now engaging both our Communions provides an unprecedented opportunity for collaboration" (n. 13).

There is no reason for Christians to worship separately when there are so many possibilities and opportunities to worship together. It is the experience of Incarnation Priory that praying the psalms offers such an opportunity.

"Praying the Psalms for Peace and Unity" originally appeared in MODERN LITURGY magazine (Resource Publications, Inc.).

The Grammar of Symbol

James O'Regan

Lent and Easter are jammed with symbolism. Any person making the journey through Lent, joining the weekly gathering for Mass and prayer, will encounter a vivid grammar of symbol continually. So, it's important that the liturgist, or liturgy team, understand the importance of symbol.

The communication and metacommunication elements of symbol are so immediate that it is conceivable that a symbol cannot weather much tinkering. What could be seen in the verbal narrative of liturgy as an interim rite, with its attendant processes for changes to shape and content, has no application to liturgical symbol. A symbol which is tinkered with can collapse or flip into a totally new symbol.

A symbol lets us know when it is complete. If changed for inorganic reasons, the symbol becomes a new symbol. A liturgy charged with symbol becomes a different liturgy and not simply an amended liturgy. It is exceedingly difficult to establish another more complete "draft" of a symbol-charged liturgy once it is complete. This is a radical point of departure in the process of doing liturgy. Liturgy will tell you when its work is finished. This finality does not of course exclude using the liturgy as a point of departure for new liturgy. But be warned, it will be new liturgy. This certainly happened when the vernacular and certain symbols were (re-)introduced after the council. In other words, while the liturgical renewal may be in progress, an individual liturgy is not. It is complete. It may not be exactly what we wanted but, if it works, it is self-sufficient.

However you put together symbols, through movement, plastic arts, masks, puppets, symbol, and/or voice, there are several key factors to remember.

Letting the Symbol Speak

Once a symbol is formed, it is possible to judge its competence for communication by "letting the symbol speak." A symbol which is self-sufficient or powerful enough to speak will do so. When it does speak, it is complete. It is finished. Further building or fine-tuning should be done with care because a symbol is a fragile construction. You must have the courage to let the symbol speak once it is capable of doing so. Explaining the symbol during liturgy only explains it away.

If a symbol does not speak, get rid of it. It is proof positive that the idea behind the symbol is weak or that your capability to bring to life is hampered somehow or that the symbol narrative cannot encompass it in the way you would like.

For a symbol to work within itself, there must be a break in the action or a proper frame in which it can sit. When a symbol is full, when it is speaking, have the courage to call it complete and break with it. When symbols, all of which speak by themselves, are pushed close together, they cease to speak. They cease to be strong symbols.

The use of a bell at the sanctus and/or consecration is often dangerously close to collapsing the moment. At the consecration, it can destroy the bread and wine symbol. I've witnessed a bell at the priest's private communion. This absolutely nips the communion into a pseudo mystery highlighting the sacred character of the "priest" in question. It says nothing about eating, communion, Eucharist. The abuse of bell ringing is the cramming together of two powerful symbols.

In a television liturgy I once saw, an otherwise evocative crucifixion painting was literally pasted on top of the act of communion. The result was most distracting. Both the breaking of the bread and the crucifixion speak to us of Jesus' death in unique ways. Crammed together, they don't speak at all.

Using the Proper Narrative Framework

Often at the Easter Vigil there are attempts to impose an alien framework on the lighting of the fire and Easter candle. This framework comes out of a verbal narrative tradition. Because we are not trained to think non-verbally, we instinctively administer verbal solutions to things we're not sure about. These mixed marriages never work: words cannot be substituted for symbols.

There are two distinct symbols (fire and candle) at the lighting of the Paschal fire, framed by prayer/reading. These are often compacted together to get at a perceived story value. The presider will take pains to explain the imagery of both and point out how each are supposed to mean something. The proper framework is removed by the over-zealous or over-pedagogical efforts of the presider. His perceived relationship is forced on the symbols by putting them in too close intellectual proximity with each other. This restricts the symbols' ability to speak by themselves. The symbols collapse. They become something totally different and quite removed from the propriety of the liturgy.

This type of instruction is unhelpful and not demanded by the liturgy nor by the symbols themselves. In other words, the two symbols may have a relation to each other. But they are kept strong and self-sufficient by being properly framed by prayer/readings.

Simply put, a symbol works within itself and is capable of speaking without a lot of background and additional material.

Symbols should be simple and are self sufficient. We must have the courage to allow them to speak. Properly framed and put into context, symbol is a powerful communications tool. We must remember that symbols will tell us how they should operate in a symbol narrative. If we try to impose an alien verbal narrative structure on them, they will collapse. We have to learn to give up control to the symbol, to trust the symbol, to listen and serve it.

If it turns out that a symbol is not speaking then there is the basis for real corrective action. We must either correct our inability to deal with the symbol or consider replacing the symbol. This decision is one that by definition can only be made a posteriori and as a result of a very long process of testing.

Redundancy

Several years ago, I read an article on religious ritual behavior which suggested that redundancy was the technique through which ecstasy was achieved by those who meditate.[1] The article reported on clinical tests measuring brain waves. The results were provocative: one side of the brain reveals a certain repeated level of activity during meditation as the result of a repeated event. This intensifies over time. At a particular moment, the other side of the brain becomes excited and both sides become simultaneously excited. The meaningful result to the meditator is the experience of ecstasy.

How Redundancy Works

Redundancy is the tool for ecstasy. This is true for religious experience. It is true for sexual experience: repeated intercourse achieves orgasm, repeated caressing achieves a sense of heightened pleasure. It is true for Bowser: when you stroke a dog's head repeatedly, he becomes content. Massage yields relaxation. It is true for the blues and rock 'n' roll: the simple repetition of a 12-bar pattern.

Redundancy not only produces ecstasy but invigorates the imagination. It offers and re-offers images to the mind's eye. This can elicit different images by virtue of the unfolding symbol narrative. A symbol placed earlier in the symbol narrative will elicit different reactions than one placed later and consequently in a different context.

Repeating something makes it redundant. Outside of the job market, redundancy is a very positive quality. In a perverse way, it makes something boring enough to elicit day dreaming.

Boredom becomes not necessarily bad but relaxing. Strong symbols put into redundancy form the basis for strong congregational imagination-at-work. It is the danger of crossing the fine line between boredom and redundancy that makes liturgy a challenge.

Not everything put into repetition will yield the intended result. Not everyone's hand will elicit ecstasy in sexuality: the wrong hand results in rape. If the wrong hand approaches a dog, there can be disastrous results. Mere repetition is not enough. Redundancy is only the tool. The task for managing liturgical symbol is to carefully choose and manipulate the symbols, which will be made redundant.

Redundancy Shapes Liturgical Symbol

Redundancy is the manipulation of content in a repetitive manner. Thus it establishes the visual grammar for the symbol narrative. It gives us the shape of the rite. It allows us to manage the story. Knowing that we can manage the "story line" of symbol, in that way, frees us to concentrate on symbol building itself. We know that the principle of redundancy will make the symbols work. That is a given. Now it's possible to work on the quality and choice of the symbols themselves.

Symbol work allows the symbols to direct us to fuller expressions of symbol and related symbols. It helps us give shape to a symbol itself much in the same way as words help shape the paragraph they form. Words help choose other words. Symbols help choose other symbols and elements of symbols.

The creative process is not mysterious in this type of work. In the partnership between author (liturgical team) and symbol is the greatest challenge to building a solid basis for the further unfolding of symbol narrative. What we discover to make redundant is the exciting unknown. By definition, we must use the human and knowable tools that we have at hand — redundancy.

Working with Redundancy

The liturgical team must ensure that the symbols are clear, strong and self-sufficient, that they are framed properly and that the redundancy works correctly. The team fine tunes the symbols and their redundant shape.

I recently read a short note on abuses of the processional for Eucharist which stated that the job of the processional is not to "single out the presider."[2] While this may be true, the note did not tell us what the procession was to accomplish other than get the ministers to the front. This wasn't very helpful.

The procession carries out one function in its basic action: to gather our focus and channel our attention and emotion to the altar. What we should see most of all in a procession is people:

that is what gives the sense of the people of God moving. This moving actually shapes the congregation into one mind and one body. This concrete and emotional identity is made redundant in the offertory procession. The repetition of the processional movement allows us to feel that it is we who bring forward the gifts.

This process of finding and building symbols, of putting them into a redundant shape, that is, finding the symbol narrative, does not fall easily into an a priori time frame. It does take a long time to build. This time must be budgeted and managed carefully.

Manipulating Symbol

"Blessed are you, Lord, God of all creation. Through your goodness, we have this bread to offer, which earth has given and human hands have made."[3] Symbol manipulation means getting your hands dirty. If you'll excuse the bastardization: symboling is a hands-on activity.

Several technical points regarding symbol manipulation have ramifications for liturgical behavior.

The Presenter

Liturgical ministers can be best thought of as "presenters." This idea of presenter has several aspects. To begin with, it encompasses more fully the range of skills needed in liturgy: acting, manipulation, voice, movement. It reflects the relationship between minister and symbol/words — service and presentation. Also, because the presenter is such an obvious part of the liturgy, the congregation will always be aware of him/her.

There are several types of activity on the liturgical stage that each presenter goes through: being him or herself, carrying the symbol, presenting or displaying the symbol, filling the symbol. Each activity is distinct and each reads for the congregation. It's important not to get them mixed up.

For example, the lector on the one hand is a particular person with a unique identity within the parish. We, the congregation, have to recognize this at liturgy, otherwise we don't know who the lector is.

The lector serves the lectionary by carrying it to its place. By carrying it, the lector can display the book to the congregation. It is enough to do that without commenting visually on the carrying of the book.

The lector also has a special relationship with the book. It is the lector's manipulation of and proclamation from the book that fills the book or allows that book to speak. When the lector is not proclaiming from the book, he/she should simply display the book.

These careful distinctions help the congregation make sense of the liturgical action.

Serving the Symbol

When working with a symbol, the presenter must be detached from the symbol. The presenter is there to serve the symbol. If the presenter gets caught up in the action or emotion of the symbol then the symbol ceases to read. When the presenter gets in the way of the symbol, the congregation is distracted by the presenter's goings on. The presenter's energy must go to the symbol and not be sent directly to the congregation. The presenter must not get in the way of the symbol. If nervous, use the nerves to feed the symbol.

I've occasionally seen an entrance procession where a minister of the word had held the lectionary high above his head, all the while gazing reverently at it and walking at the same time. Not only does this make it difficult to see where you're going but this odd stance immediately shifts everyone's attention to the minister instead of the book.

The result was that the book was incapable of speaking and the minister was saying, "Gee, look at how holy this is!" A sacred symbol doesn't need that kind of direct help. It needs proper framing not commentary.

Displaying and Filling the Symbol

A final note: when manipulating in liturgy, it is clear and perfectly legitimate to break with your symbol and reposition yourself somewhere else in the liturgical space, then represent and fill the symbol. This allows for a cleaner presentation of the situation. For example, a 20-foot walk across the sanctuary carrying a ciborium or lectionary doesn't have to be full of symbol work which might be interpreted wrongly by the congregation. Simply walk across the space as yourself, displaying the symbol, and begin new action.

The choices to be made come from the fourfold distinctions of: being oneself, carrying the symbol, presenting or displaying the symbol, filling the symbol.

Notes

1. Eugene d'Aquila & C. Laughlin, "The Biopsychological Determinants of Religious Ritual and Behavior," *Zygon* 10:1 (1975), 32–58.
2. C. Poirier, "The Introductory Rites of Mass," *Fragments* 40 (June 1986), 1.
3. Preparation of the Gifts prayer, *Sacramentary* (Ottawa: CCCB, 1974), 424.

"The Grammar of Symbol" originally appeared in MODERN LITURGY magazine (Resource Publications, Inc.).

Symbols for the Lenten Season

Catherine H. Krier

Everything conveys a message to the beholder. Beauty is an emotional reaction, a perception that conveys pleasure. A high percentage of our information comes through the visual sense as compared to our other four senses. A liturgist will do well to capitalize on this.

The following format presents colors, textures, shapes, objects, words, etc., through which some essence of the lenten season can be experienced by those who engage with the symbols on the Sundays of Lent.

Suggestions are included for all three cycles; however, the third, fourth and fifth Sundays of Cycle A are normative for parishes with catechumens.

Ash Wednesday: Violet

Have parishioners return palms on the previous Sunday. Burn a small portion of these during the penitential rite. Have the worship area arranged in simplicity. Remove flowers. Set up Lenten environment according to the year's cycle.

- **Joel 2:12–18** fasting, weeping, mourning, return, gracious, merciful, kind, relenting, bless, trumpet, assemble, bridegroom and bride, concern, praise

- **Psalm 51** mercy, goodness, compassion, wash, renew, joy, salvation

- **2 Corinthians 5:20–6:2** ambassadors, reconcile, holy, grace, salvation

- **Matthew 6:1–16, 16–18** guard, recompense, alms, merciful, deeds, secret, pray, fast, groom hair, wash face

Cycle A

First Sunday of Lent: Violet

Arrange a desert scene with cactus, sand, rock, and driftwood. A second option is an arrangement of a large clump of clay along with pottery, some fired and some unfinished.

- **Genesis 2:7–9, 3:1–7** clay, garden scene, fruit, serpent, fig leaves

- **Psalm 51** mercy, water, towel, praise, Spirit

- **Romans 5:12–19** sin, death/resurrection, gift, condemnation, acquittal, grace

- **Matthew 4:1–11** desert, Spirit, devil, hunger, stones, bread, homage, heights, adoration

Second Sunday of Lent: Violet

Keep the desert scene and add signs of life such as young plants.

- **Genesis 12:1–4** Go! blessing, curse, old age

- **Psalm 33** mercy, trust, justice, kindness, fear of God, waiting

- **2 Timothy 1:8–10** hardship, call to holiness, death/resurrection, light

- **Matthew 17:1–9** heights, radiance, dazzling sun, three altars, bright cloud, favor, listen, fear, lay hands, fear not, secrecy, death/resurrection

Third Sunday of Lent: Violet

Add a bucket of water to the scene (preferably a wooden one).

- **Exodus 17:3–7** thirst, grumbling, questioning, fear, staff, rock, water, drink, Lord's presence
- **Psalm 90** hear, harden not hearts, invitation to song, joy, rock, thanksgiving, worship
- **Romans 5:1–2, 5–8** peace, grace, boast, glory, love, Spirit, death, proof of love
- **John 4:5–42** journey, well, water, drink, bucket, thirst, worship in Spirit and truth, food, harvest

Fourth Sunday of Lent: Violet

Add a spotlight to the scene and add a few larger, more mature plants.

- **1 Samuel 16:1, 6–7** chosen king, sacrifice, rejection, ruddy handsome youth, banquet, anointing, Spirit rush
- **Psalm 23** live in God's house, shepherd, pastures, restful waters, repose, fearless, courage, table, anointed, oil, goodness
- **Ephesians 5:8–14** darkness/light, goodness, justice, truth, please, awaken, death/resurrection
- **John 9:1–41** blind (sin, God's work, night, light) mud, saliva, wash, see, signs, scorn, questions, answers, Good News, faith, worship

Fifth Sunday of Lent: Violet

Remove the desert or clay scenery from previous Sundays. Show bandages that have been thrown off of Lazarus.

- **Ezekiel 37:12–14** open graves, rise, new Spirit, life, promise
- **Psalm 130** mercy, full redemption, depths, voices, forgiveness, revere, trust, wait, dawn, kindness

- **Romans 8:8–11** flesh, please, Spirit dwells, death/resurrection
- **John 11:1–45** sick, death, asleep, comfort, rise, belief, tears/joy, prayer, resuscitation

Passion Sunday: Red

Have a glorious, triumphant procession after the blessing of the palms. You may have small groups within the parish make banners and participate in the procession in groups. The liturgy then continues in simplicity. Palms and the cross make up the simple decor. In contrast to the glorious entrance, let the recessional be silent with a feeling of incompleteness as we await the Triduum.

- **Matthew 21:1–11** colt, cloaks, crowds, branches, procession, blessed, triumph
- **Isaiah 50:4–7** well-trained tongue, weary, beating, buffets, spitting, faithfulness
- **Psalm 22** abandoned, scoff, mock, wagging heads, evil crowding, pierced hands and feet, divided garments, lots, hasten Lord, praise, glorify God
- **Philippians 2:6–11** let go, empty, obedient, exalted, bend knee, glory
- **Matthew 26:14–27, 66** thirty pieces of silver, Passover meal, garden scene, trial, journey to Golgotha, crucifixion and death

Cycle B

First Sunday of Lent: Violet

Consider the season of Lent as a whole. Is there a way of developing the season symbolically from week to week? It could begin with a simple desert scene that emphasizes the dry sand and barrenness; the scene gradually builds toward Passion Sunday.

- **Genesis 9:8–15** Noah, covenant, descendants, living creatures, animals, birds, ark, flood, sign, rainbow, clouds, no destruction
- **Psalm 25** ways of love and truth, covenant, teach, guide, saving, remember, compassion, kindness, goodness, humble, justice

- **1 Peter 3:18–22** death/resurrection, life, spirit, preach, prisoners, Noah, patience, wait, ark, baptism, pledge, angelic rulers and powers

- **Mark 1:12–15** Spirit, sent, desert, wasteland, 40 days, test, Satan, wild beasts, angels, John's arrest, Good News, time of fulfillment, reign of God, reform, believe

Second Sunday of Lent

Over the sand from the previous week, a bundle of wood and a knife may be set. Include a "dazzling white cloth." Let the simplicity speak for itself.

- **Genesis 22:1–2, 9, 10–13, 15–18** Abraham's test, call, ready, only son, loved, offering altar, wood, knife, messenger, ram offering, blessing, countless descendants, obedience

- **Psalm 116** walk, presence of the Lord, land of living, affliction, faithful, servant, loosed bonds, thanksgiving, vows, courts

- **Romans 8:31–34** unsparing God, justifies, death/resurrection, intercessor

- **Mark 9:2–10** mountain, chosen three, transfiguration, dazzling white clothes, Elijah, Moses, three booths, awe, cloud, overshadowed, beloved Son, listen, descent, death/resurrection

Third Sunday of Lent

Add a small, barren tree to the scene or perhaps something that symbolizes the commandments and law.

- **Exodus 20:1–17** commandments, only and jealous God, reverence god's name, labor, holy Sabbath rest, honor parents, no killing, adultery, stealing, false witness or coveting

- **Psalm 19** words of everlasting life, perfect love, refreshment, trustworthy, rejoicing, enlightening, pure, true, just, more precious than gold, sweeter than syrup, honeycomb

- **1 Corinthians 1:22–25** signs, wisdom, preach Christ crucified, stumbling block, absurdity, power, wisdom, wise folly, powerful weakness

- **John 2:13–25** Jerusalem Passover, sale of animals, money change, whip, spilled tables, "Out!", Father's house, zeal, sign, authority, destroy temple, raised, body temple, recollection after resurrection, believers, read hearts

Fourth Sunday of Lent: Violet

The serpent on a staff is a sign of healing. This may be displayed this weekend if it fits into the overall design of the Lenten environment.

- **2 Chronicles 36:14–17, 19–23** princes and priests, infidelity, abominations, pollutions, messengers sent, compassion, mockery, scoff, Lord's anger, fire, destruction, captives, retrieve Sabbath, charge to build home

- **Psalm 137** silence tongue, forget, streams, sat, wept, hanging harps in tree, remembering, silenced music

- **Ephesians 2:4–10** rich in mercy, great love, death/life, saved, favored, kindness, faith, gift, handiwork, created, prepared good deeds

- **John 3:14–21** Nicodemus, lifted serpent, desert, believe, eternal life, loved, saved, condemned, light, loved darkness, wicked deeds, hate, fear, truth, clarity

Fifth Sunday of Lent: Violet

Continue to build the Lenten environment as planned. If it fits into the development of the environment, something may be added using seeds on soil, saplings, fruit–bearing plants, or grain.

- **Jeremiah 31:31–34** new covenant, lead from slavery, broken, master, inner law, written on hearts, "I will be their God, and they shall be my people," all shall know, forgiven, remember not their sins

- **Psalm 51** create clean heart, mercy, goodness, wash thoroughly, steadfast spirit, renew, joy, salvation, willing spirit, teach, sinners return

- **Hebrews 5:7–9** prayers, supplication, cries, tears, save, reverence, heard, son, obedience, suffered, perfected, salvation

- **John 12:20–33** come to worship, Greeks, want to see, glorified, grain, wheat, earth, dies, fruit, loves life, losses, hates life, preserves, serve, follow, honor, troubled soul, hour

Cycle C

First Sunday of Lent: Violet

The images and suggestions for A and B should be used for this cycle also since the primary imagery for Lent involves desert. The first week of Lent this desert scene should be barren.

- **Deuteronomy 26:4–10** basket, front of altar, wanderer, alien, oppressed, hard labor, outstretched arm, sings, wonder, milk, honey, first fruits, produce, merry, offer

- **Psalm 91** presence, trouble, dwell in shelter, shadow, refuge, fortress, trust, tent, guard, bear up, foot, stone, asp, viper, lion, dragon, cling, deliver, distress, glorify

- **Romans 10:8–13** lips, heart, Word near, confess, death/resurrection, saved, rich in mercy, call

- **Luke 4:1–13** Spirit led, desert, tempted, devil, hunger, stones, bread, heights, kingdoms, power, prostrate, homage, adore, temple, parapet, throw self down, angels, support, test

Second Sunday of Lent: Violet

If you are adding to the desert scene gradually you may add a cactus or two. Be subtle with whatever you add.

- **Genesis 15:5–12, 17–18** sky, stars, descendants, faith, possess land, heifer, goat, ram, turtledove, pigeon, birds, carcasses, sunset, trance, terrifying darkness, flaming torch, covenant

- **Psalm 27** light, salvation, fear, refuge, call, pity, answer, heart speaks, glance, presence, seek, helper, bounty, courage, wait

- **Philippians 3:17–4:1** (imitators, guide, example, enemies of the cross, tears, disaster, belly, shame) citizenship, heaven, eagerly await, savior, body, power, love, long for, joy, crown, stand firm

- **Luke 9:28–36** mountain, pray, changed face, dazzling clothes, glory, deep sleep,

three booths, overshadowing cloud, fear, voice, son, chosen, quiet

Third Sunday of Lent: Violet

A bare branch or tree would be an appropriate addition. A shepherd's staff, sandals, or a bush would connect the scene to the first reading.

- **Exodus 3:1–8, 13–15** flock tending, desert, mountain, angel, burning bush, remarkable sight, command, remove sandals, holy ground, fear, affliction, complaint, slave drivers, suffering, rescue, deliver, spacious land, flowing with milk and honey, name?, I AM, sent, tell, generation

- **Psalm 103** kind, merciful, bless, benefits, pardon, iniquities, heals, ills, redeems, crowns, compassion, justice, oppressed, gracious

- **1 Corinthians 10:1–6, 10–12** remember, cloud, seas, baptized, ate spiritual food, drank spiritual drink, rock, desert, example, warning, watch, fall

- **Luke 13:1–9** bloody sacrifices, greatest sinners, suffered, reform, falling tower, guilty, fig tree, no fruit, cut, clutter, hoe, manure, wait

Fourth Sunday of Lent: Violet

The story of the prodigal proclaimed in this week's gospel is a powerful one. A pair of sandals, colorful robe, rings, or some other symbol from the story can be used if it does not hinder the development of the lenten theme.

- **Joshua 5:9–12** encamped, celebrate Passover, ate produce, unleavened cakes, parched grain

- **Psalm 34** taste, see goodness, bless, praise, glory, lowly hear, glad, extol name, sought, answered, radiant joy, shameful blush, afflicted, saved

- **2 Corinthians 5:17–21** new creation, old passed, reconciled, ministry, countering transgressions, entrusted, ambassadors, holiness

- **Luke 15:1–3, 11–32** welcomes and eats with sinners, lost, found, wasteland, dissolute living, famine, dire need, starving, squandered, caught sight, deeply moved, embraced, finest robe, fatted calf, death, life, questioned, angry, plead, obeyed, always with me

Fifth Sunday of Lent: Violet

Use the desert scene to emphasize the Gospel reading. When the Gospel acclamation is completed, the presider may silently move to the sand and make some marks in it. He can then move to the ambo and proclaim the Gospel reading. Be sure to put some small stones around the sand.

- **Isaiah 43:16–21** opens, sea, path, mighty waters, chariots, powerful army, snuffed out, quenched, remember, desert, wasteland, rivers, wild beasts, jackals, chosen drink, praise

- **Psalm 126** great things, joyful, dreaming, laughter, rejoicing, glad, desert torrents, sow, tears, weeping, carrying seed, sheaves

- **Philippians 3:8–14** loss, light, surpassing knowledge, forfeited everything, rubbish, wealth, faith, power of resurrection, share suffering, death, hope, racing, grasp prize, finish line, push ahead, run, call

- **John 8:1–11** mount, temple, teach, adulteress, stoned, trap, accuse, bent down, tracing in sand, cast stone, drifted away, straightened up, condemn?, avoid sin

"Symbols for the Lenten Seasons" taken from Symbols for All Seasons *(Resource Publications, Inc., 1988).*

Preparing a Setting for Lenten Worship

Joanne Lopez Kepes

Remember you are dust and to dust you shall return." These familiar words are one of the optional forms that are spoken as we are marked by the blessed ashes on Ash Wednesday.

A reminder that our life on earth is a measured amount of time, it also recalls our oneness with all created matter. We are shaped of the stuff of creation. That may be why we resonate so well with natural symbols such as those ashes, a tree, light, darkness and water. And that is why natural symbols can be used so effectively when we are trying to create an environment that evokes a particular mood.

For our lenten preparation we can turn to nature for inspiration, knowing such symbols will resonate. The winter/pre-spring landscape is barren and subtly hued. Yet, the promise of new burgeoning life lies just under the surface. This is a poignant metaphor for the promise of Lent. We do not need to look for themes that are literal translations of the season's readings to prepare a setting that animates the lenten journey.

A live tree waiting to bud can be an eloquent addition to the worship setting. If the available light is adequate and the tree is properly cared for it will bloom at Easter time. If blossoms begin to make an early appearance, this can be a sign of our eternity and the paschal mystery that permeates all of the Lent-Triduum-Easter season.

Perhaps in the entry or gathering area an arrangement of sand, cactus and rocks can be placed to suggest desert or wilderness.

The colors of Lent — purple, violet, gray — echo the somberness of nature awaiting spring. These will be the tones for vesture, altar and ambo paraments. A simple hanging of one of these hues can also be employed to advantage. In some places, the resurrection cross can be covered with such a hanging, thereby having it serve a dual purpose.

Waters may be drained from the baptismal font. Flowers are not used in the lenten environment but other greenery can remain, especially large plants or trees. Keep in mind that you want to create a subtly barren image.

The quiet that seems to prevail in nature during these dark, cold final weeks of winter finds its parallel in our rituals. Our lenten environment should be like a whisper in the silence.

"Preparing a Setting for Lenten Worship" originally appeared in MODERN LITURGY magazine (Resource Publications, Inc.).

Part 1

Ash Wednesday

Lectionary Commentary For Ash Wednesday

Liturgy Plus *Planning Software*

Joel 2:12–18
2 Corinthians 5:20–26
Matthew 6:1–6, 16–18

First Reading

A preacher or liturgy planner is well advised to review the assigned readings by beginning with the Gospel. The architects of the Lectionary admit that the first reading has been deliberately selected to link in some way with the Gospel. Since they have not explained the link they intended, preachers and liturgy planners must diligently seek a link even if it is not the one intended by the architects.

The reading from the prophet Joel should very likely be associated with the Gospel through verse 12: "fasting, weeping, and mourning" (compare Mt 6:16–18). A natural disaster has befallen the people. A plague of locusts has ravished the country. The prophet Joel tries to make sense of this experience for himself and his people.

Like all peasants, so too Mediterranean peasants view themselves as being at the mercy of nature. They cannot control it or predict it. They can only suffer it. However, God is definitely in control of nature, and peasants believe they have a better chance of influencing God than they have of influencing nature.

In the Mediterranean world, fasting, weeping, and mourning were effective means of stirring human beings to action. They were also considered effective for stirring God to action.

Besides, interpreting misfortune as a punishment from God, peasants naturally believe they can influence God to halt or remove the misfortune by making amends to God ("rend your hearts, not your garments; return to the Lord").

How does this all work? Cultures are value-driven systems, and the core values that drive Mediterranean culture are honor and shame. God, of course, is honor supreme! Moreover, in the Mediterranean world God is viewed as the quintessential Mediterranean. He has a keen sense of personal honor.

So the Prophet urges the people to tug at God's sense of honor. He provides the words that the people might use to activate God's sense of honor. "Make not your heritage a reproach, with the Nations ruling over them." The people are God's clients, and everyone knows it. The argument to God is: If we are placed in a shameful predicament, our shame redounds to you, our heavenly Patron! "Why should people say: 'Where is their God?'" Can't you see that your honor rating, your public esteem, God, is slipping because of our shameful predicament?

Fasting, the deliberate refusal to eat, is also a deliberate refusal to participate in a very basic social reciprocity with God. Fasting will certainly shame God into acting!

And, of course, it works! Our reading ends by noting: "The Lord was stirred … and took pity on his people."

Second Reading

This all too brief passage yanked from its larger context in 2 Corinthians appears to have been selected as a bridge between Joel's exhortation to repentance and Jesus' advice on the proper way to give alms, pray, and fast.

As the reading itself makes clear: "Now is the acceptable time! … Be reconciled to God."

Mediterranean culture is unswervingly fixed upon the present moment. The peasantry in particular has no ability to imagine any future beyond tomorrow. As the Greek text of the Our Father is sometimes translated (quite correctly on an alternate reading!): "Give us today, tomorrow's bread!" (Mt 6:11). In today's reading, Paul very obviously reflects his Mediterranean culture.

Similarly, the repeated promise of Jesus in today's Gospel: "your Father … will repay you" (vv 4, 6, 18) is understood by his Mediterranean audience to indicate that God will give a reward now, in the present. (See Mark 10:30 for a similar, present-time reward for following Jesus: a hundredfold, now, in this time!)

So it is entirely normal for Paul to repeat, daily if need be, that "now" is the acceptable time, and "now" is the day of salvation. The "now" of his exhortation is the moment at which he is writing his letter, some time around 54 CE on our calendar. Paul would be astonished that anyone living today would think he meant now, this year! The end of the *first* millennium would have been beyond his imagination, to say nothing of the second.

That mainstream U.S. citizens whose culture is primarily and very strongly future-oriented should think that Paul's "now" referred to the current year is an anachronistic interpretation of Paul. Even so, American future-orientation has much to gain by forcing itself to pay attention to its own present moment.

The second Mediterranean cultural element to notice in this selection from Paul is his plea: "not to accept the grace of God in vain." While Americans view God as the great facilitator, one who helps an individual realize personal plans and goals, Mediterraneans view God as a heavenly Patron, a type of "Godfather," who can deliver anything that one desires but which one can't get elsewhere from anybody else.

When the Patron gives a gift, it is unthinkable to refuse it or abuse it. The Mediterranean Patron's gift always has a "hook"; it binds the recipient to the giver. To reject that bond, to "receive God's grace in vain" is shameless behavior by a client who thereby shames God.

Notice that Paul calls himself an "ambassador of Christ." He is a broker, an intermediary (just like Jesus) between God the Patron and God's human clients. Thus Paul exhorts his Mediterranean listeners not to insult or dishonor God, and Jesus in Matthew's Gospel spells out the details of behavior for his disciples that will bring honor to God.

The Gospel

This passage has been carved from Matthew's version of Jesus' Sermon on the Mount, whose theme is: "Unless your righteousness exceeds that of the scribes and Pharisees, you will never enter the reign of God" (5:20).

The word "righteousness" is best understood as describing "proper interpersonal relationships and behavior between fellow followers of Jesus and God." Disciples of Jesus must surpass the scribes and Pharisees in their respective interpersonal relationships.

Scribes were commandment experts. Jesus cites the final five of the Ten Commandments (5:21–48) and presents antitheses to show how the interpersonal relationships and behaviors of his followers must surpass what is based on the Ten Commandments alone. Pharisees were outstanding laity known for their pious practices of almsgiving, prayer, and fasting (6:1–18). Jesus points out how his followers must surpass these behaviors as well. Finally, Jesus lays out a complete description of interpersonal relationships and behaviors that ought to characterize his disciples (7:1–28).

Today's Gospel focuses on the deficient behavior of the Pharisees and proposes ways in which these can be improved.

Almsgiving is a highly esteemed behavior in the ancient and contemporary Middle East. Everyone who can afford it does it faithfully and generously. Jesus does not criticize the Pharisees for their behavior (almsgiving) but rather for the way in which they do it (seeking public recognition, enhanced status, and honor for the deed). Jesus proposes that his disciples give in secret and allow God to reward in secret.

Prayer is a form of interpersonal communication by which the one praying seeks to persuade the one listening to do something for him or her. The purpose of prayer is always to get a result. Prayers that "heap up many phrases" were intended to wear down the divinity so that she/he would yield and grant the favor requested (see Luke 11:5–8). In traditional Roman and Greek prayer, the item requested had to be described as precisely as possible lest the divinity grant the wrong favor! Jesus, of course, says there is no need to ask at all, since God "knows what you need before you ask him" (Mt 6:8).

Fasting is still another form of communication, a normal part of the Middle-Eastern "protest pattern" that also included mourning and weeping. The message of the one fasting (and mourning and weeping) is a protest against the presence of evil. It says "help me in my affliction." It involves not eating, not sleeping, not worrying about how one is dressed or how one looks, because the one fasting is consumed with concern about a specific evil. Fasting is thus an extreme form of self-humiliation, and it inevitably gets a response. If human beings are moved by such behavior, surely God will be moved, too. Yet Jesus urges "clean face fasting!" Who then can notice and help? Only God, of course!

The key to Jesus' concern in these passages is the word "hypocrite" that he applies consistently and repeatedly in Matthew's Gospel to the Pharisees. Literally, the Greek word means "actor," and Jesus labels the Pharisees "actors." Like actors, they seek attention, an audience, and applause. Yet just like actors, Scripture may be the lines they quote but it is not the script by which they live!

Bible-readers sensitive to the core values of Mediterranean culture, honor and shame, wonder why Jesus condemns these very honorable behaviors. If honor is a public claim to worth and public acknowledgment of the claim by others, why shouldn't the Pharisees, or anyone else for that matter, call attention to these honorable deeds? How else can one gain the honorable acclaim that is so vital in this culture?

Jesus says such behavior robs God of the honor due to him alone. Instead of hoping for a return from the one to whom alms are given, let God reward your kindness. Instead of boring God with long reports of your needs of which he is already fully aware, be brief. Besides, the long reports are all too often intended more for human listeners than for God's ears. Finally, when oppressive troubles come, turn to God rather than to unreliable human beings for assistance. Don't try to attract the attention of other human beings with self-humiliation, but turn instead to God. These are the appropriate behaviors for a disciple of Jesus.

The Pharisees used these behaviors to gain public acclaim and to enhance their social status.

The purpose of these behaviors should be to stir God to action rather than to increase social standing and personal honor.

"Lectionary Commentary for Ash Wednesday" originally appeared in Liturgy Plus *Planning Software (Resource Publications, Inc.).*

Up in Smoke:
Preparation for Ash Wednesday

William C. Graham

Direct our hearts to better things, O Lord;
heal our sin and ignorance.
Lord, do not face us suddenly with death,
but give us time to repent
(Responsory, Ash Wednesday).

The cloud of smoke was appalling. South Bronx wasn't on fire but the church seemed to be. Last year on the Sunday before Lent, I presided at the Eucharistic table enveloped in a cloud of dense smoke that seemed unwilling or unable to disseminate. It would not go away, inviting the recollection of Isaiah 4:5:

Then will the LORD create
over the whole site of Mount Zion
and over her place of assembly
A smoking cloud by day
and a light of flaming fire by night.

We had undertaken a ceremonial making of ashes. The choir and ministers processed in and encircled the sanctuary space where the huge vat was filled with the palms that the throng of parishioners had brought from home.

In the pastor's absence, I had been asked to introduce what was happening after the hymn and greeting. Then the parish director of religious education torched the palms. Those dry branches went up in a spectacular blaze. The cantor led us in Psalm 51, and over the smoldering smudge pot I prayed the blessing appointed for Ash Wednesday's ashes. We went to our places and continued with the opening prayer for the day.

We considered ourselves ready to sing the final Gloria before Lent and to enter that holy season come Wednesday. Last year's palms were gone in a blaze, the ashes waiting. The DRE was satisfied that the teachable had been taught while the church was at prayer: some sort of new-age *lex orandi lex credendi* had been employed in service of developing sensibility.

The South Bronx and Harlem have the highest incidence of asthma in the nation. The atmosphere we created in the church that day was certainly not helpful to anyone who suffered from respiratory ailments. Had the church's interior paint not already been dingy, flaking gray, we would no doubt have seen evidence on the walls of what was happening to our lungs.

Rituals grow up to meet perceived need. Sometimes the need may be that of a DRE who wants to connect life to liturgy but does not recognize an immediate path. A ritual is then invented, a path blazed. Some such inventions work wonderfully; others don't.

Preparations for Ash Wednesday may be viewed as teachable moments for which there is no formal ritual. Most alert students believe that the Ash Wednesday ashes are the residue of last year's palms. Most pastors know that the cup of ashes they burned and pushed through a sieve in the early years of Ronald Reagan's first term may well last through the first decade of the next millennium.

What about an annual ritual burning of palms to provide fresh ash? Some say "No!" pointing for support to the fact that there is no official ritual for the making of bread or wine. On the other hand, the people of God who bake the Eucharistic bread in their homes, convents or rectories surely can and do pray and meditate over their holy tasks. The same is no doubt true for those who set the fermentation process in motion for the wine. This prayer would seem to be in the tradition of icon painters who fast and pray before and during their lovingly undertaken labors.

Our fire was something of a symbolic problem. I attempted to use it to point to the fire at Easter's Great Vigil but our pre-lenten blaze was really very different from the Vigil fire. Ours did not serve symbolically as purification from our sinfulness or as the refiner's fire, nor did it stand as the symbol of light conquering darkness or of Christ as the light of the world. It only served functionally to reduce palm to ash.

If those involved consider it important to prepare ashes with ritual activity, perhaps we might consider another model. In the Bronx, we might employ our same pot and have it burning on the porch of the church attended by high schoolers preparing for confirmation and supervised by adults. Worshipers can be alerted to bring their palms and, as they enter the church on that Sunday before Lent, either toss their palms into the fire or hand them to a student who assists.

Perhaps the ritual could be repeated for several weeks, or with certain classes or groups, to get people ready for the impending season.

Some ritual inventions that have worked, and some that haven't, become parish institutions and seem to assume the force of law after a few years. Ritual does not need tinkering or new inventions. Instead the key is proper implementation. All ideas will not be suitable. The ritual of the Church is already complete.

"Up in Smoke: Preparation for Ash Wednesday" originally appeared in MODERN LITURGY magazine (Resource Publications, Inc.).

Ash Wednesday Environment Overview

Liturgy Plus *Planning Software*

Ash Wednesday marks the beginning of the church's annual celebration of Life & Death. It is a celebration of that which is mystical *and* practical, profound *and* simple, elaborate *and* stark, glorious *and* humble. What is evident is that we are asked to consider all of the "ands" that we live with, like it *and* not, as we muddle through life.

It is easier to reflect on life in terms of "yes or no," "right or wrong," "spiritual or secular," "rich or poor," etc. And yet, as a faith community, we have been called to believe in the fundamental mystery revealed in the life *and* death of Jesus. The "and" reveals to us that life is not a series of polarities of this or that, but rather that life itself is a beautifully woven fabric, filled with innumerable "ands."

We need to reflect in our liturgical environments the ambiguities of our lives, of our world, and of our faith itself.

This means that Lent cannot be only a recalling of the *death* of Christ, with Easter the celebration of *life*. In fact, Lent recalls the essence of the mystery, in which death and life are woven together.

Art is often judged by "polarities." The decor for the environment may be viewed as "dramatic or subtle," "bright or dark," "ornamental or practical," "good or bad," "right or wrong," even "feminine or masculine!" As ministers of the environment, we need to remember that many people will not be able to readily understand how creative energy expresses itself as both: "dramatic and subtle," "harsh and soft," "bright and dark," "ornamental and practical," "masculine and feminine," and of course "cost-efficient and costly."

Our task is to express through our lives the fulfillment, peace, and prayer that we experience, through acceptance of the multitude of contradictions that make up life.

There is wonderful theology written in regard to the Liturgy and Environment. However do not neglect your intuitive sense and common sense. We need to consider theology, current events, the Universal Church, the Local Church, our community, and finally our own experience.

If your parish has a lot of retired persons and your church is Baroque, a 16-foot rough-cut pine cross may not help your parishioners to pray. It might instead serve as a "seasonal distraction." This is not to say that if a 16-foot cross is fundamentally significant that it should be ignored. However, we can choose to exercise the same patient-acceptance that our God exercises with us. You might need to begin with a smaller cross this year, gently providing a means for people to develop an understanding of what you already appreciate. With patience, we find ourselves able to minister more effectively.

"Ash Wednesday Environment Overview" originally appeared in Liturgy Plus *Planning Software (Resource Publications, Inc.).*

Ash Wednesday Liturgy

Stephen R. Kuder, SJ

Editors Note: The content presented in this liturgy would appear dated if presented exactly as written here. It is important for the liturgist to add new content as needed and to make the liturgy relevant to the local parish.

I. Liturgy of the Word

The room is without furniture save two benches, one for the Chorus and one for the celebrant and deacon (which stands behind a low table to the left of the fireplace containing a barely smoldering fire). The room is dark except for three circles of light: the Chorus alcove, the instrumental group, and the table. The deacon, in alb with black stole, and the celebrant, in black cope, enter and seat themselves on their bench; the Chorus consists of four people.

> **Chorus … entrance:**
> Here let us stand close by the ashes.
>   Here let us wait.
> Are we drawn by death? Or is it the
>   knowledge of life-from-death that
>   draws our feet
> Towards the coals? What death can come
> For us, men and women of _____
>   What dying
> With which we are not already familiar?
>   There are many deaths
> For us, and there is a little warmth from
>   the fire. Some premonition of an act
> Which our eyes are compelled to witness,
>   has called our feet
> Towards this room and table. We are

here to remember and bear witness;
To share a meal and begin anew.

Deacon … theme:
It has been a year since the Ash Wednesday
Peace-Liturgy on Golden Gate Bridge,[1]
A year since Joe Wall wore this same
  black cope.
In the meantime we have struggled
  through another winter.
The rains have quenched our fires,
left us cold and waiting amid the ashes.
It has been a season of vague discontent.
We have glimpsed the face of death in a
  hundred windows and mirrors;
Branches stripped from dead eucalyptus
  trees; bombs raining on home and hospital;
Floods, earthquakes, and fire; political
  greed and terrorism;
Through it all the Church's silence,
Our own smoldering hopes and loves.
The fire we kindled once in good faith
Dies down as winter drags on.
We look to its ashes for hope
And listen for God's Word:
"Turn to me and you will be rekindled."

Celebrant … collect:
Let us pray for hope in the face of death.

(Pause for 30 seconds)

Lord, we spend our days amid decay,
We taste the ashes of death in our
  mouths,
Give us the hope and the faith to turn
  to you
For the life that is without end.
This we ask of you, Father,

In the name of your Son Jesus,
Our Brother and Lord,
Who lives and reigns with you
And the Holy Spirit, one God,
Forever and ever.

People:
Amen.

Deacon … introduction to the first reading:
How do we taste death here before
   the hearth?
How do we encounter the defeat
Which threatens us as we wait
Like a smoldering fire?
Hear the voice of the Psalmist:

Chorus … first reading:
Psalm 102:1–11

Deacon … rite of ashes
To signify our participation in the
   mystery of death yielding to life,
Take the ashes from this hearth and sign
   the person next to you,
Then touch some ashes to your own
   tongue for a taste of death's certainty.

*(The deacon takes cold ashes from the fire and puts
them in several dark ceramic chalices. He then
hands one of the cups to the celebrant, who marks
the deacon's forehead with ashes in the sign of a
cross, saying loudly: "Remember, Man (Woman),
that you are dust and into dust you will return."
He then touches some ashes to his own tongue.
The deacon takes the cup and does the same to the
celebrant. The Chorus members come forward and
take the remaining cups to the various parts of the
room. Each member of the congregation receives
ashes on his forehead and tongue, then passes on
the rite. Throughout this period there is flute music
in a minor key.)*

**Deacon & Chorus … dialogue on death
and ashes:**

Deacon:
We are signed with ashes and
   taste them in our mouths.
We must stand and wait,
   meditating on the ash heap
   of our days and ways.
What of our lives is in ashes
   at the beginning of this
   lenten season?
Where has the fire of life
   been stamped out in us?

Chorus 1:
I taste the ashes of patriotism,

the dead and maimed in
   Southeast Asia.

Chorus 2:
I taste the living dead in
   Bangladesh and Pakistan.

Chorus 3:
I taste the defeat of so many
   peace lovers and political
   hopes.

Chorus 4:
I taste the ashes of my
   righteous causes, the
   private crusades that
   seemed so important at
   the time.

Chorus 1:
I taste the death of family and
   friends, of Joe Wall
   especially.

Chorus 2:
I taste the imprisonment of
   Carmichael Peters.[2]

Chorus 1–6:
I taste the ashes of my whole
   life: its futility, its
   failures, its weaknesses.

(Pause for 10 seconds.)

Chorus 3:
Sometimes I taste even the
   ashes of prayer, the
   religious life, priesthood.

Deacon:
How can we move beyond
   ashes and death
Beyond the poison or urban
   despair
Beyond the paralysis of
   suburban joy
Beyond the impotency of
   liberal outrage?
How can we rise like a phoenix from these
ashes?

Chorus 2 … second reading:
Joel 2:12–17

Celebrant … third reading:
Matthew 6:1–18

*(At verse 9 the Deacon and Chorus interrupt the
reading and lead the congregation in recitation of
the Lord's Prayer; the celebrant resumes at
verse 14.)*

Deacon & Chorus … service of repentance:

Deacon:
The Lord our God has spoken
　　to us:
"Turn to me now with all
　　your heart,
with fasting, with weeping,
　　and with mourning;
rend your hearts, not your
　　garments."

To each of the following prayers all respond:

We turn to you now, Father,
　　and ask forgiveness.

Chorus 1:
Father, we have gazed on
　　life and beauty, and on all
　　that you have made,
But we have refused to see you
　　working among us, and
　　refused to give you praise
　　for all that you have given us.

Congregation:
We turn to you now, Father,
　　and ask forgiveness.

Chorus 2:
You call us to greatness, and we
　　choose mediocrity;
You place your trust in us,
　　and we mistrust each other,
　　ourselves, and you.

Congregation:
We turn to you …

Chorus 3:
You bid us spread peace,
　　and our actions divide;
You call us to build up, and
　　our efforts tear down.

Congregation:
We turn to you …

Chorus 4:
You bid us spread your
　　message of life, and we
　　stockpile weapons of destruction;
You give us cause to hope
　　in man, and we blind our
　　eyes with despair.

Congregation:
We turn to you …

Deacon:
Father of mercy, and Father
　　of love,
Look on us with kindness now
As we turn our gaze to you.
We have taken upon us this
　　sign of repentance,
Proclaiming as we do that
　　we are nothing
If we are not yours.
Ashes we were, and ashes we
　　will be;
But you, our God, are God
　　forever and ever.

Congregation:
Amen.

Deacon … rite of cleansing and peace:

(*Two large bowls of water are brought in and placed on the table.*)

As a sign of our change of heart
And the cheerfulness of our Lenten fast.
Let us prepare for the Eucharist by
　　cleansing ourselves of these ashes.
Wash the forehead of the person next
　　to you
With the towels which will be handed
　　around.
Then let us greet each other with the
　　greeting of peace.

(*The celebrant takes a towel, dampens it in one of the bowls of water, and washes the ashes from the forehead of the deacon. The deacon then does the same to the celebrant. They then give each other an embrace of Christian peace. The Chorus members take towels and pass on the cleansing rite. As this is taking place, the celebrant and deacon go to the table and begin washing, rinsing, and drying the chalices which have held the ashes. Meanwhile, the chorus members are rekindling the fire and lighting two candelabra on the mantle above the fireplace. The deacon and celebrant then exit to vest themselves in white albs and purple stoles. The congregation sings Psalm 51.[3] The Chorus members spread a purple cloth over the table, and then bring forth a large loaf of black Russian-rye bread, the newly cleansed chalices, and a large carafe of wine. The deacon and celebrant re-enter as the congregation begins the last Verse of the psalm: "Now I am clean, I will go up.")*

II. Liturgy of the Eucharist

Celebrant … prayer over the gifts:

(The celebrant prepares the gifts in silence by filling the chalices with wine. He then prays:)

O Almighty Father,
You have cleansed us
of ashes and despair.
You have promised us life;
Now let us share this life-giving meal
As a sign of our community moving
    beyond death to life.
We ask this through Christ,
    your Son our Lord.

Congregation:
Amen.

Celebrant … preface:
And now may the Lord be with you.

Congregation:
And also with you.

Celebrant:
Lift up your hearts.

Congregation:
We lift them up to the Lord.

Celebrant:
Let us give thanks to the Lord
    our God.

Congregation:
It is right to give him
    thanks and praise.

Celebrant:
We thank you, Almighty Father,
    and we give you praise because
    you are Lord of our deserts
    and our ashes.
You loved us and sent your Son
    to turn our deserts to gardens,
    our ashes to his new fire.
He has given us Life and taught us
    to hope, because he has shown
    that you are our Father, and so
    we give you thanks and join your
    whole creation in a hymn of
    praise singing:

Congregation: Holy, Holy, Holy Lord, God of
    power and might …[4]

Celebrant … Eucharistic prayer:

We thank you Almighty God,
    because your works among men
have from the very beginning
    given us the promise of death
    from life.
As Father, you have not neglected our
    plight nor left us to die by the wages
    of our sin. You have not given us
    ashes to eat like bread nor tears to
    mingle with our wine.
Despite our sins, you have called us
    from slavery to a promised land,
    from exile to a New Jerusalem,
    from Law to freedom.
Finally, though we set our hearts
    against you by sin and idolatry and
    despair, you did not turn away
    your face but promised us a Messiah.
And so you sent your only Son to share
    all our sorrows of desert and ashes
    and death. He centered our hopes
    by his works and words among us.
And then on the night before he died
    he called his friends together a final
    time. He took bread and wine,
    blessed and broke it, saying:
This is my Body, broken for you,
and my Blood, shed for you and
    all so that sins may be
    forgiven.
Whenever you do this, you will do
    it in memory of me.
And now, Lord, we remember
    and celebrate how Jesus
    conquered death by his own
    passion and dying and how he
    gave us life by his resurrection
    and gift of the Spirit, the
    promise of the glory which
    awaits us.
Let us proclaim the mystery
    of our faith:

Congregation:
Dying you destroyed
    our death,
    Rising you restored our life,
    Lord Jesus, come in glory!

Celebrant:
Send your Holy Spirit, Lord, to
    breathe upon our gifts and meal
    which we share in your sight.
May we share this living bread and this
    living cup as people unified with the
    one Church of Christ, hoping in your
    covenant, in the Spirit's new fire of
    love, and in the brand new creation
    of Christ Jesus our Lord.

Through him, with him, in him, in the
    unity of the Holy Spirit, all glory
    and honor is yours, Almighty
    Father, forever and ever.

Congregation:
Amen!

Deacon:
This bread which we break is the
    new manna in the desert.
Though death stalk us like a Lion or
    despair like a wolf, still this bread of
    life will be ours to bless, break,
    and share.
Let us now pray to the Father:
    Give us this day our daily bread.

Congregation:
Give us this day …

Chorus:
When we are led into the desert, and
    our spirits wither like grass …

Congregation:
Give us this day …

Chorus I:
When the fire of love dies
    down in us, and ashes
    threaten to choke our
    souls…

Congregation:
Give us this day . …

Chorus I:
When we forget your promise,
    Lord, and our hope
    vanishes like smoke …

Congregation:
Give us this day …

Chorus 3:
When we are tempted to turn
    our faces and look away
    from our brothers in need …

Congregation:
Give us this day …

Chorus 4:
When we taste the ashes of
    sorrow and forget the
    bread of life …

Congregation:
Give us this day …

Chorus 1–4:
When we drift from this

table of fellowship,
    and starve in the desert of
    selfishness…

Congregation:
Give us this day …

Celebrant … communion rite:
Take now, and receive this meal
Given to us by Jesus for the
    forgiveness of sins.
Happy are those who are called to
    this supper.

Congregation:
Lord, I am not worthy to receive you,
but only say the word and I shall be
    healed.

*(Celebrant and deacon receive the Eucharist and
pass baskets and chalices to the congregation. A
duet sings Psalm 121 as a meditation hymn during
communion.[5])*

Deacon … concluding prayer:
Let us pray for new life and hope.

(Pause for 30 seconds.)

Blessed are you, Father, that you
    have given us
A share in the body of your Son,
In his life and his death,
And in the victory which he has won.
Fill us once more with new life and
    hope during this Lenten season.
We ask this in the name of Jesus
    Christ,
Your Son and our Brother,
For by the power of his name
You have lifted us from the ashes
    of death
And called us to new life in Him.
In his name we give you praise,
Forever and ever.

Congregation:
Amen.

Celebrant: … blessing:
May God bless you and keep you.

Congregation:
Amen!

Celebrant:
May God let his face shine on you and
    be gracious to you.

Congregation:
Amen!

Celebrant:

May God uncover his face to you and
   bring you peace.

Congregation:

Amen!

Celebrant:

May almighty God bless you, the
   Father, and the Son, and the
   Holy Spirit.

Congregation:

Amen!

Deacon … dismissal:

Go with God; enkindle the world
   with your hope.

Congregation:

Thanks be to God.

*(A very brief minor key flute arrangement, ending
with a rising note of hope, is played as the deacon
and celebrant retire.)*

Ash Wednesday Editorial Notes

1. This thematic statement includes a number of references quite specific to the congregation. A special ecumenical Liturgy of Peace had been held on the Golden Gate Bridge, Ash Wednesday 1972; Fr. Joseph B. Wall, SJ, had presided. Several months later, Father Wall, who was especially beloved of the members of the Berkeley Jesuit community, died suddenly.

   The 1972–73 winter in the San Francisco Bay Area had been especially harsh, with unusually heavy and prolonged periods of rain and extraordinary frosts; the former provided a dreary setting for the academic year, while the latter caused the death of large numbers of eucalyptus trees. This particular type of tree is especially common in the area, and when dead presents a significant fire hazard; the situation was serious enough to draw attention of national news media and environmental agencies.

2. Carmichael Peters was a student at the Graduate Theological Union, and well known to the congregation. His imprisonment followed what friends considered an irregular and unjust trial for a crime for which he had been "framed."

3. "Psalm 51" as arranged by Paul Quinlan, *Hymnal for Young Christians* (Chicago: F.E.L. Church Publications, 1966), page 71.

4. "Holy, Holy, Holy" as arranged by Peter Scholtes, *Hymnal for Young Christians*, op. cit., page 110.

5. "Psalm 121" as arranged by Paul Quinlan, "This Life Goes On."

"Ash Wednesday Liturgy" originally appeared in Service, Resources for Pastoral Ministry, *© Copyright 1976, Paulist Press, New York, N.Y. Reprinted by Permission.*

A Service of Ashes

James Notebaart

Editors Note: For the sake of making this service more inclusive you might elect to have both men and women repeat the sections which are, in this format, specified for one gender or another. Of course it could be meaningful as written. However, by both genders repeating the parts of Adam and Eve it would help us to understand the responsibility all humans bear for the destructiveness of our sin.

The purpose of this service is to experience the rite of ashes more powerfully. It is also the belief of this author that a rite of ashes is more appropriate on Ash Wednesday than the eucharistic celebration. The rite includes the burning of palms, lists of one's sins, etc., so that the power of the image can instill in us what "return to dust" means. This service is more experiential than intellectual. Because of this, the author used some of the images of poet Nikos Kazantzakis.

Introductory Dialogue

Leader:
God created us in the image of himself; in the image of God he created us; male and female he created us. The man and woman heard the sound of Yahweh God walking in the garden in the cool of the day, and they hid from Yahweh God among the trees of the garden. But Yahweh called to the man. Where are you?

Men:
I heard the sound of you in the garden; I was afraid, so I hid.

Leader:
Have you been eating from the tree I forbade you to eat?

Men:
It was the woman you put with me; she gave me the fruit and I ate it.

Leader:
Then Yahweh God asked the woman, What is this you have done?

The woman replied:

Women:
The serpent tempted me and I ate.

Leader:
To the woman he said: I will multiply your pains in childbearing, you shall give birth to your children in pain. To the man he said: Accursed be the soil because of you. With suffering shall you get your food from it every day of your life. It shall yield you brambles and thistles, and you shall eat wild plants. With the sweat of your brow shall you eat your bread, until you return to the soil, as you were taken from it.

Men:
For dust you are and to dust you shall return.

Women:
For dust you are and to dust you shall return.

All:
For dust you are and to dust you shall return.

Song:
Psalm 51 or other typical selection

The Word of God

Reading 1:
(Choose one of the following.)
Joel 2:12–18; Exodus 20:1–21;
Deuteronomy 6:4–9; 2 Samuel 12:1–9,13;
Isaiah 53:1–12

Response:
(Choose one of the following.)
Psalm 13, 25, 31, 32, 90, 123, 139

Reading 2:
(Choose one of the following.)
2 Corinthians 5:20–6:2; Romans 3:22–26;
Romans 6:2b–13; 2 Corinthians 5:17–21;
Ephesians 4:1–3,17–32; Ephesians 5:1–14;
1 John 4:16–21

Gospel:
(Choose one of the following.)
Matthew 4:12–17; Matthew 5:1–12;
Matthew 5:13–16; Matthew 18:21–35;
Mark 12:28–34; Luke 15:1–10;
Luke 15:11–32; John 15:1–8; John 15:9–14.

(An examination of conscience follows. Symbols of sin are gathered, possibly including written texts of our sins.)

Confession

Leader:
We confess to you, our Creator, to one another, to the whole of creation and to the ancient ones that we have sinned through our own fault, in thought, word and deed, by what we have done and by what we have left undone.

All:
Jesus, remember me when you come into your kingdom.

Leader:
We have not loved you, God, with our whole heart, mind and strength. We have not loved our neighbors as ourselves. We have not forgiven others as we have been forgiven.

All:
Jesus, remember me when you come into your kingdom.

Leader:
We confess to you, Lord, all our past unfaithfulness: the pride and impatience of our lives, our misuse of others, our anger and frustrations, our envy at those more fortunate than ourselves.

All:
Jesus, remember me when you come into your kingdom.

Leader:
For all false judgments, for uncharitable thoughts toward our neighbors, and for prejudice and contempt toward others. For our negligence in prayer and our failure to live the faith that has been given to us.

All:
Jesus, remember me when you come into your kingdom.

All:
We commit ourselves to God. Let us be like rays of light, like a great tree mighty in its roots, mighty in its top that reaches the sky, where the leaves catch the light and sing with the wind the song of the circle. Let our lives be like the rainbow whose colors teach us unity. Let us follow the great circle, the roundness of power, and be at one with the moon and the sun and the circling ripples of the water. For all my relations.

Kindling of the Fire

Leader:
The matter gathered here is a sign to us of the frailty of all matter. For from matter, stuff, earthen dust are we born. From things of darkness and no life at all, from things of pain and sadness, we make our lives. It is the stuff of matter that we impress with our image. We form; we make; we use to our own purposes, the earth from which we came. We are creatures here only for a while. We are transformers, here only for a while. We are part of the purity and part of the death of our planet, of our lives, of others' lives. In the beginning there was not darkness, there was not coldness, there was fire. In the beginning there was chaos. It was out of the womb of darkness that light emerged, patiently, to eliminate the dark frailness of our lives. Flames which flood the room, transform, purify, return everything to dust to make again freedom and life from ashes. And in the ashes a new humanity is begotten. Today, the word of God prolongs our birth, gives us new life. For dust we are and to dust we shall return.

(The gathered symbols of sin are now burned. Appropriate chant asking for mercy is sung, e.g., Taizé style music, American Indian penitential music, Gregorian chant, etc. The idea is to provide a mantraic text to focus the assembly on the need for mercy as the fire reduces all to ashes.)

Blessing of the Ashes

Leader:
(A sung presider's text may be used acclaiming our identification with the ashes.)
Blessed are you, our eternal God, for the fire which purifies. Blessed are you for the reminders of our frailty. Blessed are you for telling us now what we are to become. Blessed are you in the ashes of our lives, for we return to you with all our hearts. We will take upon us now this sign of our repentance, proclaiming as we do that we are nothing if we are not yours. Ashes we were and ashes we will be: But you, our God, are God forever.

All:
(may be sung response) Amen and amen and amen.

Leader:
May God our Father have mercy on us, forgive us our sins, and bring us to everlasting life.

All:
Amen.

Leader:
And may the God of mercy and the God of love grant pardon and freedom from all our sins.

All:
Amen.

Leader:
Marked with these ashes, under the sign of death and a new mercy, let us pray to our God. During the distribution of ashes the prayer of the faithful will be said.

The people's response:
We ask forgiveness.

Distribution of Ashes

Receive the ashes of our sorrow, the pain we have caused. They are the rubble of good intentions gone wrong, ashes of war and intolerance, signs of our frailty and mortality. Let our sorrow mingle with these ashes that they might become new medicine for the world's survival. For we are dust and unto dust we shall return.

(The ashes are distributed by various members of the assembly. Bowls made of wood or some other humble material is used. Appropriate music is chosen.)

Ending Prayer

Leader:
May God stretch out his hand over the good and the bad, over the honorable and the dishonorable. How many times it is that Satan takes on the face of God. Our eyes are clay, dirt, and tears. How can they distinguish? Take a sponge, Lord, take a sponge and erase.

Our Father/Sign of Peace

Dismissal

You are invited to take each other's burdens home for this Lent in the form of ashes to bear each other's sorrows, for we have mingled together our sinfulness and failings. Let the ashes remind us that together we have sinned and together we are healed. Then at the Easter Vigil bring the ashes back to be cleaned in the new fire of Christ's resurrection. *(Leave in silence.)*

"A Service of Ashes" originally appeared in *MODERN LITURGY magazine (Resource Publications, Inc.).*

A Eucharistic Prayer for Ash Wednesday

Leo P. Dressel, SJ

Although this is not an approved Eucharistic prayer, it has many traditional qualities about it. The absence of the Eucharistic narration places the Eucharistic prayer in the model of the Didache which reflects the tradition of the immediate post-apostolic community. The question of the narration of the last supper may not be overlooked today although the Didache is a precedent. The prayer might be used most appropriately in non-Eucharistic prayer services on Ash Wednesday, although this may not be the author's intent.

> We thank you, Father, for you have shown us
> mercy.
> You are a kind God.
> You have overlooked our sins and spared us,
> for you are our loving Father,
> our faithful God.

Response:
Now is the acceptable time! Now is the day
of salvation!
You are a kind and merciful God.
We marvel at the riches of your kindness:
the warm light of sun and moon,
the cool shadows in the hills,
the peaceful soothing of the rain,
the mighty sea's magnificence.
We marvel at the lives you have given us,
and the lives which we in turn
have given to each other.

Response:
Now is the acceptable time!
Now is the day of salvation!

You are a kind and merciful God.
We marvel at your richest kindness:
the gracious gift of your son,
Jesus Christ,
a brother of compassion for each
of us.
Your mercy knows no limits
Your kindness has wiped out our offenses,
for you love all things you have made.
Our brother Jesus has conquered all
our sin and even our death,
creating a new heart and life
for us,
and bringing us again to your
presence as your children (sons
and daughters).

Response:
Now is the acceptable time!
Now is the day of salvation!
You are a kind and merciful God:
Jesus has walked among us,
touching us, healing us.
He has lifted our sins from our
weak shoulders.
He has restored life to our
weak hearts.
He has given us the only food
and drink
which satisfies the hunger of
weary despair
and quenches the thirst of
pained and painful cynicism.

Response:
Now is the acceptable time!
Now is the day of salvation!
We shout praise and thanks to our

merciful God,
   and we call to mind the saving
   actions of our brother Jesus:
      He has died so death itself has ceased.
      He is risen so life does indeed prevail.
      He will return so his glory will
      be ours forever.

Response:
Now is the acceptable time!
   Now is the day of salvation!
You are a kind and merciful God.
   We still thirst in need of your kindness.
   Send us your willing spirit to sustain us
      as ambassadors for Christ,
      as doers of his word.
   When we are hypocrites,
   humble us with new signs.
   When we wound each other,
   heal us with your love.
   When we despair, save us with your hope.

Response:
Now is the acceptable time!
   Now is the day of salvation!
You are a kind and merciful God.
   Bind us together so we can be
   signs of your mercy:
      hopeful people in the face of despair.
      loving people in the face of hatred,
      joyful people in the face of sadness,
      living people in this land of death.

Response:
Now is the acceptable time!
   Now is the day of salvation!
All things we ask and celebrate
through Jesus Christ,
   your great gift of mercy,
   with him and in him,
   in the unity of the Spirit,
   this day and all days.
Amen.

"A Eucharistic Prayer For Ash Wednesday" originally appeared in MODERN LITURGY magazine (Resource Publications, Inc.).

Part 2

Sundays of Lent

Lectionary Commentary for The 1st Sunday of Lent

Liturgy Plus *Planning Software*

Cycle A

Genesis 2:7–9; 3:1–7
Romans 5:12–19
Matthew 4:1–11

1st Reading

Read in context, the second reflection on creation concerns the implications of creation and the destiny of humanity. The issues are ones that involve humankind's faithful responses and effective coping. The focus is not on the origins of evil or death but on troubled, anxiety-ridden life. Chapters 2 and 3 of Genesis portray a drama in four scenes. The first scene (2:4b–17) describes the placement of the man in the garden. The second scene (2:18–25) tells of the formation of a "helper." The third scene (3:1–7) explains the disruption of the garden, and the final scene (3:8–24) speaks of judgment and expulsion. The texts for this Sunday, then, are found in the first and third scenes of our drama. In scene one, a creature is formed out of the clay of the ground who is totally dependent upon God. There is the planting of a garden as a good place for the creature and identification of the two trees as one of life and one of knowledge. Our Sunday text leaves out the concluding verses that are crucial to the whole drama of the second reflection on creation. Verses 15–17 state the reason for being in the garden and the conditions placed on the creature. First, there is a vocation for the human creature: to care for and tend the garden.

Second, there is a permit and a prohibition given to the human creature. Everything is permitted, except the eating from the tree of knowledge. In other words, there is freedom, but there is also a God-imposed limit on human freedom. Scene two tells of the creation of a "helpmate" for the man, and scene three (3:1–7) now moves quickly to a new agenda. As the scene opens, we are reminded of the prohibition from scene one. The serpent must not be confused with Satan or evil. The serpent is a figure used as a literary device to move the plot of the story along. The serpent is a player in the dramatic presentation and proposes some dangerous theological questions: "Did God really tell you not to eat of the tree of knowledge?" The prohibition or limits imposed in scene one are now scrutinized as optional. The question is, are the boundaries or limits set by God to be accepted and respected? Or, are they, in an age of great technological advancement, to be seen as a barrier to be overcome and gotten around? The language of fidelity is taken over by the language of analysis and calculation. God is now a barrier to be circumvented. As the drama plays out, the man and woman creatures see the tree as "good for food, pleasing to the eyes, and desirable for gaining wisdom." As each one consciously chooses to ignore the boundary, their eyes are opened, and the floodgates of anxiety, competition, envy, and sexual distinction are released.

In his commentary on Genesis, Walter Brueggemann relates that one of the agendas of this drama is how to live with the creation in

God's world on God's terms. Recognizing and honoring the boundaries lead to well-being. Rationalizing and circumventing those boundaries lead to anxiety.

2nd Reading

Romans can be very difficult, for Paul is presenting an argument to get the Romans to accept his interpretation of the effects of Jesus' death on the cross. What would be the purpose of Jesus' death if the act of salvation did not somehow change, alter, restore the balance of creation disrupted in the second and third chapters of Genesis? Paul uses that drama as the basis for a type of Rabbinical argument to get his point across. Unfortunately, if understood within the context of the full Hebrew scriptures, the second chapter of Genesis does not state that death is the result of the man and woman's action, for they continue to live after being sent out of the garden. Paul is thus merely using the Genesis story as an example, not as a proof text, for original sin or death as a punishment for disobedience. Death is a reality in human experience. But Jesus' death is unlike anything in human experience, for through his death humanity receives the gift of God's grace. Through the action of the first man and woman, humanity received only a continuing struggle to survive which ends in death. Paul speaks of an overflowing grace and gift of justice through the death of Jesus. Thus the death of Jesus restores the imbalance initiated in the action of the man and woman creatures by establishing once again the boundaries of God's justice.

Gospel Reading

Matthew's gospel, like Luke's, begins with an infancy narrative that establishes Jesus' origins and identity. Matthew then returns to, or starts to follow, Mark's basic narrative form. We have the Baptism scene, which Matthew expands to set the distinction between Jesus and John the Baptist, and then we have the temptation scene (which Mark gives only one verse to). Matthew's expansion of the temptation scene is meant to say more than that Jesus was tempted. If one were to ask about Matthew's community, about what they needed to hear and understand, not only about Jesus but also about their own Christian lifestyle, we might begin to understand Matthew's expansion of Jesus' temptation. Matthew's church is a Christian community struggling to maintain its Jewish roots and traditions. He needs to tell his community that they are struggling with many of the same things that Jesus struggled with.

Matthew does not intend his account of Jesus' temptation to be an historical account (compare Mark and Luke, and the lack of a temptation scene in John for proof of this statement). Rather, it is his way to teach his community about very important values, and to encourage them in living those values. The Roman world of the first century of the modern era offered many opportunities and gave many promises and hopes of glory. Who would not, especially if you happened to be of the lower classes, jump at the chance of being rich, powerful, and successful? In an eclectic world of many gods, who would not latch on to the god that would enable you to get want you wanted? Without diminishing the power of Matthew's narrative, this background can give a good insight into the impact of Matthew's narrative upon his community.

The interplay of Satan and Jesus is a marvelous dialogue of one-upmanship. First Satan quotes scripture and then challenges Jesus to accept his interpretation. Then Jesus counters with another quote and rejects Satan's interpretation. Interestingly, all Jesus' quotes come from Deuteronomy, which the Jewish community believed to be the very words of Moses. As will be seen in chapter 5, Matthew will again hint at Jesus' Mosaic connections. In the final supreme statement, Jesus quotes the commandment and silences Satan. Jesus, the Son of God, descendent of David and Abraham, stands victorious over the false interpretations and offers of Satanic power and success.

The first Sunday of Lent begins the final stages in the catechumenal initiation process. The rite of election of catechumens and the call to continuing conversion for the candidates can overwhelm and consume the focus of the liturgy. Thus the pastoral implications which the scriptures present for the first Sunday of Lent must take into account the tug and pull of the ritual celebrated within the liturgy. The first Sunday of Lent begins the period of purification and enlightenment. It is meant to be a time of intense spiritual preparation that is meant to enlighten the minds and hearts of the elect with a deeper knowledge of Christ the Savior (*Rite of Christian Initiation of Adults*, nos. 138–139).

I might be tempted, then, to choose one focus from the gospel, or Romans, or Genesis to proclaim. What I would be doing is limiting the power of the interplay between the three readings. I would be choosing black and white over the full glory of living color. Our tendency has been to moralize and capsulize the scriptures by focusing on sin and temptation with a pulpit-pounding kind of homily. This is not the intention of the scriptures. The second reflection on creation found in chapters 2 and 3 of Genesis was written at a time in Israel's history when there was a struggle going on in their religious circles. The establishment of the monarchy under David and Solomon brought great political, cultural, and social advances to a nomadic people. In contrast to the story of Exodus and the Mosaic tradition, the period of the monarchy played human freedom and advancement against the will and command of God. The story of Exodus, on the other hand, places emphasis on the community and the right ordering of the community through the commandments. The Exodus experience places complete dependence on God and the individual's "submission" to the will and purpose of the community. The monarchy, however, glorified the individual and sought to break through the barriers of community, so that the political, economic, and social good of the individual could be advanced. The problem encountered in Genesis is one of boundaries and limits and the tension between the individual and the community's desires and goals. In modern terms: is it me first, then the community? When science and technology promise unlimited potential to the human individual, what happens to the community? Life comes not from "autonomy" but from participation in the community and from sharing in the goals of the community. Thus we are molded into the image of the community, not the community molded into our image.

What Genesis and what Paul are ultimately hinting at is that the boundaries and limits of the community are non-negotiable! When the man and woman viewed or rationalized the limits as negotiable, death entered into human history. Here death is to be understood as more than physical death. Death comes through competition; success at all costs; inequality that must be covered in fear; power grabbing; and so forth — all the deaths that rob humanity of value, worth, and dignity, destroying community in the process. Freedom and justice are not found in exerting individuality over community. Freedom and justice are found in taking on the death of Jesus as lived within the Christian community. This is what the rite of election and the final stage of purification and enlightenment are all about. Initiation into the Christian community is not like joining another social club. Initiation is first into the life, death, and resurrection of Jesus Christ, a dying to self and being born into the person of Jesus.

This challenges those of us who consider ourselves already initiated, for we are called to continuing deeper conversion into the life of Jesus. Here the story of Matthew and Jesus' temptation might illuminate the rite of election and the challenge of continuing conversion. Matthew begins by saying that Jesus was led by "the Spirit" into the "desert" to be tempted. Could the "Spirit" be the "Ruah" of God that breathed life into the human creature in Genesis? Could the desert be the place of purification as Israel experienced it in their time of liberation from slavery? If this be true, then the rite of election and our continuing journey of Christian faith echoes once again the question of Genesis: "Did God really tell you…Not on bread alone are you to live but in every utterance that comes from the mouth of God…You shall do homage to the Lord your God; God alone shall you adore!"

Accepting the ways of the Christian community by taking on the death of Jesus presents tough, dangerous choices with hard and difficult decisions. Even for us who are already members, the continual evaluation and our deeper incorporation into the community's plan of life confronts us with the same dangerous choices and difficult decisions. The boundaries of our Christian community are non-negotiable. Live within them, and we will experience well-being. Circumvent them, and we will live in anxiety and fear.

Ultimately, the figure of Jesus (as Matthew shows us) illuminates our purification and conversion as we seek to be incorporated into his community of faith.

Cycle B

Genesis 9:8–15
1 Peter 3:18–22
Mark 1:12–15

In the season of Lent, the architects of the lectionary have assigned a series of readings for each cycle that presents the main elements of "salvation history" from its beginning until the promise of the New Covenant. This poses two new challenges. First, it may not be possible to draw any but an artificial link between the Old Testament selection and the Gospel; it is quite possible that the links may have been contrived or forced. Second, the notion of "salvation history" as a distinct set of divine interventions on behalf of Israel, making it unique in its historical and cultural setting, has now been modified significantly.

What is a preacher to do? At the very least, let us seek to respect the assigned texts in their cultural dimension. Pastoral applications will still be possible.

1st Reading

One tenuous link between the Noah story and the Gospel is that both Noah on the Ark and Jesus in the wilderness got along well with the animals, the wild beasts and the tame, just like Adam and Eve in paradise before their fall. This, however, does not seem a sufficient foundation for a homily. Another possible link is that both Noah (Gn 6:8) and Jesus (Mk 1:11) were exceptionally pleasing to God, outstanding among their peers. Perhaps more can be mined from the text.

These verses of the Noah story focus on God's covenant with Noah. In God's first speech to Noah, verses 9–11, God introduces the topic of the covenant and its content: the future stability of the cosmos. God promises that he will never again use a flood to thwart human efforts to increase and multiply and fill the earth.

In God's second speech, verses 12–16, God places a rainbow in the clouds as a sign confirming the covenant he has made with Noah and his descendants and the animals. There are many signs in the Bible, but most if not all remind human beings of God's presence. Here, most unusually, the rainbow is a sign seen by human beings but reminding God of God's own promises!

Recall that Mediterranean peasants had no control over nature but rather yielded submissively to it and were subject to it. God, of course, has complete control over nature. So if a rainbow follows a storm, even a devastating flood, God must be saying something.

Babylonian mythology regarded the rainbow as the bow with which God shot his gleaming arrows (lightning) in anger against his creatures. That God hung it in the clouds meant that he would not use it this way again.

Scholars reject this interpretation of this biblical text. Instead, they take a cue from Ben Sirach 43:11–12: "Behold the rainbow! Then bless its Maker, / for majestic indeed is its splendor; / It spans the heavens with its glory, / this bow bent by the mighty hand of God." Even more directly does Ezekiel relate the rainbow to the Lord enthroned above his creatures: "Like

the bow which appears in the clouds on a rainy day was the splendor that surrounded him" (1:28).

A culture believing that it is at the whim and mercy of nature but that God has control over nature easily concludes that God can occasionally be whimsical and capricious. However, if God promised Noah he would never behave like that again and put a rainbow in the clouds to remind God of his promise, that is sufficient for the peasant.

Another noteworthy cultural aspect of the Noah story is the strong Mediterranean communal dimension that it reflects. Noah found favor with God, but his entire household was saved (his wife, his sons and their wives, and all their children even if not mentioned). In like manner, when Paul is miraculously freed from prison in Philippi, the frightened jailer decides to convert. Paul instructs him: "Believe in the Lord Jesus, and you will be saved, you and your household." Here is a stark cultural contrast with mainstream U.S. individualism.

2nd Reading

The second reading is addressed to "resident aliens" in Asia Minor, a class of people generally considered inferior to the full citizens and therefore acknowledged to have only limited legal and social rights. They could not vote or own land. They were also restricted in marriage opportunities, in inheriting property, and in commercial transactions with full citizens.

The resident aliens who converted from both Jewish and Gentile segments of that society found that Christianity provided them the social unity and acceptance that wider society did not. Besides, they were told that the God of Israel looked kindly on them. But Christian identity brought other hardships along with these benefits. Converts experienced an increase in social conflict with their neighbors.

In these verses assigned for today's liturgy, the author of 1 Peter seeks to explain to these innocently suffering resident aliens the reasons for their mistreatment and suffering.

To make his point, the author, drawing on Genesis 6–9, relies on the common, widespread, and strong Mediterranean belief in mischievous spirits who make life miserable for human beings. The "sons of the gods" (Gn 6:1–4) sowed evil among human beings at the beginning of time. Noah resisted these evil impulses. Christ, who also suffered innocently, preached to disobedient spirits and turned them back to obedience to

God. Jesus' victory over death through his resurrection is now available to all who submit to baptism. This awareness should fortify those who suffer innocently to bear their wrongs patiently, for in the end they will conquer.

The imagery is this: God once saved a faithful minority (Noah and his family) while he destroyed all else in a deluge. In Asia Minor he saves a believing minority through the deluge of its baptism. This baptism is no mere cleansing bath but rather fosters steadfast commitment to God's will.

Gospel Reading

Cultural specialists point out that the circum-Mediterranean region was characterized by a vivid belief in a spirit world. Mediterraneans believed that the air, the atmosphere, was densely populated with all kinds of capricious spirits, good and evil. These spirits are ever ready to interfere in human life because they seem to have nothing else to do. Consequently, Mediterranean natives took all kinds of precautions against these spirits.

The color blue is one powerful safeguard against evil spirits. Window frames and door jambs are routinely painted blue in the Middle East. Blue ribbons or other articles of clothing are worn for the same reason. Many people wear a blue amulet with an "eye" on it to foil any potential attacks from evil spirits.

This spirit-belief is one reason compliments are very carefully phrased before they are expressed. It is in fact better not to express a compliment at all. Remember Jesus' response to the man who addressed him as "Good Teacher" (Mk 10:17–18)? Jesus denied the compliment: "No one is good but God alone!" Besides being an acceptable expression of cultural humility, Jesus' denial is an attempt to confuse the spirits in the atmosphere who upon hearing this might decide to do something to test whether Jesus really is good or to cause him to fall from goodness.

This is precisely the point of the temptation of Jesus (Mk 1:12–13). Jesus has just been baptized by John in the Jordan (Mk 1:9–11). When he emerges from the water, the heavens open and a voice says: "You are my beloved Son; I am well pleased with you." Certainly the spirits hear this declaration from God. Now it would be necessary to see whether this really is God's Son. Is this Son dutifully obedient or not? Can he hold up under pressure? Satan pulls out all the stops. Because Mediterranean readers of the Gospel know and

assume this fact, Mark doesn't bother to spell out the details of Jesus' temptations.

In other words, to the Mediterranean mind, the temptation of Jesus is a natural and understandable sequel to God's declaration about his son. This combination of stories (baptism and temptation) also helps us understand Jesus' reaction to the compliment later in Mark 10.

Preachers and liturgy planners are encouraged to be respectful readers of Mark's text and to resist the "temptation" to introduce the three temptations reported by Matthew and Luke. Mark's sparse report offers the opportunity instead to consider the wilderness or desert. Like many other images in the Bible, it too is polyvalent.

The wilderness was where the fidelity of God's chosen people was tested but found wanting (Ps 78:17–18; 106:13–33). The wilderness was also where God made his covenant betrothal with his chosen people (Hos 1:14–15). Mark's readers would be familiar with such contrasting possibilities and would naturally applaud the report that Jesus passed the test!

After the Baptist is removed from the scene, Jesus, his erstwhile disciple, begins his own preaching ministry. Jesus' message has four elements:

1. "This is the time of fulfillment." Here, Jesus expresses something obvious to his listeners. Mediterranean culture recognizes two seasons in its climate: a rainy or wet season and a dry season. The tempo of life in the Mediterranean world is set by the rhythm of rainfall and prolonged sunshine. The rainy or wet season is the time for sitting home, a time for limited social interaction. The dry season allows wars to be fought and journeys to be made. According to the Synoptic Gospels, the period of Jesus lasted for a single dry season that ended with the close of the rainy season after the celebration of a Passover. The activity of Acts of the Apostles started right away for another dry season allowing travel and public interaction.

2. "The reign of God is at hand!" The Greek and its underlying Hebrew word is best translated as "reign" rather than "kingdom." Jesus was not talking about a place but, true to his Mediterranean culture, was eminently concerned about a person and relationships. "Reign" specifically means the "active ruling of

God." The teaching and healing activities of Jesus about to take place in the Gospel stories are signs of God's active ruling, his reign, his way of dealing with people.

3. "Reform your lives." "Repent" is a traditional exhortation among the prophets (Hos 6:1; Is 1:10–20; Jl 2:12–13). It suggests a change of heart, a broadening of perspectives, a transformation of horizons—all leading to a new way of life.

4. "Believe in the good news!" The change of life leads inevitably to belief. Faith, however, entails two things: obeying the word of God proclaimed by Jesus and accepting the role and life of discipleship.

Cycle C

Deuteronomy 26:4–10
Romans 10:8–13
Luke 4:1–13

Every garden requires preparation before planting. The soil may need to be turned over, rocks cleared, weeds removed, and compost added. Without this work the garden may fail to produce a good harvest.

1st Reading

The book of Deuteronomy is a retelling of the Israelites' journey from slavery in Egypt to life in the promised land. Written several hundred years after the original events, the authors of Deuteronomy looked back on the beginning of the nation and the covenant. The reading is a description of the offering of the "first fruits," a ritual that dedicated a portion of the initial harvest to God. This feast was not original to Israel. The Canaanites also observed a harvest rite and offered tribute to the gods who granted them rain, the land, and the mysterious quality of fertility. Israel adapted this ritual to its own faith.

The content of our reading today is regarded by some scholars as a short creed that was part of the liturgy of the ancient sanctuary. The creed may come from a much earlier period than the book of Deuteronomy itself. A major theme is God's faithfulness in fulfilling promises. The people cry out in their distress and the cry is heard by God; God then acts decisively in history to save them. Salvation takes the form of a new home in a fertile land. God's faithfulness takes the form of liberation from oppression.

Through the offering of the first fruits, each Israelite claimed ownership of the story. Each became the wandering nomad, the oppressed slave, and the blessed recipient of the land. The first reading of Lent does not proclaim doom and gloom. It invites us to reflect on what we have received and to rejoice.

2nd Reading

Like the reading from Deuteronomy, the verses from Romans also present in condensed form the essence of Christian faith, "Jesus is Lord." The reading is taken from a section of the letter in which Paul contrasts the way of law and the way of faith. This is central to Paul's theology. Paul wants to convince the Romans that with Christ a new age has arrived. Formerly the "word is near you, on your lips" (v 8) applied to the Law; it is a passage encouraging obedience from Deuteronomy 30:11–14. Now the "word" is not the Law, but Christ. Faith in Christ and in his resurrection is the way to attain right relationship with God (justification) and ultimately eternal reward (salvation).

In verse 11 Paul quotes from another passage, Isaiah 28:16. In Isaiah, God establishes a cornerstone for Zion; the one who trusts in God will not be disappointed. Through this quote from Isaiah, Paul alludes to the new cornerstone, Jesus the Lord, in whom all are called to place their trust.

The Law was something that divided Jew and Gentile; Paul maintains this division has ended. The way to God is faith in Christ. The final quote is from Joel 3:32 and it applies to the final days: "'Everyone who calls on the name of the Lord shall be saved'" (Rom 10:13). The original message referred to the God of Israel; here Paul applies the meaning of "Lord" to Christ. The resurrection of Jesus begins a new age of universal grace.

Gospel Reading

In all three synoptic Gospels, the temptation of Jesus by the devil follows the baptism and God's declaration that Jesus is the beloved Son. Thus the temptations present a challenge to God's declaration, to Jesus' understanding of himself, and it sets the direction his ministry will take.

There are many interpretations to the meaning of the three temptations. The first temptation (vv 3–4) is a suggestion by the devil to turn the stones into bread. Presumably Jesus was hungry after his desert stay. Yet the bread may symbolize more — the desire for bodily comfort, material security, vanity, wealth or luxury. Jesus reveals his priorities in his response.

The second temptation (vv 5–7) may be to misuse the power he now can claim. Might it be a temptation to control people, to establish the Kingdom of God through power rather than suffering, to break the first commandment, the commandment to worship God alone? Jesus' response is to set God before anyone or anything else.

The third temptation (vv 9–11) may be that Jesus ask God for a special sign. Jesus has learned that he is the Son. Does he trust what that means? Will he still trust God when faced with suffering and death? This temptation prepares him for the isolation of the cross.

The tempter will return again in Luke's Gospel (v 13). Evil returns to infect the heart of Judas (22:3), and at the cross, various people challenge Jesus to prove his messiahship (23:34–39). While the temptations are overcome in the beginning of the Gospel, we know that at another time and place they will surface again. Like Jesus, Christians learn that the struggle to remain faithful is not a one-time decision but an ongoing commitment.

Before beginning his ministry, Jesus withdrew to the desert, where he was vulnerable. Jesus took time to prepare himself for the task that lay ahead. We, too, can take time to prepare for the tasks that lie ahead of us, no matter what they are. Jesus struggled to remain faithful to God and through the power of the Spirit he emerged victorious. Jesus trusted in God's power to provide for him. That same power will provide for us. We are invited to trust in his victory.

"Lectionary Commentary for the 1st Sunday of Lent" originally appeared in Liturgy Plus *Planning Software (Cycles ABC) (Resource Publications, Inc.).*

Lectionary Commentary For The 2nd Sunday of Lent

Liturgy Plus *Planning Software*

Cycle A

Genesis 12:1–4a
2 Timothy 1:8b–10
Matthew 17:1–9

1st Reading

The first eleven chapters of Genesis tell the drama of the universe's origins to the establishment of the human community. These stories are not meant to be understood as literal fact, but, like a dramatic presentation that is colored and shaped by a deeper level of meaning, they go beyond literal historical fact.

With the story of Abraham and Sarah, however, we move from a narrative that shapes history to a narrative shaped by history. The stories of the patriarchs are stories that proclaim family history and tradition. They are also stories revealing the saga of a people who struggle and persevere through history.

Abraham bursts upon the scene in unequivocal terms as one chosen, called, and set apart from all other peoples. In straightforward, simple words, God says to Abram, "Go forth...to a land I will show you." Nothing prepares us for this momentous occasion except the certainty that God's voice as heard in the act of creation carries power and a promise of obedience (as seen from last week's Genesis reading). We are told very simply that Abram goes as God has directed. Abram's response is quick and trustworthy.

The verses in the middle of this narrative speak more to the people of the time in which this narrative is put together. In Solomon's day, the court writer (Yahwist writer) needs to confirm and legitimize Solomon's expansionist claims. Through Abraham, all succeeding generations receive the blessings of God. Through Abraham all the "nations" shall receive blessings, but only if they are incorporated into the "family of Abraham."

The contrast is theological rather than historical. What is contrasted is the family story and the greater saga of Israel the nation. Like a finely woven tapestry, Solomon's court writer claims as his own Abraham's story. The writer applies the blessing given to one family (Abraham's) to the whole nation. "All the communities or peoples of the earth shall find blessing in you." Thus Solomon's expansionist designs are given legitimacy.

Promise and blessing are characteristic of the narratives drawn together by Solomon's writer. The narratives reach far back into family/tribal memory. They are, however, molded and shaped for a new purpose with a new meaning given to them. Abraham responds to the directive of God and receives blessings in return. So too the nation/people of Israel are to respond to God's call, and they will receive blessings in abundance.

2nd Reading

In chapter 4 of 2 Timothy, the writer exhorts Timothy to preach the word whether it be convenient or inconvenient (4:2), for a time will come when they (the community) will not endure sound doctrine but will go after those who tickle their ears with fancy teachings (4:3). The whole of 2 Timothy carries the force of exhortation and diligence in proclaiming the gospel. The reason for this focus was the need of the community to locate itself within the tradition of the larger church community. As each generation found itself one step further from its historical origins, it found that it had to be diligent, had to persevere in its traditions and teachings, or lose contact with its roots.

Written some 30 years after Paul's own martyrdom in Rome, 2 Timothy is a letter written with all the authoritative force of Paul's spiritual leadership. But the time and case of its writing raised new questions that needed different answers. The question becomes, how can the second and third generation be sure that its faith is in continuity with the apostolic witness of the first generation? This question is especially pertinent when all those original apostolic witness have died. Who can the community turn to for assurance and guidance under those circumstances?

The answer to the first question is found in verse 13 of chapter 1. Assurance and guidance come from holding fast to the gospel as it has been handed on (by Paul himself) through the laying on of hands (1:6). The question of continuity, then, is answered by the continuing teaching and preaching of the community's leaders, Timothy being one of those leaders. The second question is answered by the first. Continuity with tradition is exemplified in the leaders and the scriptures which are held to be inspired by God. The leaders and the scriptures are the spiritual and moral guides for the community.

In the passage chosen for this Sunday, the writer builds upon the prayer of thanksgiving (1:3–5). Because of his deep-rooted faith, Timothy is instructed to preach the gospel fearlessly with a "spirit of power and love and self-control" (1:7). Timothy is to follow the example of Paul (who boldly proclaimed the gospel) and ultimately the example of Jesus Christ, who gave his life for others. By reflecting upon the gift God has given through Jesus, Timothy will deepen his love and faith for Jesus, whose gospel he preaches. He and the community will be assured of guarding the truth that has been entrusted to it (1:14).

Gospel Reading

Starting with chapter 14, Matthew follows closely the Markan narrative, inserting little beyond his stories about Peter (14:28–31; 16:16–19; 17:24–27) and the discourse on church life in chapter 18. From chapter 14 on, Jesus begins the formal prophecies of his passion, death, and resurrection. For Matthew, the community is being prepared to carry on after Jesus' departure.

The context for the transfiguration scene begins with chapter 16:13–28. In the region of Caesarea Philippi, Jesus poses the question to his disciples, "Who do men say that the Son of Man is?"

Some respond that the Son of Man is John the Baptist, others say Elijah, others Jeremiah. Jesus then asks, "Who do you say I am?"

Peter responds, "You are the Christ, the Son of the living God."

This statement of Peter's is Matthew's solemn confessional formula of faith. Authority is then conferred upon Peter (16:17–20) and the disciples. This is followed by the first passion prediction in Matthew (16:21–23), and the example of discipleship (16:24–28). In a sense the narrative of the transfiguration, within Matthew, confirms Peter's confession of Jesus as Son of the living God and serves to anticipate the resurrection and parousia.

It also shows the connection between Jesus as the Son of God and the Son of Man. For Matthew, going up the mountain is a favorite symbolic place of revelation. On the mountain in chapter 5, the new law is revealed. On the mountain in chapter 15, the bread is blessed and broken and given (prefiguring the Eucharist).

In the transfiguration, revelation comes to the disciples as a foretaste of the vision of the Son of Man promised in 16:28. Moses and Elijah, both of whom received revelation from God on mountaintops (Sinai/Horeb), are speaking with Jesus. This is another symbol of the days of fulfillment. Jewish expectation was to look for the return of Elijah in the advent of the final days.

Peter proposes that they build three tents for the heavenly trio. But, while Peter is still speaking, the revelation reaches its climax, as a radiant cloud of God's presence descends upon and envelopes the scene. From the cloud, God's voice is heard (as it was heard at Jesus' baptism), "This is my beloved Son, with whom I am well pleased; listen to him." In response to this proclamation, the disciples fall to their faces in fear. Only in Matthew, however, does Jesus touch them and raise them up. The Son of the living God, who gives life to the dead, raises up the cowering disciples and delivers them from their fear.

The concluding statement places the whole scene as a true revelation (vision) of what is to come. However, even though the disciples have been initiated into the vision, others have not, and will not understand until Jesus has completed his own mission in death and resurrection (17:9).

The climb to the top of Mount Tabor leaves one breathless and sweaty. With one's heart pumping fast, anyone would see visions in the sky. The response of Peter to build three tents because it is good to be on mountaintops would sound more like a plea to stay put for a while. There are cool breezes and a great view up there. Besides, who wants to go back down the mountain knowing that the road leads to Jerusalem and death!

The transfiguration has been called a misplaced resurrection appearance. Such appearances, as found at the end of Matthew, Luke, and John, identify Jesus as the divine Son of God glorified through the resurrection. The voice from the heavens proclaims that Jesus is the beloved Son whose words must be heard and listened to. All the evidence is there for interpreting the Transfiguration as a resurrection appearance.

However, the breathless, sweaty walk up the mountain and the fear or anxiety about the journey to Jerusalem cannot be so easily dismissed. There is a struggle in this narrative between the recognition of the revelation and the reality of the journey ahead that leaves one with fear and anxiety.

I wonder how Abraham felt when confronted by the voice of God promising blessings in abundance. In the hot Negev desert, people could think they were just hearing things or the heat had gotten to them. I wonder if those words satisfied Abraham, who was still childless? Did the promise of many descendants take away the anxiety or emptiness of childlessness? Words and promises can comfort, but they do not necessarily take away the doubts and fears.

This is what 2 Timothy says. Believing in the gospel entails hardships. Even with the announcement that death has been robbed of its power, that life has come into clear light, does not diminish the hardships which the gospel entails. The picture here is a contrast between the revelation of glory and the hardships and anxieties that remain. Leaving father and mother and all that defines home, as Abraham had to, does not instill too much confidence, even in a nomadic tribe. The voice of God telling of blessings and descendants is a revelation of promise and hope. It does not take away the anxiety of being uprooted, but it does hold out a beacon of hope that can guide the journey to the new home.

Thus the transfiguration is a beacon, a beacon pointing to Jerusalem with full understanding of what is to take place there. It is also a beacon of hope in the face of the difficult road ahead. No one said the road was to be easy. It is a hot, sweaty, and at times breathless route that leads across deserts and up to mountaintops. The beacon of glory and the promise it holds guide the way.

Cycle B

Genesis 22:1–2,9a,10–13,15–18
Romans 8:31b–34
Mark 9:2–10

1st Reading

This story of another covenant that God strikes with a human being, Abraham, is certainly linked with today's Gospel by the common theme of a "beloved son." Here are two sons "obedient unto death."

Mainstream U.S. citizens who train their children from an early age toward autonomy, to stand on their own two feet, to work toward independence from the home setting, and who train them in self-defense as well as warn them against abuse, especially from relatives, find the sacrifice of Isaac a baffling tale. Why did the boy not flee for his life? Or why did not Jesus, who sensed the danger lurking in the garden, stir a diversion and escape? What kind of son, young or adult, submits meekly and obediently to such physical punishment?

Only a son reared with regular physical punishment, as is customary in Mediterranean culture, could be so docile. Read and ponder the advice for childrearing in Proverbs 13:24; 19:18; 22:15; 23:13–14; 29:15,17,19; and Sirach 30. Recall that heroes of this culture include the suffering servant (see Isaiah). Notice the New Testament echoes in 1 Corinthians 11:21–30 (Paul's boastful list of suffering) and Hebrews 12:3–11 (God treats us as Mediterranean fathers treat their sons).

Mainstream U.S. Bible readers are puzzled by the ending of today's reading from Genesis. Is God really pleased by this kind of obedience?

Keep in mind a basic principle of theology: everything we think and say about God is rooted in human experience (i.e., all theology is analogy). And human experience is conditioned by culture.

Contemporary U.S. parenting styles are significantly different from that recommended by Proverbs and Sirach. If Jesus had been a U.S. native, salvation might have taken a different shape. But in the end, contemporary believers of any culture can rest secure in the covenant made by God with our Mediterranean ancestors in the faith. As their spiritual descendants we are grateful for God's fidelity and for the redemption won by Jesus. Yet our task is to live in fidelity to God within our culture, facing its challenges, perhaps learning how to draw victory out of defeat, how to gain success from apparent failure once our values are appropriately clarified.

2nd Reading

These concluding verses of chapter 8 are a hymn-like celebration of the reality of the power or force of the risen Jesus present upon the earth. The word "spirit" is intensely concentrated in this chapter of Romans. It appears twenty-nine times! This spirit is a vital force in human life. Being subject to the Spirit results in becoming a true son (or daughter) of God. The indwelling Spirit makes it possible for a person to call God "Abba/Father" in a very real sense.

Recalling what was just said about Mediterranean parenting styles, especially as reflected in Proverbs and Sirach, note how matter-of-factly Paul states: "Is it possible that he who did not spare his own Son but handed him over for the sake of us all will not grant us all things besides?"

From this perspective we can see added reason scholars now recognize that the Aramaic word "Abba" does not mean "daddy." It is not a tender, loving title but a formal, aloof, and respectful title, "Father," as one might expect to be used toward a harsh disciplinarian.

Nevertheless, Paul's point, "If God is for us, who can be against us?" makes these verses a fitting bridge passage between the sacrifice of Isaac and the transfiguration of Jesus. God was surely on the side of Isaac and Jesus, two beloved sons.

Gospel Reading

The core values of Mediterranean culture are honor and shame. Honor is a public claim to worth and a public acknowledgment by others of this claim. If the acknowledgment is withheld or denied, the claim is worthless and the claimant is shamed.

Mediterranean culture recognizes at least two kinds of honor: acquired, which generally is inherited, and achieved, which usually derives from competition in honor-and-shame contests.

The heart of the Gospel transfiguration story is in verse 7. A voice out of the cloud (definitely the voice of God) says: "This is my Son, my beloved." This statement explicitly presents Jesus' acquired honor-status.

But preachers and liturgy planners are fully aware of the prevailing contemporary scholarly opinion that the transfiguration story is an authentic resurrection appearance of Jesus deliberately retrojected into his lifetime by the evangelist.

In Mark's story-line, Jesus' acquired honor-status is stated at the very outset (1:1) and again at his baptism (1:11): he is the Son of God. But as the story proceeds, few human beings acknowledge this status. Instead, many disbelieve the claim and refuse to grant him honor. Recall that Jesus is declared a blasphemer when he accepts this title (14:61). Only demons and unclean spirits (3:11; 5:7) and a pagan centurion (15:39) acknowledge this honor-claim.

To avoid conflict and quite in accord with the Mediterranean cultural penchant for secrecy and deception, Jesus tries to silence those who publicly proclaim this honor (sometimes called the messianic secret). If people don't know his true identity, they will be stymied in attempts to harm him.

When Jesus' life ends with an ignominious death on the cross, his enemies seem to have won. Son of God, indeed, they would scoff. God didn't come to help him in distress. But by raising Jesus from the dead, the Father validates Jesus' identity and bestows upon him honor far superior to any human accolade. Thus, just past the mid-point of Mark's Gospel, as Jesus is already on the way to meet his shameful death, the evangelist deliberately retrojects this post-resurrection awareness into the earthly life of Jesus as an assuagement for the difficult events that are still to come and as a "preview" of the final outcome. No matter how bad it looks, Jesus remains an honorable person whose ministry will have an honorable outcome.

Cycle C

Genesis 15:5–12,17–18
Philippians 3:17–4:1
Luke 9:28–36

The transfiguration is a glimpse of Jesus and a glimpse of ourselves. Jesus reveals, for an instant, what he is like. His appearance changes, and though it is confusing, the disciples know that they have witnessed a privileged event. The change Jesus reveals is the change we will experience. One day we will no longer be on the "outside" but will enter fully into the reign of God and ourselves be changed in appearance.

1st Reading

The storytelling tradition of Israel kept alive an ancestor named Abram or Abraham. Connected with this memory were stories of infertility and a nomadic lifestyle. How is it, later people wondered, that our great nation emerged from a wandering, childless shepherd? The answer, the faith answer, is given in the reading from Genesis.

Israel understands that it is God who transforms Abram from childless to "child-full." He will have more descendants than there are stars. Abram's most important contribution in the process is faith.

For the people who told the story of Abram, many hundreds of years later, the primary category of life was the Law. Abram's faith is interpreted according to the standards of Law. His trust in God is as important as an act of obedience to the covenant of Sinai (v 6).

Israel also knows that God gave them the land. The land is a gift from God. Because the history of them as a people begins with Abram, so too does their land story. God transforms Abram from land-less to landlord. The sign of this promise is an ancient ritual of covenant. The parties of ancient covenants evidently passed between the severed pieces of the animals to seal the pact and invoked upon themselves the same fate of those animals should the covenant be violated. It is God and not Abram who promises to keep the agreement. The burning coals and fire that move between the animals symbolize God's commitment (v 17). God will be faithful.

In this narrative, the land promised to Abram uses the boundaries marking the kingdom of David a thousand years later (v 18). In other words, David's kingdom, won by battle and alliance, is not David's accomplishment but a sign of God's continuing faithfulness to Israel. The biblical authors at the time of David knew that God transformed the puny tribes into a kingdom. They wrote down the story of their ancestor Abram to reflect this truth. God is committed to Abraham, to Israel, and to us.

2nd Reading

Paul writes to urge the Christian community to follow his example. Because he has aligned his life with Christ, he can boldly beseech the Philippians to imitate him (v 12). Part of this letter attempts to counterbalance the false teachings surrounding the community. Some people wanted Christians to be circumcised, according to the practice of Judaism (3:2). Just who the "enemies of the cross of Christ" are (v 18) is unclear. Paul condemns those with false values but he is not saying that creation or human beings are evil. What he is writing against is some unknown distortion within the community that reverses the priorities of Christian life.

Paul promises the Philippians that their true citizenship is found with God. Because Philippi was a Roman colony and subject to Roman law, it had a superior political status. Paul assures the community that they will have an even greater position in Christ. Further, their bodies will be transformed into the likeness of the risen Lord. All of this is assured if they, like Abram, stand firm in faith (4:1). Faith leads to transformation into glory.

Gospel

It is important to recall that in the three synoptic Gospels, Jesus' transfiguration is preceded by the prediction of his suffering and death. Jesus finishes teaching his disciples that they will have to take up their crosses and follow him (Lk 9:23–27) and then is transfigured. The low point is followed by the mountaintop. The disciples are shown what they can expect if they remain faithful. In the midst of Jesus' journey to Jerusalem and the cross, the disciples get a glimpse of future glory.

In this passage Jesus withdraws and goes to a mountain to pray and teaches by example that prayer is essential. While praying, Jesus is transformed before the disciples' eyes and filled with light. Elijah and Moses, two important leaders who also experienced the glory of God on mountains, are present. They represent the Law and prophets and they speak of Jesus' exodus. This exodus is Jesus' "passage" through death to new life. Jesus' destiny will follow an ancient pattern: suffering, exodus, and then freedom. Peter's offer to set up three shelters may be a reminder of the Jewish harvest feast of Succoth, a feast that also celebrates the exodus.

From a "cloud" (v 34), one sign of God's presence at the time of the exodus, a voice is heard. Just as at the baptism (3:22), Jesus is claimed with divine authority as the Son. This voice reaffirms Peter's confession (9:20). The voice tells the disciples to listen to Jesus. Finally, Moses and Elijah withdraw and Jesus, the one with greater authority than the prophets, remains. He is to be the focus of their attention.

Transformation requires faithfulness, even if the faithfulness leads to the cross. We can be sure that God is faithful. God did not abandon Abraham; God raised Jesus from the dead and will one day raise us. Do we have faith? If we "stand firm in the Lord" (Phil 4:1), we, who are called to share his suffering, will also share his glory. We will be changed in appearance.

"Lectionary Commentary for the 2nd Sunday of Lent" originally appeared in Liturgy Plus *Planning Software (Cycles ABC) (Resource Publications, Inc.).*

Lectionary Commentary For The 3rd Sunday of Lent

Liturgy Plus *Planning Software*

Cycle A

> Exodus 17:3–7
> Romans 5:1–2,5–8
> John 4:5–42

1st Reading

The story of the Exodus begins with the enslavement of the Israelites and their struggle for liberation from Pharaoh's control and domination. The Israelites cry out for release (2:23), and their cry is heard by God, who remembers the covenant with Israel's ancestors. God witnesses their affliction, is moved by their oppression and pain, and rescues them from the hands of the Egyptians.

As the story continues, Pharaoh's heart is hardened; this is followed by a series of plagues meant to bring Pharaoh's empire to its knees. The final blow comes with the death of Egypt's firstborn, and Pharaoh concedes defeat, giving release to the Israelites.

As the Israelites approach the sea, faced with possible destruction, the Israelites cry out in complaint. Out of their fear, they seem to desire slavery over death (14:12). But Moses proclaims that God will win for them a victory over Egypt! Moses says, "The Lord himself will fight for you." With tremendous power, God splits the sea in two, and the Israelites cross through unharmed.

One would think that this would calm the Israelites' fears and complaints. As Exodus continues, we see that they cry out not once (15:24), not twice (16:3), but three times (17:3–7). There is great contrast between the acts of God, which rescue, quench thirst, and satisfy hunger, and the constant complaints of Israel that doubt and question God's plan of action. The answer to the question, "Is the Lord in our midst or not?" seems obvious: God has acted powerfully and dramatically for the people of Israel. This is proof enough of God's presence in their midst!

2nd Reading

In the opening chapter of Romans, Paul boldly proclaims that the gospel reveals the justice of God, which begins and ends with faith, for the just person shall live by faith. Romans continues with Paul's detailed argument that what has taken place in the death and resurrection of Jesus supersedes the Law, for faith and acceptance of salvation through Jesus fulfills the Law. Paul goes on to say that Abraham was justified by faith (Genesis 15:6), and so everything depends on faith and everything is grace (4:16).

Through Jesus' death we have gained access by faith to the grace of God, which now becomes our boast. Paul then states in 5:3–4 that he can even boast in his afflictions, for this makes for endurance, which makes stronger virtue, which leads to hope. In verse 5, then, Paul says that the hope we have gained does not leave us disappointed. Rather it gives us a deeper, fuller experience of God's love poured out in our hearts through the spirit.

Finally, Paul concludes that the tremendous gift of salvation has come to us, even while we are powerless and sinful. At the appointed time, Christ died for us. In this death God proves how much we are loved. The passage culminates with the assertion that because God has loved us so, God has become our boast through Jesus Christ, through whom we have now been reconciled.

Paul's argument has stated emphatically that salvation/reconciliation has come to us as an absolute gift from God. What is important about Paul's statement is God has given this gift not to perfect, sinless creatures. Rather, God's salvation comes to powerless, sinful people.

Gospel Reading

Following the Prologue and introductory material involving Jesus' baptism and the call of the first disciples, John's "Book of Signs" begins with the miracle at Cana. Each of the signs Jesus reveals challenges the observer to believe and accept Jesus, or to reject him. Witnessing the sign at Cana, Jesus' disciples become the first to accept and believe in him (2:11).

In contrast to the sign at Cana, the cleansing of the temple (2:13–17) leaves some questioning and doubting Jesus' authority. Jesus' encounter with Nicodemus (3:1–21) leaves us hanging, for at the end of the story we do not know if Nicodemus is ever "born again by water and faith" (3:5).

In the middle of Nicodemus' story, we hear in John's discourse that "God so loved the world that the only Son is given so that whoever believes in the Son may have eternal life" (3:16). This thought is further elaborated upon by John when he says, "Whoever accepts this (Jesus') testimony certifies that God is truthful" (3:33). Believing in the Son and accepting the Son's testimony will bring eternal life (3:36). These statements are important in illuminating the Samaritan woman story.

As the story opens, we are told that it is the hottest time of the day, noon. A Samaritan woman comes to draw water from the town well. John has set the story well, for we are told that the town is Shechem (which has strong patriarchal connections), and the well is Jacob's well. These facts add to the double level of meaning that is working in the story. On the one hand, we have the dialogue between Jesus and the woman, and on the other hand is our own recognition of Jesus' real identity.

In the first exchange between Jesus and the woman, Jesus asks for a drink. This violates the social custom of the day. The woman is startled by his address and reacts with understandable alacrity. His attitude toward women is probably different than any other man she has ever met.

Jesus then issues a two-part challenge to the woman: If she recognizes who is speaking to her, she will ask him for living water.

In the second dialogue the woman misunderstands Jesus' offer, viewing things only on an earthly level (vv 11–12). Jesus clarifies that he is speaking on a heavenly level by offering the water of eternal life (vv 13–14). The woman is intrigued and asks for water, fulfilling one of Jesus' challenges (v 15).

The second scene in the story now moves to the question of worship. In the first dialogue Jesus takes the initiative by leading the woman to recognize who he is by referring to her personal life (v 16). The woman gives an ambiguous answer (v 17), and Jesus then uses her answer to tell her the truth about herself (v 18).

The second dialogue begins with the woman moving closer to the light and truth (vv 19–20). Jesus explains that true worship can only come from those begotten by the spirit of truth (vv 21–24). The woman finally recognizes, as far as possible at this point in the story, who Jesus is (vv 25–26). This fulfills the second part of Jesus' challenge in verse 10.

The story concludes in verses 39–42 with the woman and the townspeople affirming who Jesus is. This time they believe in Jesus' own word that he is the savior of the world. The woman has moved from unbelief to belief, and her conversion is complete.

The first scrutiny is celebrated today, and the story of the Samaritan woman could not be more appropriate. The goal we are working toward is a recognition of the truth that Paul proclaims in Romans. While we are still sinners, God proves how much we are loved by sending the Son to us. The ultimate meaning of this truth is that we do not have to be perfect or holy to accept salvation or God's love.

Our acceptance of this truth is only the beginning, however. The process of accepting the gift of new life leads through many stages in the formation of faith.

Jesus' loving response to the woman speaks to the longing in each of us. To have the fountain of youth welling up within us is a dream many have! The search for the Holy Grail is a quest centuries old. Our hearts should quicken and our blood race. To have the opportunity to drink of the fountain of eternal life is the chance almost everyone would grab for. My first thought would be, where do I sign up? What do I have to do?

This is why the woman so quickly responds, "Give me this water so I will not grow thirsty!"

With the celebration of the first scrutiny, we must consider that the first barrier that must come down, and one of the levels of conversion that must be made, is intellectual superiority. Belief in Jesus Christ is not a head trip! It is a life commitment. Many of us who are cradle Catholics still have our faith on a purely intellectual level. We got the answers right in the *Baltimore Catechism*, and that was all we had to know. Maybe those of the elect have already experienced this conversion, but the barrier of intellectual superiority might remain.

Thus, the scrutiny or exorcism is meant to be an experience of the power of God within the community that brings release from the barriers in our lives. It is an experience of moving deeper into the mystery of Jesus Christ by letting our faith move from our heads to our guts. This is the experience of the "Living Water" welling up inside, giving life.

We could stop there and think that once intellectual conversion has taken place, that is as far as we need to go. The second scene in the gospel does not allow such a shortsighted conclusion. Jesus poses a moral question to the woman. Jesus does not tread lightly here, and it takes the woman by surprise. She can no longer deal with Jesus purely on an intellectual level. She calls Jesus a prophet, one who can see into hearts. This would scare the hell out of most people, but the woman plunges on by asking a question about worship. This is not a question about the place of worship (e.g., Jerusalem or Samaria); it is a question about "authentic" worship. Authentic worship is genuine worship, worship that involves the whole person, worship that involves lifestyle and faith commitment. Authentic worship comes from the gut and involves values and moral choices that are in accord with the motivating principle of the Gospel.

It is interesting that Jesus does not judge or condemn the woman for her lifestyle. Instead, he persuasively calls her to a deeper faith, from which she will make the choice herself to change her life. This is what takes place with the first scrutiny. We, the community, are persuasively calling the elect and our entire community to turn away from "inauthentic" worship or lifestyle to the genuine life of Jesus Christ. We are calling them to let go of the barriers that prevent them from living the "authentic" life and choose the values of the gospel. We are calling them to make the moral choices that are contrary to the society in which we live. These values and morals come from the gospel of Jesus Christ, from his life and the witness of those who walk in his footsteps.

Cycle B

Exodus 20:1–17
1 Corinthians 1:22–25
John 2:13–25

1st Reading

The architects of the Lectionary propose this version of "commandments" as yet another stage in the "history of salvation." Experienced Bible readers also know lists of commandments in: Ex 34:14–26; Lev 5:6–21; 18:6–17; 19:2–18; Dt 27:15–16; Ps 15; Ez 18:5–9. It is the Deuteronomist (Dt 4:13; 10:4) who applied the number "ten" to our familiar commandments. Even so, the actual numbering is different among Catholics/Lutherans, other Protestants, and Jews.

The context of these commandments in Exodus 20 is a theophany, that is, an appearance or revelation of God-experience, rather than a covenant.

The preamble (20:2a) identifies the name (Yahweh) and title (God) of the one laying down these stipulations. The historical prologue (20:2b) gives the reasons: Yahweh emancipated these people from slavery.

Three general stipulations (20:4–6: no other gods; no images; no worship of other gods) exclude (but don't deny) other superhuman authorities. The reasons? Yahweh is jealous; he punishes those who hate him but is full of loving-kindness ("hesed") to those who love him.

The subsequent set of specific stipulations obliges free, adult, Israelite males: perjury; Sabbath; parents; revenge-killing; no sexual relations with another's wife; no kidnapping of a fellow free Israelite male; no false witnessing in court; no stealing a fellow free male's wife; no stealing anything of his at all, listed in degree of importance.

A detailed exegetical study of the various lists of commandments would be very interesting but lies beyond the scope of this Lectionary overview.

It is important to note that the morality taught by Jesus goes beyond the commandments but presupposes them as valid. The challenge faced by contemporary believers is: if one does not reach the level of the commandments, is a new covenant morality possible? What is one "going beyond"?

At base, one must recognize that discussion about the role and relevance of the decalogue is posed quite differently in the New Testament and in the Western Christian tradition. In Jesus' day, the problem was "pharisaism," a legalism that states that a person is good if she or he does nothing wrong (thou shalt not). In contrast, Jesus urges that the good person is characterized as one who does what is right positively!

In Augustine's time and later, Christians of the West were already normatively legalistic: a good person was one who did nothing wrong. Augustine explained that Jews did nothing wrong out of fear, but Christians are motivated to do nothing wrong out of love. Augustine failed to recognize or recall that the context of the commandments is covenant, grace, love, yes, even in the Old Testament.

Even in contemporary, mainstream U.S. culture, the prevailing normative Christian tradition among most believers seems to be the "pharisaic" negativism, minimalism, obligationism, legalism or moralism. This is the tradition that Jesus and Paul have specifically rejected. Neither of them rejected the commandments, only the negative approach to keeping them. The preacher and liturgy planner sensitive to the distinctive context of each worshipping community will know how to make the appropriate adaptation.

2nd Reading

These verses, torn from the larger context of Corinthians, are nonetheless a marvelous example of Paul, the typical Mediterranean male. The key point of the passage is Christ crucified, or how God turned shame into magnificent honor.

In the context of honor and shame, the core values of Mediterranean culture, crucifixion is a shameful death. Jesus, who throughout his career achieved many grants of honor because he successfully warded off verbal attack from his various enemies, got tripped up at his trial. Here, shameful labels were applied to him and stuck: blasphemer and throne pretender. The negative labels led to his execution.

This explains why the crucified Christ is a stumbling block and foolishness to any Mediterranean person, Jew or Gentile. But Mediterranean believers know that God raised Jesus from the dead and bestowed honor upon him that has no parallel in human terms. Only God could so manipulate a culture as to draw honor out of its most shameful elements.

Paul was positive that this argument was convincing to a Mediterranean reader or listener. He was correct in his judgment. However, the Mediterranean Jesus of the Gospels, in western culture, is less often viewed as a stumbling block than he is dismissed as irrelevant. The contemporary preacher will have to determine how to make an analogous cultural argument for believers living in a culture in which honor and shame are not pivotal.

Gospel Reading

For the next three Sundays of Lent in Cycle B, the architects of the Lectionary have assigned readings from John to show Christ's coming glorification through his cross and resurrection.

Guided by this hint from those who arranged the Lectionary readings, the preacher and liturgy planners can see that verses 19–22 about Jesus' death and resurrection are central.

Jesus' "cleansing" of the Temple is best understood as a prophetic symbolic action. A symbolic action is a deed performed by a prophet that conveys meaning and feeling and invariably effects what it symbolizes. When Ezekiel (ch 5) cut some hair off his head and face, the audience knew this was not a haircut and shave. They also knew that this action was not just a cleverly concocted audio-visual strategy to illustrate a point. God communicated to Ezekiel both the action and its explanation. Ezekiel pointed to the hair and said: "This is Jerusalem." The hair symbolized Jerusalem. He then proceeded to do away with the hair in three different ways. Finally, he concluded by giving God's explanation of the symbolic deed.

Jesus directs his "cleansing" deeds against people who performed legitimate functions in the Temple. They provided the requisite animals for sacrifice and exchanged coins for the specifically required coins. By rendering these special services, these functionaries enabled the performance of proper sacrifices as commanded by God in the Torah. By driving them away, Jesus has put a halt to divinely willed Temple sacrifice. As justification for this deed, the Evangelist John (who himself is one of the staunchly anti-Temple authors in the New Testament) says that the disciples remember Psalm 69:9, "Zeal for your house will consume me."

Jesus himself is reported to say: "Stop turning the house of my father into a house of market" (marketplace; the play on the word "house" reflects a language style that Jesus typically enjoyed using and in which he excelled). That statement borrows from Jeremiah 7:11, a prophet with whom the Synoptics often associate Jesus.

What then did Jesus intend with his prophetic symbolic action? In actuality he disrupted legitimate Temple sacrifice. The symbolism of his deed initiated the forthcoming end of legitimate Temple sacrifice. The person of the risen Jesus will be the new Temple of sacrifice pleasing to God. "Destroy this temple and in three days I will rebuild it."

Cycle C

Exodus 3:1–8,13–15
1 Corinthians 10:1–6,10–12
Luke 13:1–9

We cannot experience God's forgiving love until we admit our need for forgiveness. We cannot know mercy until we have to ask for it. We cannot begin new life until the old is relinquished.

1st Reading

Abram experienced God through a burning brazier. God appeared to Moses in the form of a burning bush. Both men had encounters with God that changed their lives and the lives of the people of Israel.

The call of Moses, which is the reading for this Sunday, comes while Moses lives as a fugitive in the wilderness (2:16). He left Egypt because he killed an Egyptian for mistreating a Hebrew slave. Just prior to the call of Moses (3:1ff), "the Israelites groaned…and cried out" (2:23). Their experience of suffering calls out to God and will call out to Moses. Someone must do something.

Moses' call is sometimes regarded as an archetype of religious experience. It contains elements that are common to most calls from the Lord. First there is a revelation in nature, the fire in the bush, that signals the presence of God. Second, a message comes through God's Word. Third, Moses expresses unworthiness and raises objections but his call is followed by affirmation of God's presence and power. Moses is called to liberate the people.

Thousands of years of religious experience taught the biblical writers that calls from God are neither easy nor foolproof. An authentic call will raise doubt and fear in a faithful person and needs to be tested. God responds to Moses' fear with the revelation of a divine name, formed from four letters of the Hebrew verb, "be." The letters are YHWH. It can be translated several

different ways: "I am who am," "I will be who I will be," "I cause to be what comes to be." (The reason for so many variations is that Hebrew does not contain vowels. Depending on the vowels added in translation, the form of the word changes. But whatever the form, the name is clearly an assurance of God's power and presence. Orthodox Jews will not speak this word because it is so holy. They often refer to God as *ha shem*, "The Name.")

The name is the sign Moses needed. Moses listened to God and responded with faith to God's grace. Moses, a murderer, will become God's chosen leader.

2nd Reading

Paul warns the community not to be overconfident in God's mercy. Apparently some Corinthians believed that because they were baptized and participated in the Eucharist, they would not face the consequences of sin. He challenges their thinking by means of a comparison with the people of Israel. Israel was baptized by the passage through the sea. Christians are saved by the waters of baptism. Israel ate manna and drank from the rock, just as Christians share in the Eucharist. (A rabbinic tradition held that the rock [v 4] accompanied the people through the desert.) Despite all of this, Israel desired evil things, worshipped idols (v 7) and was punished for sin. Paul warns the community that they, too, will be held accountable for their actions, even if they have participated in the sacraments. Love and judgment are not opposites but part of one another. God's grace brings us to judgment so that we may repent and be reconciled with God.

Gospel

The first part of the reading for this Sunday is almost like a news bulletin. "Pontius Pilate murders Galileans, tower at Siloam falls." These incidents are recorded only in Luke and we cannot be sure what historical incidents may underlie the text; nevertheless, the evangelist's description of Pilate's action of mingling blood "with their sacrifices" (v 1) seems to indicate that the Galileans were murdered during the sacrificial ritual itself. Whatever the background of these incidents, their mention not only gives some sense of life in the first century but also reveals how events were interpreted. Pontius Pilate violates God's law and an important building collapses.

In the Gospel, as Jesus travels to Jerusalem and the cross, he uses every opportunity to preach repentance. Popular belief considered suffering to be a punishment for sin. If something bad happened, it was because the person did something wrong. In Jesus' allusion to these two examples of suffering, however, he does not judge either innocence or guilt. Instead he uses the occasion to challenge his audience to examine their own sinfulness and the consequences of their unwillingness to repent.

The message of repentance has a softer tone in the parable about the fig tree. The fig tree is in a vineyard. The reason it is in a vineyard and not an orchard or field is that a vineyard is a symbol for the people of Israel and for the church (Is 5:1–7, Lk 20:9–19). Fig trees are expected to produce fruit in three years. If they do not produce by this time, they may never produce. The message here, like the "news bulletins," is about time. The fig tree is granted a reprieve. It has another chance to produce fruit.

Learn a lesson from events and nature. Those who have not yet repented have time; there is still another chance to produce good fruit. God's judgment is present, but God's graciousness prevails.

"Lectionary Commentary for the 3rd Sunday of Lent" originally appeared in Liturgy Plus *Planning Software (Cycle ABC) (Resource Publications, Inc.).*

Lectionary Commentary For The 4th Sunday of Lent

Liturgy Plus *Planning Software*

Cycle A

1 Samuel 16:1b,6–7,10–13a
Ephesians 5:8–14
John 9:1–41

1st Reading

The context of David being chosen as king begins with the downfall of King Saul. In chapter 10 of 1 Samuel, we are told that Saul is anointed commander over Israel (v 1), and the spirit of the Lord rushed upon him (v 6). But by chapter 15, Saul is reproved by Samuel, and the Lord regrets having chosen Saul (15:10–11). So Samuel is sent to Bethlehem to choose a new king.

The story of David and Samuel works on many levels. God initiates the action and commands Samuel to stop grieving for Saul. But Saul objects and questions how he might be so bold to undertake such a dangerous mission. God tells Samuel to lie about the purpose of his visit (16:2). Samuel does as God commands.

In the second scene, Samuel arrives in Bethlehem and is confronted by the elders of the village on the purpose of his visit. Has he come on peaceful terms, or is he a spy for Saul? Samuel, as directed by God, lies to the elders and sets the ruse for God's choice of a new king. In the third scene, each of Jesse's sons comes before Samuel.

Samuel asks himself the question, "Surely the Lord's anointed is here before me?" Each son is judged, but God's voice says to Samuel, "Do not judge from appearance…not as man sees does God see…the Lord looks into the heart." Saul was judged by appearance. The next leader of Israel was not to be chosen in this way. As the scene continues, all seven sons are brought before Samuel, but none are chosen. Samuel then asks if there are any more sons. Jesse replies that one remains, the youngest, who is tending sheep. David is brought before Samuel, and the Lord announces through Samuel that this, the youngest son, David, is to be anointed king. Thus, in the midst of his brothers, David is anointed, "and from that day on, the spirit of the Lord rushed upon David" (v 13).

The ways of God are not the ways of humankind. There will not be a second mistake, for God will do the choosing. What is interesting is that God chooses a shepherd to now shepherd Israel. David also stands outside the normal structures, for he is the eighth son and does not stand to inherit anything, except the very leadership of God's people.

2nd Reading

The scope of Ephesians is cosmic in vision. "God has put all things under Christ's feet and has made him, thus exalted, head of the church, which is his body: the fullness of God who fills the universe in all its parts" (1:22–23). In God we have been chosen (1:11–13), and we are no longer strangers or aliens (2:19). We are united into one body (4:4) and must continually live as the new creation in God's image (4:24).

At the beginning of chapter 5, the author urges the reader to follow the way of love and turn away from conduct unbecoming to a follower of Jesus Christ. The author then goes on to say that since we share in the life of Christ, we no longer walk in darkness but in the light. "Light produces every kind of goodness, justice, and truth" (5:9). Therefore, the author says, "Take no part in deeds done in darkness" (5:11).

While not a direct quote, the author seems to draw from Isaiah the image of an end to the darkness of exile and the recognition of the light of God now giving restoration or salvation (Is 60:1–4). The author's tone of voice is more like "Wake up, you fools! Christ has brought you light, and you're still sleeping! What is wrong with you?"

Ephesians goes on to encourage the community to walk not in ignorance but in a discerning spirit (5:17), to be filled with the spirit (5:18) rather than acting like ignorant fools (5:15). The point is that if we have been chosen to be holy and blameless (1:14), then we should be acting like it!

Gospel Reading

Structurally, the story of the man born blind is found in the section of John's gospel called the Book of Signs. It comes in a series of stories, beginning with a cure Jesus reveals on the Sabbath (5:1–47), that relate to the major Jewish feasts. Each sign is connected with a major feast, and through the discourse that follows each sign, we are instructed in the way that Jesus stands superior over the feast. The Sabbath is meant to renew life, and Jesus gives life to the man at the pool of Bethesda (5:1–47). The Passover celebrates the salvation of Israel from slavery, and now Jesus gives the Bread of eternal salvation (6:1–71). The water and light ceremonies of the Feast of Tabernacles are now replaced by the Light of the World (7:1–10:21). Finally, at the Feast of Dedication, Jesus is consecrated in place of the temple altar, as Messiah and Son of God (10:22–42).

The blind man's story comes in the reference to the Feast of Tabernacles. Originally the feast was an agricultural feast that arose at the time of the Deuteronomic reform in the seventh century B.C. Its ritual is found in Numbers 29:12–38 and is also mentioned in Deuteronomy 16:13–17.

Chapter 7 begins the section with a statement from the disciples that Jesus should go to Judea, so that his disciples there could see the works he was revealing (7:3). Since the Feast of Booths

(Tabernacles) was a feast of pilgrimage, it would have been appropriate for Jesus to go to Jerusalem. With the festival half over (7:14), Jesus finally arrives in the temple but is immediately embroiled in controversy. On the last day of the festival (Num 29:35–38), Jesus proclaims that he is the source of the water that quenches thirst (7:37) and the light of the world (8:12).

While the connection is not perfectly clear, the story of the man born blind flows from Jesus' statement of his being the Light of the World. The sign is Jesus' miraculous healing of the man born blind (9:6–7). A series of interrogations ensue: a questioning by neighbors and friends (vv 8–12); an interrogation by Pharisees (vv 13–17); the man's parents are questioned by the Jews (vv 18–23); and finally a second interrogation by the Jews (vv 24–34).

The final scene is the dialogue between Jesus and the man (vv 35–41). Hearing of the man's expulsion from the synagogue, Jesus asks, "Do you believe in the Son of Man?" The man answers simply, "Who is he, sir, that I may believe in him?" "You have seen him," Jesus replies. "He is speaking to you now." The man proclaims his belief and worships Jesus. The man has moved from blindness to faith and belief in the one who quenches thirst and gives light to the world. In spite of all the interrogations and controversy, the man moves calmly through the rough waters to the calm harbor of faith in the Son of Man.

Some people like to read books by going to the last chapter first to see how it all turns out. That way, if things do not work out for the main character, they do not bother to read the book. In the same way we could approach the story of David and the blind man from the result: David is anointed as the next shepherd of Israel, and the man who once was blind professes his faith in the Messiah. This is the cut and dried, straightforward approach. We know how the story ends, and that is all that matters. But there is much great drama going on in each of these stories.

Amid the tension and decline of Saul's reign as king, God commands Samuel to act in a subversive way. In those dangerous moments of entry into Bethlehem, the elders question Samuel's intentions. We who are the readers know that God has commanded Samuel to choose a new king. The participants in the story do not. This dual level of recognition or action is present within our own lives. What we see on the surface is not always what is on the inside. There is a need for a critical or discerning attitude. This is the attitude of village elders. Is Samuel's mission from God or from Saul?

To put it in terms of this Sunday's celebration of the second scrutiny, we are forced to discern whether our choice to follow Jesus is a mere social convention or a personal decision to change our life and goals. If we have a discerning spirit, we will be able to look at the surface features and see through to the deeper reality of faith and God's presence. This is what happens as Samuel assays each of Jesse's sons. Not by appearance does he choose, but by the presence of God within the heart of the individual.

This process is part of the blind man's story. In his story the stakes and risks are higher, however. It is easy for Jesus to come along and give the man sight. But what happens to the man as he returns to his family, who still think of him as blind and treat him accordingly? He is questioned, grilled, and eventually ostracized by family and friends.

The process of initiation may lead along paths that are unfamiliar. It does not say in David's story how he reacted to being chosen and anointed. But I am sure that it was no easy transition from a shepherd to an anointed king. When the spirit rushed upon David, his life was not instantaneously changed. Rather, his life was set on a course known only to God. In the same way, the life of the man born blind was changed in ways that he could not imagine. What is interesting is that the man did not even ask for a miracle (like David who did not ask to be chosen). He was once blind, dependent on others, and enslaved to darkness. After his encounter with Jesus, his eyes are opened, and he is free to walk his own path. One would think his family and friends would be happy; however, they physically and verbally abuse him. Some response to a miracle!

This Sunday the elect take one more step in their journey of initiation. With them the whole Christian community is called to a deeper faith. The stories of David and the man born blind are stories about the way God acts in the lives of people. The stories also tell us that when God acts, lives are changed, and that once one embarks upon the path chosen by God, nothing assures easy passage.

Cycle B

2 Chronicles 36:14–17,19–23
Ephesians 2:4–10
John 3:14–21

1st Reading

Preachers and liturgy planners are undoubtedly familiar with the biblical "tool" known as a synopsis, a book that places the synoptic Gospels in parallel columns in order to align corresponding passages. A similar resource exists for comparing Kings and Chronicles.

Comparing 1 Chronicles 36:11–16 with 2 Kings 24:18–25:17 reveals that the Chronicler adds a comment lacking in Kings. Verses 12b–14 give as a reason for Judah's destruction the fact that Zedekiah did not humble himself before Jeremiah, who spoke on behalf of the Lord.

Therefore this passage assigned for today generalizes that the people's ultimate sin was their failure to respond to the prophetic voice by repenting. In his mercy, God sent prophet after prophet to his people, but the prophets were scorned and disregarded until finally there was no more forgiveness.

Finally God selects a pagan, Cyrus, to whom he gives all the kingdoms of the earth. Surprisingly, he also commands Cyrus to build a Temple in Jerusalem!

One common thread linking this passage with the Gospel is the theme of rejecting God's salvation. In spite of such rejection, God never gives up but makes his salvation ever available.

2nd Reading

This passage from Ephesians was probably selected because of the author's statement that God brought us to life with Christ when we were dead in sin.

The statement that Christians have already been saved, raised, and enthroned with Christ moves far beyond Paul's statements (e.g., Rom 5:9–10). The author of Ephesians, likely a disciple of Paul, has drawn on the ready language of preexistent hymns which praise God as if his mighty deed of salvation has already been completed. Still, the Pauline touch is evident in the assertion that this salvation comes through faith and is not due to human effort.

This latter statement is of special interest from a Mediterranean cultural perspective. In general, Mediterranean peasants place little to no stock in "doing." Since they have no control over nature, they feel as if they have no control over any part of life. Therefore the standard posture is "being," that is, spontaneously responding to whatever happens, as it happens, moment by moment.

Those who did not have to rely on nature for subsistence, such as the elites which included priests and Pharisees, would definitely emphasize "doing." The Pharisees' designation of 612 commandments that ought to be "kept" or "done" is evidence of that. Paul himself was not a peasant but an artisan or craftsman and should logically favor the "doing" posture. However, a key element in his conversion was the realization that nothing he had done had gained the grace God bestowed upon him. It was a very pivotal awareness for a Pharisee. This is what his disciple reflects in these verses from Ephesians.

Gospel Reading

This reading's central point is that the "Son of Man" must be lifted up so that those who believe in him may have eternal life. Once again, let us explore the insights that Mediterranean cultural sensitivity can highlight in this text. This passage reflects an "us" and "them" perspective that characterizes John in a way that sets him off from the Synoptics: those who believe in Jesus, and those who don't; those who love light, and those who love darkness. John's community has a strong sense of separation from every other social group at the time, and the notable groups they oppose are "the [this] world" (a phrase used 79 times in John but only 12 times in the Synoptics) and "the Jews" (71 times in John; 12 times in the Synoptics). John's is clearly an anti-societal group.

Anti-societal or anti-social groups develop a language of their own and in fact overuse the language. Count the various and diverse usages of "believe" in this brief passage. Essentially all occurrences carry the same meaning, but the varied usage tends to confuse and turn off an "outsider," one who is not part of the anti-social "in-group."

Because such groups are strongly anti-social, they tend to develop a high sense of individualism. John uses the Greek pronoun "I" 146 times compared with 18 in Mark, 23 in Matthew and 26 in Luke. Jesus repeatedly makes "I am" statements in John (6:35,41,48,51; 8:12,18; 9:5; 10:7,9,11,14; 11:25; 14:6; 15:1,5), even though the items with which he identifies himself he previously offered to other persons in John's narrative. Jesus individualistically overcomes "the world" in which he is constrained and enveloped. He breaks the fetters of his social group ("his own") and stands out uniquely, alone.

Yet this Mediterranean individualism is quite exceptional, for it tends to occur only in anti-societal limbo. Jesus and other members of this group are perceived as "generalized individuals." This perception finds expression in Pilate's identification of Jesus: "Here is the man!" (19:5). Mainstream U.S. individuals are institutional individuals, set distinctively and contrastingly apart from and over against other individuals. This concept is rather peculiar among the world's cultures and different from John's Mediterranean perception.

In his Gospel, John explains how and why it all turned out: Jesus overcomes the world and is exalted above it in the end. He overcomes evil; light overcomes darkness. The tragic aspect of this is that human beings, in John's view, are stuck in a somewhat subhuman, unnatural condition. By dying on the cross, Jesus is exalted and points to a higher order principle that can endow life with meaning and draw people out of their ruts.

What is the point of it all? While the Synoptics' Jesus refuses to offer signs to anyone, John's Jesus liberally overwhelms the reader with signs. They are intended to give direction to the individual hearer or reader of the story. The signs show that Jesus is uniquely the Christ, and the individual who commits self to Jesus gains eternal life.

What should the reader or hearer do about it? Remove self from society and find a safe haven in this loving anti-societal and anti-social group. This involves total social transcendence, with full disregard for existing institutions, especially those from whom John's group has broken off, namely, "the world" and "the Jews."

The value of these insights generated by sensitivity to John's cultural dimensions is to highlight one distinctive response to Jesus. There have been times in history, even in American society, when religious, enthusiastic groups have behaved just like John's group. Suffice it to say that this posture adopted by some of our ancestors in the faith is not customary, nor was it of lasting duration in that culture. Neither could it be of lasting duration in our culture. Even so, notice that faith generates many different responses.

Cycle C

Joshua 5:9,10–12
2 Corinthians 5:17–21
Luke 15:1–3,11–32

The point of all gardens is to get something good to eat. By the fourth Sunday of Lent, Lent is more than half over. Just as the first strawberries, first peas, and first leaves of lettuce can be sampled before the harvest, the readings offer us a taste of joy before Easter.

1st Reading

God's faithfulness to the covenant promises and God's care for the people of Israel continue to be the theme for the first reading this Lenten season. The book of Joshua tells the story of the conquest of the land of Canaan. Like much of the Bible, this book came together over a long period of time and contains not only accounts of actual events but also the circumstances and concerns of the later authors and editors. Their additional insight is apparent in the passage for this Sunday.

The forty-year travelers, at the edge of the Promised Land just outside Jericho, pause and celebrate the Passover. The authors of this book, looking back years later, understood that the entry into the land was an important turning point. The first Passover feast recounted in Exodus marks the liberation from slavery; this feast commemorates the transition from a nomadic life to that of a settled people. It marks another passing over. This ritual event formally closes the forty years of wandering in the wilderness with thanksgiving for deliverance from slavery and the entry into the land. The promise made by God to Abram is fulfilled.

The transition is symbolized by the food the Israelites eat. In the desert, they lived on manna. When they enter the land, the manna ceases and the people live on grain, an agricultural product. God provides both kinds of food. As long as they remember that the land is a gift, they will remember that the grain the land produces is a gift as well.

2nd Reading

Paul describes the transformation that occurs with the coming of faith as a "new creation" (v 17). The sign of this new world order and new life is reconciliation. Christ, who became identified with sin so that everyone could receive forgiveness, also shares this mission. Paul wants the Corinthians to realize that their experience of salvation does not end with themselves. The Corinthians are agents, representatives of forgiveness. Because of Christ, the world is different now. Paul expresses the beautiful idea that God reaches out to others through us (v 20). Reconciliation is not forced or required; it comes by invitation. Those who accept this invitation are transformed and become like God; they share in "the righteousness of God" (v 21). Everything sinful and weak now touched by God is restored to wholeness.

Gospel Reading

The reading is a story of almost inexhaustible meaning. It is found only in the Gospel of Luke. The setting of the story is significant (15:1–3). The outcasts of the day, the toll collectors and assorted disreputable types, were drawn to Jesus. This causes the religious leaders to complain that Jesus eats with the riff-raff—thereby implying Jesus is himself disreputable. In response to this criticism, Jesus tells three parables about being lost: The Lost Sheep, The Lost Coin and The Lost Son. For those who have ears to hear, it is obvious that in the last parable, the sinners are represented by the younger son, while the elder son reflects the attitudes of the religious leaders.

The story implies that both sons rejected their father's love, the younger by wasting his inheritance, the older by loveless obedience. In a sense, the father suffers most in the story. He loves both sons but is caught in the middle and cannot please either. Clearly the overflowing love of this father is a symbol of God's love.

The change and transformation of the younger son, when he realizes what he has done (v 17), is the realization that his father is just, even to the servants. The son gets back in touch with the real world, with the world of love. His perception is confirmed before he even reaches home—his father is out looking for him. The father pours out his love and concern, which the son now can recognize. He receives all of the signs of sonship: clothes, shoes, and a ring. The reconciliation is sealed with a meal and a banquet.

Both sons are invited to the party, yet the elder son, despite his father's pleading, is bitter and angry. This elder son does not see himself as an heir but as a servant. He has always done what his father asked, but now it is revealed that he acted out of obligation. The story ends with the father's explanation that his younger son's return is like someone returning from the dead. This son is a new creation.

What are some possible meanings of the story? Is this really about a wasted inheritance? Or is it about a man who lost a son and gained him back again only to lose another son? Or is it a story about love and forgiveness? Or a story of repentance? One scholar tells us that there were many folk tales circulating in that time about sons who left home, made good, and returned as conquering heroes. The surprise in the parable, then, is the graciousness of the father. His son returns disgraced, penniless, and hungry, but he throws a party anyway. In this father, we see imaged the graciousness of God, who accepts us even when we are unacceptable.

The ending of the story is incomplete. The father invites the older son to join in the party. Whether he accepts or not is not told. It is for us to decide the outcome. Do we identify with the younger son, who lived foolishly in a far country, or the one who stayed home and became bitter and self-righteous? God invites all of us to the great banquet. Will we accept or reject the invitation?

"Lectionary Commentary for the 4th Sunday of Lent" originally appeared in Liturgy Plus *Planning Software (Cycles ABC) (Resource Publications, Inc.).*

Lectionary Commentary For The 5th Sunday of Lent

Liturgy Plus *Planning Software*

Cycle A

> Ezekiel 37:12–14
> Romans 8:8–11
> John 11:1–45

1st Reading

The scene from Ezekiel is a field of dry bones. It is unfortunate that the lectionary does not include the vision of the dry bones. Only the concluding prophecy is proclaimed. The context of this scene is the exile and the experience of the destruction of Jerusalem. This experience was as if the very heart of the people had been ripped out of them.

While later writers will see in the transformation of the dry bones a foreshadowing of resurrection, the story tells of Israel's restoration and revival following exile. The prophet is led out to a plain filled with dry bones. He prophesies that life and flesh will cover the dry bones. The point is (37:6) that once restored, Israel (the dry bones) will know once again that God is their Lord.

We hear and see the bones come to life as they rattle and shake with sinews and flesh beginning to form on them (37:7–8). In verse 11 the voices of Israel in exile cry out like the dry bones, "Our hope is lost, and we are cut off." But God's voice answers back that they are not to remain in exile. They shall be brought back to the land (37:12). The spirit of God will be placed in them, and they shall know the Lord (37:14). The final thought of verse 14 is most telling, "I have promised this, and I will do it, says the Lord." While exile was God's ways of disciplining the people of Israel for their disobedience, restoration is also God's promise. The dry bones (death) of exile shall be turned into an army filled with God's spirit and life.

Paul's argument states that with sin's entrance into God's created order, death became a part of human history (Rom 5:12–14). But God did not intend for sin and death to be the way of humanity. So out of God's gracious love, Christ died for us (5:8), so that grace might overflow upon all humanity (5:17). In this way grace now reigns by way of justice, leading to eternal life through Jesus Christ our Lord (5:21).

2nd Reading

If death has been conquered, Paul continues, then sin also has been overcome. "Sin will no longer have power over you," he says, "You are now under grace" (6:14). With the freedom won by the death of Jesus, we should then be compelled to live a life exemplifying the presence of grace. Paul, however, is very much aware that conversion from a life of sin to a life of grace is a continuing struggle. He himself admits to the struggle to live the life of grace (7:15–24). The struggle is confusing and downright frustrating (7:24). However, Paul once again emphatically states that "the law of the spirit, the spirit of life in Christ Jesus, has freed us from the law of sin and death" (8:2). Thus the choice before us is to live either by the spirit of Christ or according to the flesh (or sin). If we lean towards sin, then we must know it will lead to death. If, on the other hand, we lean towards the spirit, then we will have life and peace (8:6).

The point of the following verses (9–11) is not to set up a black and white contrast. Rather, it is once again Paul's voice of exhortation. The "If...then" clauses build in a progressive series of statements. "If Christ is in you..." demands a response from the hearer. Maybe it should be "Is Christ in you?" The response should be a rousing shout, "Yes!" "Then you are dead to sin; so stop sinning....Is the spirit of God who raised Jesus from the dead in you?" The rousing response should again be, "Yes!" "Then," Paul states, "that same spirit will bring about a transformation in you enabling you to experience the freedom and power of God's grace" (8:14–17).

Gospel Reading

The raising of Lazarus from the dead in the gospel reading is the final sign of Jesus' power and divinity. It is also the sign whose direct result is Jesus' own death (11:46–53). As stated previously in Nicodemus' story (third Sunday of Lent), there is a twofold response to the signs: faith and disbelief. The raising of Lazarus brings many to faith (11:45) but also brings many to plot Jesus' death. In a sense, Lazarus' story is not only a story that shows Jesus' power with the response of faith but also a story that prefigures Jesus' own death and resurrection. Hence John's passion narrative follows immediately upon the raising of Lazarus.

If the story is read in its entirety, it presents some confusing elements. We are told in verse 2 that Mary, the sister of Lazarus, is the one who anointed the Lord's feet. This story, however, does not come until the next chapter (chapter 12), thus suggesting a misplacement or insertion of Lazarus' story into a later edition of the gospel. We are also told that Jesus loved Martha, Mary, and Lazarus very much; yet he stays on where he was while Lazarus dies (11:5–6). Strange behavior for intimate friends! We are told that through Lazarus' sickness, God's glory will be revealed and the Son of God will be glorified.

Another confusing exchange comes between Jesus and his disciples. When Jesus states that he must return to Judea, the disciples protest (11:8). This dialogue works on two levels. It hints that Jesus' hour has arrived (cf. 2:4), and it echoes a previous theme of light and darkness (3:19–21; 8:12; 9:5). On a deeper level the hearer is pushed

to remember Jesus' identity as "light of the world" and thus is challenged to turn away from the darkness. However, the disciples miss the point (vv 12–13). Jesus' response is a bold statement that Lazarus' death will become a test of faith for them. Unwittingly Thomas voices the hallmark of a true disciple, "Let us go along to die with him" (11:16).

The main part of the story now begins with Jesus' entry into Bethany, where he is met by Martha. The statement that Lazarus had been in the tomb four days (v 17) takes away any doubt that Lazarus was physically dead. The center of the story is Martha's dialogue with Jesus. She approaches Jesus first with a little anger and unbelief. Then she expresses her confidence that God will accomplish a miracle through Jesus. Jesus' response is not in reply to Martha but to a deeper question of resurrection.

Martha is first asked if she believes her brother will rise again. Yes, she says, on the last day. Then Jesus utters John's pre-eminent theological statement. Jesus states, "I am the resurrection and the life!" Even though one should die, he says, with faith and belief in him, one will never die, but will come to life. This statement parallels Jesus' statements in the Bread of Life discourse (6:35,51), the Feast of Booths discourse (8:12), and the Good Shepherd discourse (10:11–14). Martha's response suggests she has come to the deepest level of faith, "I have come to believe that you are the Messiah, the Son of God: he who is to come into the world" (11:27).

The narrative now focuses on Jesus' reactions and those of the crowd standing around the tomb. Most translations relate that Jesus was deeply moved in spirit and troubled. This translation does not fully convey the Greek word. On the surface it shows the human side of Jesus. His tears are for his most loved friend. On another level it expresses Jesus' sadness in the face of human death, in the face of its darkness and its distress. On a much deeper level, it expresses Jesus' anger as he comes face to face with the realm of Satan and its link with the powers of death. It also, perhaps, expresses his anger with the bystanders' lack of faith (11:37). With that, Jesus orders the stone to be moved from the tomb's entrance and cries out, "Did I not tell you that if you would believe you would see the glory of God?"

Following a prayer of thanksgiving, Jesus cries out in a loud voice, "Lazarus, come out!" (11:43). In a full expression of Jesus' divine power, Lazarus hobbles out of the tomb. With symbolic meaning, Jesus orders that Lazarus be unbound and set free. This is the true significance of resurrection.

It must be kept in mind that Lazarus is resuscitated, not resurrected. Lazarus is brought back to life so that God's glory may be revealed. This sets the stage for Jesus' death and resurrection, which will be the ultimate revelation of God's glory.

With the fifth Sunday of Lent, we have come within sight of the gates of Jerusalem, the City of Zion, the heart and soul of Israel. Jerusalem will also be the place of God's revealed glory in the death and resurrection of Jesus. But we are not there yet! We have one more scrutiny to celebrate. The words of Ezekiel are our guide, for God has promised us life. The third scrutiny becomes the final step leading to initiation and the gates of the New Jerusalem.

The reading from Romans can enlighten us about the implication of this Sunday's readings. For Paul, the life of sin (flesh) is evidence that a person has not accepted the gift of salvation. Any behavior that is contrary to the life of Christ or the gospel is a sign that the person has not allowed the death and resurrection of Christ to be the instrument of transformation or conversion. Sin is not supposed to have power over us. But as Paul himself relates, the life of grace is not an easy life to live. Even he has trouble choosing the way of Christ. Thus if Paul had trouble, we are bound to have similar trouble.

While not described in detail, the process of conversion does not mean an instantaneous turning away from old ways or old habits. The wisdom of the *Rite of Christian Initiation of Adults* provides three opportunities for us to let go of the old, to purify ourselves.

This is what Paul is suggesting when he says that the spirit of God who raised Jesus from the dead will bring our mortal (sinful) bodies to life. This is echoed in Ezekiel. The dry bones are brought to life by the spirit of God. No matter how many times we profess our faith, there is always a little more that we have to do to experience full conversion. All the principles that motivate our lives must conform to the way of Christ. By allowing the power of Christ to dwell in us, the process of conversion will be energized and completed.

It would be easy to jump the gun this Sunday and preach on resurrection. But, as seen from Romans, the point is not resurrection. The focus is on the power of Jesus Christ that brings life from death! As the source of life, Jesus is the resurrection. By believing and accepting Jesus, one will have eternal life. So the idea that energizes this Sunday is the transforming power of Jesus Christ. The elect and the entire community is being called to accept this power into their lives, so that they will be set free from the dark powers of Satan.

Cycle B

Jeremiah 31:31–34
Hebrews 5:7–9
John 12:20–33

1st Reading

As honor and shame are pivotal and core values in the Mediterranean world, economics is the pivotal and core value in the mainstream United States. In fact, economics as we know and live it does not exist in the ancient world. Economics there is embedded in their two explicit social institutions: kinship and politics. One made a living or got by in life through an intricate network of relationships between equals (kinship) and by the benevolence of people in power (politics). The reality behind the word "covenant" borrows from both these social institutions.

Most Middle Eastern covenants are made between equals. Terms are drawn up and sworn to, and then a ritual is observed (walking through carved carcasses, or the like) to insure keeping of the covenant. "May God do thus and so to me if I don't keep this covenant." The agreement between Jacob and Laban about the proper treatment of Laban's daughters by Jacob is a good example (Gn 32:43–50).

But the covenant between God and human beings is between non-equals. Humans are duty-bound to accept and observe the terms imposed in order to enjoy the benefits promised. Such are God's covenants with Noah (the sign of which is the rainbow), Abraham (the sign of which is circumcision), and Moses for Israel at Sinai (the sign of which is the Sabbath).

It seems clear that participants in the covenants concluded that mere outward observance might fulfill the conditions. Performing the agreed rite and ceremony was expected to satisfy God and keep his benefits coming. Of course, the prophets saw through this sham and noted that there would have to be a new and better covenant that did not rest exclusively in rite and ceremonies but in inward conformity to the will of God. This in effect is what Jeremiah is projecting.

The elements of the covenant described by Jeremiah are: both Israel and Judah will be included; it will not be like the old covenant because people will know the stipulations in their hearts and not have to be taught; Yahweh will once more be their God, and they God's people; God will forgive their past sins; and, by implication, this covenant will last forever.

Upon closer inspection, this covenant clearly is not completely "new." It revises the Sinai covenant that required obedience to God's stipulations. But Jeremiah preferred this kind of covenant to the unconditional and one-sided covenant of royal ideology that he staunchly opposed (7:1–15). Note well that the people who favor the royal ideology express their culture's primary value orientation, "being," that is, spontaneous response to their experience. In effect they say: "We are the chosen people; God is our king. What is there to 'do'? All that is necessary is that we 'be'." As a remedy to this attitude, the prophets like Jeremiah urged that people adopt the culture's secondary value orientation, "doing" as a necessary supplement to "being." It is not enough to "be" objects of God's predilections. God's people must "do" God's will and "keep" God's commandments and covenant stipulations. Jesus urged the same cultural value rearrangement in the Gospels.

2nd Reading

This passage serves as an admirable bridge between the reading from Jeremiah and the gospel. The New Covenant, like the Old Covenant, requires obedience, but this should now come easier since God will implant it in the human heart. How "easy" it is to obey God is then demonstrated by Jesus in John's gospel: "My soul is troubled now, / yet what should I say— / Father, save me from this hour?" And it is again illustrated in the reflection recorded in Hebrews: "…Christ…offered…loud cries and tears to God,…[but] Son though he was, he learned obedience from what he suffered."

The author of Hebrews shines through the letter as a typical and representative Mediterranean male. Boys are a treasure in the Mediterranean family, but after birth they are reared entirely by the womenfolk and in the company of women. They are pampered and pleasured. At puberty, the boy must be pushed out into the harsh, hierarchically arranged male world, and the boy is confused and terrified. He repeatedly runs back to the women, who continue to expel him until he stays with the men.

There he is no longer pampered, nor is his every whim and desire fulfilled. He learns obedience through repeated physical punishment, which he is expected to bear without flinching or crying. The proof of his manhood is the ability to bear pain and punishment without complaint. Having had no male model to emulate in his childhood, he now learns what his culture expects of men.

As the Mediterranean author of Hebrews matter-of-factly informs his readers, Jesus learned obedience from what he suffered. Even if obedience to Jesus brings pain and suffering in its wake, the obedient believers will gain eternal salvation. Like all Mediterranean young men, so too Jesus is not delighted with pain and suffering. In the Synoptics Jesus asks his Father that the cup of suffering might pass. This aspect of the garden scene is lacking in John. Instead, John's Jesus asks: should I ask the Father to spare me this hour? No! And the commentary from Hebrews is a fitting expansion and Mediterranean pastoral application of Jesus' behavior.

Gospel Reading

Very likely the verses that prompted the selection of this Gospel passage for this Sunday of Lent are those that speak of the seed dying but especially Jesus' statement about being lifted up and drawing all to himself. Once again have the architects of the lectionary highlighted the significance of Jesus' death and resurrection.

Recall that John's gospel was intended for an anti-societal group, for "us" and not for "them." Note the indicators in this passage that "they" fail to understand. The voice from the sky was interpreted by some as "thunder" and by others as the voice of an "angel." John's Jesus sarcastically comments that he didn't need an interpretation; "they" did! Note also the editorial comment at the end of today's passage, just in case some of "us" fail to understand what was just reported. The tension that fills these verses makes a reader uneasy.

Further, scholars offer these additional enlightening contrasts between the Synoptics and John. In the Synoptics, Jesus speaks in aphorisms and in parables. In John, there are no parables but rather long, involved discourses, and only occasionally is an aphorism buried deeply in an extended discourse. In the Synoptics, Jesus is presented as a sage; in John, he is presented as a philosopher, lecturer, and mystic.

One of John's rare aphorisms appears in today's reading: the one who loves life loses it, while the one who hates his life in this world preserves it to life eternal. This aphorism echoes Matthew 10:39; Mark 8:35; Luke 9:24 and 14:26. All these passages are variations on something Jesus said that described the jarring human experience of being reoriented through disorientation. How can hating one's life in this world save it for life eternal?

Such a saying pulls a hearer up short. Essentially, John simply says "this world" and life in it are problematic. Therefore, hating life in "this world" gains life eternal, a much better deal. This is perhaps easier said than done, especially when one takes seriously John's difficult if not risky black-and-white attitudes on reality.

Even so, the most important point is "honor." Jesus prays: "Father, glorify (honor) your name!" God bestows honor unsurpassable. In whatever culture they find themselves, God's creatures must do whatever glorifies or gives honor to God. The process often involves a reversal of accepted outlooks and values.

Cycle C

Isaiah 43:16–21
Philippians 3:8–14
John 8:1–11

"New" has a sense of wonder attached to it. It means "never seen before." "New" has a sense of hope attached to it. It implies, "this is what we've always wanted to happen." The new leaves on the trees, the new buds on the rose bushes, and the new sprouts in the garden are promises of spring.

God is the creator of new. God is the inventor of all we see. God is the one who makes everything we've always hoped for happen. Jesus revealed God's creativity by forgiving and healing. In Jesus, God did something new. The forgiving love revealed in Jesus is the promise of an eternal spring.

1st Reading

The setting for the reading is the Babylonian exile (587–537 BCE), a time when the Jews lived as captives, hundreds of miles away from their land. As time passed, they lost hope of ever returning home. They looked back to the exodus from Egypt as just a glorious event of the past, without significance in their present difficulty.

Into this hopeless group came an unknown prophet, someone who carried on the tradition of the great prophet Isaiah. Chapters 40–55 of

Isaiah are referred to as Second Isaiah because these chapters come from a time much later than chapters 1–39. When the book of Isaiah was formed, the editors combined these two prophetic collections (as well as a third, chapters 56–66), perhaps recognizing a similar spirit in all.

First the prophet calls to mind the events of the exodus and the memory of God's help. This memory is meant to strengthen the exiles because their fate is similar: they, too, are captives. God helped their ancestors and God can help them. The powerful army whom God snuffed out (v 17) is that of Egypt. Yet God's actions are not just something in the past but point to expectations for the future. What happened to Egypt will be repeated to Babylon. This will result in a new remembrance (v 18).

"I am about to do something new!" (v 19). God will again create a path through the desert, not the desert of Sinai but the desert that stretched between Babylon and Jerusalem. God will provide water for the travelers, not simply a drink from a rock (Ex 17:6) but an entire river (Is 43:20). For Second Isaiah, to receive the blessing of God's Word is like drinking water (55:1). In the final verse of the reading (v 21) Israel is told that it was created, "formed," by God as a people of praise. The prophet encourages the people to trust in the Creator's help and to believe that God will act again.

2nd Reading

Paul wrote the letter to the Philippians from prison. It may be that this setting provided a unique opportunity for him to reflect upon the changes in his situation, his previous dependence upon the Law and his new life in Christ.

In the first section, Paul wants to convince the Philippians that the Law, even for him, is now worthless because of Christ. Some people in the community endorsed circumcision and other observances. Just preceding the reading (vv 5–6), Paul explains that as a Pharisee he, too, was circumcised and lived a life of zealous obedience. Now Paul is different and looks upon his past life with new eyes, eyes formed by faith in Christ. The Law will not bring salvation (v 9). Paul's only desire is to come to full communion with Christ, to "know Christ" and to live a life similar to his (v 10).

His argument then flows to a familiar metaphor for Greek citizens, sports. He compares his striving to know and imitate Christ with a foot race. Although Paul tries to imitate Christ more deeply (and grasp this prize), in reality he himself has been grasped by Christ (v 12). Paul assures the Philippians that he, too, must struggle forward. He doesn't have it any easier than they do. What enables him to push on is the goal of the race, life eternal, the prize that God will award at the end of the race. He tells them to continue on, look at the end goal, just as a runner does in a race.

Gospel Reading

The gospels are full of stories about people whose lives seem finished until they meet Christ and discover they are only beginning to live. In this week's passage, a woman accused of adultery is a person at the end and beginning of life.

The story comes after a series of conflicts about Jesus' teaching and authority. According to the Law (Dt 22:22) a woman accused of adultery must be put to death (as must the man). The Gospel writer notes the purpose of the encounter of the Pharisees, Jesus, and the woman: the religious leaders need some kind of reason to condemn Jesus (v 6). The woman is being used in this sense by the Pharisees.

Jesus avoids the trap laid by the leaders by refusing to judge the woman himself. Instead, he challenges the accusers to judge. The Law stated that the witnesses of a crime should be the first to raise their hands against the offender (Dt 17:7). He carries this injunction a bit further by suggesting that only those without sin are really qualified to punish this woman.

Obviously Jesus is not saying we ought not judge unless we are perfect. That would nullify the office of every magistrate in our country. He is dealing here with self-righteous zealots who have taken upon themselves the enforcement of the Law. Jesus knows that their motives are less than honest. The circumstances of her arrest and the spiritual state of the woman are not even considered by them.

The story, which until now has really been about the Pharisees and Jesus, shifts to the woman herself, who to this point has not spoken. Alone with Jesus, she still does not speak until he asks her a question. The one person qualified to judge her does not condemn her, but neither does he condone her sin. Jesus' response is a blend of mercy and justice. The woman is simply asked to avoid sinning again. She makes the journey from death to life in a few short verses. Not only is she reprieved from physical death but also from spiritual death. She can forget her past and begin life anew.

The Law could not bring life to this woman. Forgiveness and mercy are the creative forces at work in this story. These qualities have the power to make someone new.

"Lectionary Commentary for the 5th Sunday of Lent" originally appeared in Liturgy Plus *Planning Software (Cycles ABC) (Resource Publications, Inc.).*

Lectionary Commentary for Passion Sunday

Liturgy Plus *Planning Software*

Cycle A

> Isaiah 50:4–7
> Philippians 2:6–11
> Matthew 26:14–27:66

1st Reading

The historical background of Second Isaiah includes the destruction of Jerusalem and the Exile with its suffering. Themes of comfort and salvation permeate its poetry. God is presented as creator and is an active force in history, both as redeemer/savior and as creator. The poetry of Second Isaiah is filled with the language of the Psalms that proclaim salvation. For Second Isaiah there is an unbreakable bond between creation and salvation. The poet sees fulfillment of the divine purpose for God's holy, covenanted, chosen, called, redeemed people.

The Servant Songs (42:1–4; 49:1–6; 50:4–9; 52:13–53:12) are an integral part of Second Isaiah's prophetic poetry. The servant symbolically represents the whole of Israel. The servant is not an individual; rather, the servant is the community of Israel that is struggling to redefine itself in Exile. In the first Song (42:1–4), Israel/servant is called the chosen one who will reveal God's law to the nations. Unlike a king, who uses all the means of public announcement, the servant/Israel will speak quietly, respecting the faint glimmers of hope within the community.

The second servant song (49:1–6) is similar to Jeremiah 1:4–10. Israel (like Jeremiah) is called and chosen by God. Israel is to fight with the word that is as sharp as a sword that penetrates like a polished arrow. Like Jeremiah, the servant protests, "I have labored in vain...spent my strength for nothing and vanity." Perhaps this protest comes out of the frustration of exile and the struggle to accept the difficult life in Babylon.

Isaiah 50:4–7 represents the third servant song. In verses 1–3, God is accused of divorcing Israel (God's spouse) and of selling her to a creditor. God responds that it was their iniquities that were the cause of Israel being sold into exile. God asks, where is the bill of divorce? Who is the creditor? Verses 4–7, the third servant song, is the response of the prophet in words of defense of God.

God has called the servant (vv 4–5a) and, despite opposition, Israel (at least Second Isaiah's community) has remained faithful and kept to the task. As John Scullion points out in his commentary on Isaiah 40–66, God is the prime mover and is four times the subject of a series of three verbs. God has given (v 4a), has opened (v 5a), and helps (vv 7a, 9a) (*Isaiah 40–66*, no. 12, *Old Testament Message* [Wilmington: Michael Glazier, 1982]). The community of Second Isaiah proclaims their unshakable confidence in God.

While the tradition of Christianity identifies the Suffering Servant with Jesus, we should not be too quick in making this identification. To see the "servant" as the community of Second Isaiah expands the image and enables our contemporary communities to more closely identify with the struggling, suffering community of Israel.

2nd Reading

Paul founded the Christian community of Philippi around A.D. 50 on his second missionary journey. It was a Roman colony (originally founded by Philip of Macedonia in the fourth century B.C.), and its citizens enjoyed full Roman citizenship.

In Philippians 1:21, Paul says that the essence of life is Christ, and so in 1:27–30 Paul urges the Philippians to conduct themselves in a way worthy of the gospel of Christ. They are to have the one love, united in spirit and ideals (2:2). They are to think humbly of others (2:3) and carry the attitude of Christ (2:5). What follows is an ancient hymn incorporated by Paul into his letter.

Verses 6–11 stand out in Christian literature as a pre-eminent statement of Christ's self-emptying gift of life. Jesus emptied himself, taking the form of a slave (v 7). He humbled himself, obediently accepting even death (v 8). Because of this, Jesus is exalted by God (v 9) and given the name of Lord (v 11). The hymn expresses a high christology, and yet it focuses on the humanity of Jesus as he takes on death in order to bring exaltation to all humanity.

Gospel Reading

Donald Senior's book *The Passion of Jesus in the Gospel of Matthew* (Wilmington: Michael Glazier, 1985) is a very good resource for getting into Matthew's Passion. Senior comments that the Passion in Matthew, as it is in the other evangelists', is the climax of Jesus' entire mission. "Theological motifs that run through the gospel find their resolution and most eloquent expression in the dramatic events of Jesus' death and resurrection" (p. 11). Senior goes on to say that "the Passion of Jesus was not simply a story of suffering out of the past but a point of identification for the Christians of Matthew's own time, who struggled to find meaning and purpose in the cross they now had to take up" (p. 13). Ultimately what we come to understand about the Passion is that it reveals for us the cross that must be endured and actively and deliberately taken up (p. 8).

Matthew's Jesus is presented firmly embedded in Israel's sacred history and tradition. At the same time, Jesus is the explosive force for the new and decisive age of salvation (p. 18). Senior also notes that the Passion story is not simply an account of Jesus' suffering and death; it is also an account of the Christian community's encounter with the Passion (p. 40). Thus the pattern of the cross is the pattern of Christian existence (p. 43).

The Passion begins with a prelude in which Jesus' opponents devise a death plot for him (26:1–16). Our text begins in the middle of this prelude with a secret meeting between Judas Iscariot and the chief priests. This secret meeting contrasts with Jesus' open announcement of his own death (26:1–2). Matthew's portrayal of Jesus has him in full control of the events that are about to play out. Jesus moves forward in fidelity, while his opponents are oblivious to the great act of salvation in their midst. In verses 14–16, Judas represents the dark side of discipleship, the potential for betrayal possible in every believer who faces crisis (Senior, p. 55).

Following the secret scene of Judas are four scenes that relate to the last Passover meal that Jesus celebrates with his disciples. This meal is not just a Passover meal that becomes our Eucharist. It is a meal that interprets Jesus' death (26:28). In the first scene (vv 17–19) we hear Jesus instruct the disciples on how to prepare the meal. We see the disciples respond in obedience (v 19). In the second scene (vv 20–25) the secret betrayal of Judas is made public. With mounting tension Jesus confronts Judas, who responds to the question of betrayal, "It is not I, is it, Rabbi?" (v 25). Judas unwittingly sets his plan in motion to destroy Jesus.

In scene three (vv 26–29) we stand at the heart of this section of the Passion narrative. The Passover meal, rich in tradition and symbolism, celebrates the liberation/salvation of Israel (the Exodus account of Passover will be used on Holy Thursday). Thus the meal Jesus shares becomes an experience of liberation and salvation. Drawing from the rich tradition of Exodus, Matthew interprets the cup that Jesus blesses as the cup of the new covenant and Jesus' blood, poured out for many, as the new covenant of redemption.

The final scene (vv 30–35) completes the poignant story of the disciples' failure. Not only does Judas betray Jesus, but Peter and the other disciples also betray Jesus. In the midst of the singing of triumphant songs, Jesus predicts their betrayal. This strongly contrasts Peter's profession of faith near Caesarea Philippi (16:16,22–23,35).

The next section of the Passion is the scene in the garden of Gethsemane (vv 36–56). The first part of the scene finds us in the midst of Jesus' anguished prayer (vv 36–46), and the second finds us witnessing Jesus' arrest (vv 47–56). Senior (p. 74) comments that "with the prayer of Jesus preparation for the Passion ends; the arrival of Judas and the mob begins the tortuous events of Jesus' suffering and eventual death." All that takes place in the scene fulfills the scriptures, as Jesus says. From Matthew's perspective the words of the prophets are fulfilled (5:17). All the sacred history of Israel is compressed into Jesus, God's Son (p. 89).

The next scene in the Passion narrative moves from the Mount of Olives to the house of Caiaphas, the high priest (26:57–27:10). The focus of the encounter between Jesus and his opponents is on Jesus the Messiah, the Son of God. From the interrogation and mockery before the Sanhedrin (26:69–75) to the final verdict and handing over of Jesus to Pilate (27:1–2), Jesus stands confident and resolute. In contrast to Jesus' resoluteness is Peter's denial that draws us into the story. When Peter weeps, we weep with him. Verses 3–10 in chapter 27 are unique to Matthew. The tragic fate of Judas points out his lack of reconciliation (in contrast to Peter) instead of turning to Jesus. He returns to the chief priests, which leads Judas to despair for his betrayal.

The next scene is Jesus' trial before Pilate (27:11–31). There are three episodes in this section of the Passion story: an interrogation of Jesus by Pilate (vv 11–14); the choice between Jesus and Barabbas (vv 15–26); the mocking of Jesus by the Roman garrison (vv 27–31). The major issue of the Roman trial revolves around the question of whether Jesus is the king of the Jews (v 11). The narrative carries many images with it. From the suffering servant songs, Matthew wraps Jesus in a traditional cloak of the faithful servant who suffers for his obedience to God.

Senior (p. 112) comments that the most important episode in the trial scene is the choice posed to the people of Barabbas or Jesus. Confronted with the person of Jesus and his message, we are forced to accept or reject him. Matthew interprets the death of Jesus in line with the death of the prophets, and so various images and symbolic actions (Pilate washing his hands, cf. Dt 21:1 ff) describe the rejection of Jesus by the people of Israel. In this section caution must be taken to avoid any anti-semitic overtones in blaming the Jews for Jesus' death. All references must be kept in context and historical circumstance.

The next section of the Passion story brings us to Golgotha and Jesus' death (27:32–56). There are two episodes here: Jesus' crucifixion and final mockery (vv 32–44) and death (vv 45–56). Matthew's description of crucifixion is swift and to the point. Matthew draws heavily upon the Psalms in describing the lament and intensity of Jesus' death. Surrounding his suffering is further mockery and betrayal, with Matthew drawing the final words from Psalm 22, "He committed his cause to the Lord; Let him deliver him, let him rescue him, for he delights in him!"

The eerie stillness of the ninth hour is broken by the heart-clutching scream of Jesus: "My God! My God! Why have you forsaken me?" (Psalm 22). As Senior notes (p. 137), "only the first line (of the psalm) is quoted but the spirit of the entire psalm is behind the lament in which the psalmist weaves together hoarse cries of pain with tenacious assertions of faith." The moment of Jesus' death comes with stunning quickness. With his final breath, Jesus yields up the spirit that has been entrusted to him since the beginning of the gospel. Here can be heard the words of Philippians, for Jesus is obedient unto death. At the instant of Jesus' death various signs occur, from the tearing of the curtain in the temple, to an earthquake, to the opening of tombs and the resurrection of saints. All these signs bring the execution detail, most specifically the gentile centurion, to acclaim, "Truly this was the son of God!"

The Passion narrative concludes with the burial of Jesus and the vigil at his tomb (27:57–66). The drama and intensity of Jesus' death are now followed by a quiet reflective mood. Both the burial and the vigil lead us to the resurrection. We have to wait in vigil as the women waited at the sepulcher.

Passion or Palm Sunday has always been a difficult day for me. I have not gotten into Lent yet, and now the pressure of Holy Week bears down upon us. The greatest difficulty is that so much is going on, and the reading of the Passion so long, that the homily either gets dropped or is cut down to a bare minimum. People scramble for their palms, but take little time to hear and reflect upon the scriptures.

Passion Sunday is not as stark as Good Friday, because we start with the triumphant entrance into Jerusalem. With shouts of Hosanna we enter Jerusalem and moments later our shouts become "Crucify him! Crucify him!" We seal Jesus' fate. It has always struck me how similar these two acclamations are. The tension between our acceptance of Jesus and our refusal or betrayal is a tension we live with.

As Don Senior said, the pattern of the cross is the pattern of Christian existence. The challenge is not to rush past the Passion just to get to the resurrection. To feel the pain and intensity of Jesus' suffering might be too much for some, but if the cross is the pattern of Christian existence, then we have to stop our palm grabbing and stand beside the cross for a while (this opportunity will come on Friday). Here the choice of the Philippians reading is important. The Passion is not just suffering; the Passion and cross also witness to the obedience, humility, and self-sacrificing of Jesus.

Walking with Jesus to Golgotha can be a lonely, painful walk. It is a walk surrounded by mockery, betrayal, and the sounds of despair/anguish. The focus is not on palms but on the way we find the Passion and death of Jesus making sense in our lives. This is especially true when Jesus screams from the cross, "My God! My God! Why have you forsaken me?" The depth of anguish takes us into the heart of Jesus' humanity, where the certainty of God's presence is a real uncertainty. The feelings of abandonment and failure are some of the deepest feelings we can have. When we come to this point in the Passion, our oneness with Jesus' suffering should be most intense.

In triumph and failure, in anguish and exultation, we walk with Jesus the final steps to glory!

Cycle B

> Isaiah 50:4–7
> Philippians 2:6–11
> Mark 14:1–15:47 or 15:1–39

1st Reading

This passage is one of the so-called Suffering Servant songs. Contemporary scholars prefer to keep these passages well integrated into the whole of Isaiah, and many scholars apply the passages to Israel rather than to a single individual.

Be that as it may, by pairing this text with the Passion story, the architects of the lectionary have left themselves open to the charge of disrespecting the Old Testament. One gets the impression that the Old Testament has its sole purpose of existence in being fulfilled in the New Testament. Preachers and liturgy planners would do well to avoid strengthening that mistaken impression with regard not only to Isaiah but to all of the Old Testament. God's interpersonal relationship with Israel as reflected in Isaiah ought to be respected in itself, and the text deserves respect as it stands, on its own terms.

From the cultural perspective, the speaker in this passage reflects typical Mediterranean male obedience. The speaker boasts of his ability to tough it out, to accept what is dished out to him. Shameful though this treatment is, the speaker

has absolute confidence that God is on his side. Therefore what seems like shame will turn out to his credit and honor. Since God is on his side, he is "not disgraced." This confidence gives the speaker all the more courage and determination to stay the course. He knows he will not be put to shame.

From this perspective, a respectful link of this passage to the Gospel is obvious. In an honor and shame culture, absolute trust in God allows one to believe with confidence that shameful treatment can truly have honorable outcomes. This interpretation of the Isaiah passage and Mark's Passion story make both messages culturally plausible rather than culturally unusual.

2nd Reading

The key to understanding this familiar passage lies in appreciating the Mediterranean value known as "humility" (see verse 8: "he humbled himself"). In an honor and shame culture, one's chief honor derives from birth (acquired honor) and one is culturally duty-bound never to surpass this status. To get ahead, to better oneself, and similar strategies are very shameful in the Mediterranean world. Indeed, even the suspicion of such a strategy is so potentially shameful that normal people genuinely try to stay one step behind their rightful status. (See Mk 1:7, the Baptizer's self-humiliation relative to Jesus.)

Proverbs 15:33 and 18:12 teach that humility takes precedence over honor. In concrete terms, to humble or humiliate oneself means to declare that one is powerless to defend legitimate status, a fundamental cultural obligation. This is what this Philippian hymn expresses. Such self-humiliation before God is praiseworthy and obtains God's help. (See Prv 3:34.) This is what Jesus himself urges upon his followers (Mt 18:4) and what this hymn tells us he himself practiced.

The result is obvious: "Because of such humility, even to the extent of dying on the cross out of obedience, God exalted him."

This all fits perfectly well with Mediterranean child-rearing practices as well as the honorable behavior expected of adult males. Proverbs and Sirach are the implied background behind such sentiments.

Gospel Reading

The gospel Passion narratives have their roots in the tradition cited by Paul in 1 Corinthians 15:3b–5: Jesus died in accord with the scriptures, was buried, was raised on the third day in accord with the scriptures, and was seen. Recorded by Paul more than twenty years after Jesus died, this passage already reflected a hardened tradition.

Newcomers to the faith would want to know more. Why did this good man die? Well, he was put to a trial, found guilty, and sentenced to die. This series of stories was appended to the tradition in Corinthians, itself gradually expanded with detail. Essentially, this short narrative was kerygmatic in nature. It presented the "facts" of the Passion story in the light of prophecy. Specifically, the Suffering Servant would be glorified.

But why was Jesus brought to trial? Because he was betrayed by an intimate friend after sharing a very special meal with his friends. As he was at prayer in his favorite garden, the betrayer arranged to have him arrested. Then followed the trial, etc. And thus did the basic Passion story evolve from the tradition in 1 Corinthians to its longer form.

As time passed, the basic story line evolved in two further directions. Matthew and Mark essentially shaped their narratives to demonstrate the fulfillment of Suffering Servant themes. Luke and John were more rooted in the "pietistic" element and reported more words of Jesus. Luke moved the table talk of the supper onto the road to Gethsemane. And John 13–17 so expanded the table talk that the supper disappeared!

In recent years, scholars have turned fresh attention to the Passion stories. To these many fine studies, the following insights from the Mediterranean cultural perspective can be fruitfully added.

Another way of looking at the events of the Passion narrative is to see in them a series of status-degradation rituals. Throughout the Gospel, Jesus has gained an honorable reputation as teacher and healer. He has engaged in argument with his opponents and won (or honorably evaded) each encounter. Those who are not persuaded about his ministry and reputation resolve to put him down a notch or two. Jesus, of course, opens himself to this risk by leaving the hinterlands of Galilee and coming right to the center of action, the Jerusalem Temple.

Here Jesus provokes the chief priests and the scribes by disrupting Temple sacrifice (11:15–19). More, he publicly discredits them (see 11:27 and 12:12). In the view of these authorities, Jesus is no hero. He is rather a disrespectful deviant, a social upstart, and he must be arrested, tried, and punished if not destroyed. Keep in mind that the Gospels are a form of propaganda literature written by admirers and believers and intended to be favorable to Jesus. A mirror-reading of the same texts helps one to appreciate the other perspective. Mark calls the witnesses "false" (14:57–61) and says their testimony did not agree. Matthew omits these Marcan evaluations in his version. The statement against Jesus may well mirror the honest convictions of people who consider Jesus to be deviant and dangerous.

He has, after all, disturbed the operation of the Temple. Now in reply to a direct question: "Are you the Messiah, the Son of the Blessed One?" Jesus merely repeats what has already been proclaimed at his baptism and transfiguration: Yes! But the authorities cannot square his disregard for the Temple with the status of Son of God. So they pin the ultimate deviant label on him: blasphemer! "They all concurred in the verdict 'guilty,' with its sentence of death."

Remember, too, that the Gospel versions of Jesus' arrest, trial and execution are in fact retrospective interpretations of the close of Jesus' career. Even if one can claim that Mark reflects the actual events and charges, it is also true that Mark has manipulated them to redound to Jesus' credit and honor rather than to his shame. Mark's Jesus does not shy away from the charges of deviance but rather accepts them as true and authentic titles: "I am [the Messiah]; and you will see the Son of Man seated at the right hand of the Power and coming with the clouds of heaven." Thus Mark uses the degradation process (the trial) as an occasion for letting Jesus prove his prominence!

In his culture, Jesus was not the equal of his accusers. Only equals may engage in the game of honor and shame. Superiors (like the chief priests) should disregard inferiors (like Jesus). Inferiors are only a nuisance but not a serious threat. Yet, in taking Jesus to trial, the chief priests and scribes were taking a big risk. And in Mark's story line, they lost the gamble. Jesus beat them at their own game. Christians, of course, are not surprised because Jesus already instructed them on how they would win their trials (Mk 13:9–13).

Jesus' strategy is interesting: he makes no reply to "charges" (threat to destroy Temple; accusations to Pilate) but speaks only when a question gives him an opportunity to promote his prominent status ("Are you Messiah? Are you King?"). Actually, the charges have been successfully deflected earlier in the Gospel narratives.

True enough, the authorities succeeded in having Jesus put to death. But his resurrection was something they didn't expect. Though Mark does not report a resurrection appearance of Jesus, the messenger will make it explicit in next week's reading: "He has been raised up; he is not here." (The passive voice, "has been raised up," is a way of talking about God without using the word.) The retrospective rehabilitation of Jesus to honor after his shameful trial and death validates and reconfirms the honor Jesus achieved during his ministry. Without an explicit resurrection appearance, however, Mark's readers and listeners are now thrown back on their faith in the word of promise. Here is a point that preachers and liturgy planners can highlight to advantage among mainstream United States citizens who generally insist on scientific proof.

Cycle C

Isaiah 50:4–7
Philippians 2:6–11
Luke 22:14–23:56

Barren branches in winter help us appreciate the green leaves of summer. We cannot reflect on the triumph of the resurrection without encountering the mystery of the crucifixion.

1st Reading

The four "suffering servant songs" found in Isaiah are in the lectionary for Holy Week. In this third song, the servant is speaking. He describes himself as a student, someone whose ear is open to God and is trained by God. The student learns from God how "to sustain the weary with a word" (v 4). Written during the time of the Babylonian exile, "the weary" are the people of Israel in captivity who have lost hope. The servant did not listen to the voices of despair around him but to the voice of God.

The servant/student is able to withstand the insults and abuse of others, possibly those who refused to listen to his message. Unlike some, this servant has not turned away from God; the servant is faithful, even when it results in personal injury (vv 5–6). Pulling out someone's beard was not only painful but was considered particularly insulting. Despite the abuse, the servant of God is at the core unaffected; the servant's face is "like flint" (v 7). The reason for this confidence is the servant's faith in the future, "I shall not be put to shame" (v 7). God is in control of events, and despite the difficulties of the present, the future is secure because God is faithful.

Though these songs come from the sixth century before Christ, they provided for the early church and provide for the church today a way of speaking about the innocent suffering of Christ. They are not so much predictions of Christ as they are means of approaching the mystery of Christ's death. The songs give Christians a way to speak of the suffering of a blameless person in religious language with ancient roots.

2nd Reading

The selection from Philippians for this feast is based on an early Christian hymn which scholars believe Paul inserted into his letter. Paul includes this liturgical piece to encourage the church to be humble and unselfish, as Christ was (v 5). Christ is the example to be followed. The hymn describes Christ's humiliation and exaltation. He freely takes the form of a slave. Even more, he endures an ignoble death as a common criminal (v 8). Despite this humiliation, he is glorified and exalted. Christ is now the Lord of all. The Philippians, who shared in Christ's glory through faith, must also share Christ's attitude. They are not to seek positions of power for its own sake but must live as humble servants. Service and humility are to be their ways to glory.

Gospel Reading

Each Gospel presents the passion in a unique way. Luke's account of Jesus' final days carries forward some of the concerns of his Gospel. Table fellowship, forgiveness, and Jesus as the innocent man are given a special dimension.

The Last Supper is the context for Jesus' teaching on service and discipleship (22:24–30). Both Matthew and Mark tell this incident in the course of Jesus' journey to Jerusalem. (In John, Jesus illustrates this same point through the footwashing.) Of the three synoptic gospels (Matthew, Mark, and Luke), only Luke speaks of the new covenant (v 20), a reference to Jeremiah 31:31–34. Luke sees Jesus' death as the fulfillment of prophesy and as the beginning of a new relationship with God.

The Last Supper also looks forward in anticipation of the final banquet in the kingdom (vv 16, 18). Meals are important in Luke's gospel. The meal is a place where the reality of Christian life is expressed. Who is invited, who gets to sit where, etc., all reveal the hidden values of the participants (14:7–11). For Luke, the eucharistic table is the place where sinners are invited. It is where the community expresses its life in Christ. This life and unity must be nurtured through loving service.

Luke's gospel can be called the Gospel of Forgiveness. All the gospels record that the slave of the high priest had his ear cut off during Jesus' arrest (Mt 26:51, Mk 14:27, Jn 18:10), but only Luke records that Jesus healed the man (22:51). After Peter's denial of Christ, Luke with touching insight includes this line: "The Lord turned and looked at Peter" (22:61). On the cross Jesus asks that the crucifiers be forgiven (23:34). Only Luke tells the story of the two criminals at the cross (23:39–43). At the hour of his death, Jesus reaches out in forgiveness to the man who recognizes his own sin. Luke understands Jesus to be the compassionate and merciful Lord, a man capable of deep feeling. His death is a moment of glory.

Luke wrote for a predominantly Gentile community. At the close of the first century, religion and sedition were sometimes seen as close neighbors. Luke carefully portrays the passion of Christ as the suffering of an innocent man. Neither Herod nor Pilate find anything to condemn in him (23:14–15). At the crucifixion, it is a Roman centurion who in the end declares, "Certainly this man was innocent" (23:47). For Christians, living under Roman rule was a given. Luke's portrayal of Christ as legally innocent gave them hope. Their faith in Christ was not just faith in a political revolutionary. Their faith was in someone much greater.

The passion story is almost overwhelming in its detail. Where do we find ourselves on the Way of the Cross? Who are we in the passion story?

"Lectionary Commentary for Passion Sunday" originally appeared in Liturgy Plus *Planning Software (Cycles ABC) (Resource Publications, Inc.).*

Planning Guide for Lent — Cycle A

This year's Gospel readings are normative for the catechumenate; they give substance to this final lenten leg of the catechumenal process, the Period of Purification and Enlightenment. Each Gospel depicts a particular aspect of the journey in faith.

Penance and penitential practices are not ends in themselves but characteristics of the Christian journey. Lenten penance is not only an individual spiritual discipline; it is also the community's way of making room for neophytes — sort of the church's "spring cleaning."

The length of the readings poses a pastoral problem that must be dealt with by effective proclamation, not by abbreviating them (even though lectionaries appear to legitimize this). We print here the references to the longest version in each case.

Note how often the Common Lectionary (ecumenical) is longer than the Roman selections. If we consider greater length an enrichment rather than a burdensome imposition, then we're led to proclaim them accordingly. Lenten readings might call for a lector's renewal and refresher program, which of course will include priests and deacons since they must proclaim lengthy Gospels in a way that conveys their drama and awakens faith-commitment in the hearers.

Ash Wednesday

Jl 2:12–18
2 Cor 5:20–6:2
Mt 6:1–6,16–18

After all the effort we put into coercing people who want ashes to come for Mass, maybe we should reexamine whether the Eucharist really is appropriate today. As noted in the introduction, the Eucharist is not a penitential act but a celebration of the paschal mystery. Those who seek ashes today need to be nourished by the proclaimed word; we should insist on that. But perhaps we should begin to see non-Eucharist as well as ashes today as a sign that we are beginning a season that is very definitely not "business as usual" for the church. This approach should be considered carefully and discussed with others.

For many Catholics, Eucharist is the center of their spirituality and to cut these persons off from the saving mystery could be problematic.

The readings are a radical call to conversion from the depths of our hearts, not merely to engage in a particular set of practices. Yet the internal can only be expressed and proven externally. The focus is on the threefold discipline of prayer, fasting, and almsgiving as necessarily complementary to each other. Distortions arise when any one is emphasized to the exclusion of the other two.

Liturgy Notes

Simplicity — back to the basics — is the order of the day. The gathering rites consist of hymn, sign of the cross, greeting, and collect.

Following the Joel lesson, you may wish to sing Psalm 103:8–14. Psalm 51 may then be sung in its entirety during the giving of ashes procession.

RCIA Thoughts

Candidates for full communion may celebrate a rite of "Entering the Penitential Period" with the rest of the Christian community. See the (Episcopal) *Book of Common Prayer* and the *Lutheran Book of Worship* (Ministers Edition) for additional sources for designing this ritual.

One may question the appropriateness of signing catechumens with ashes and calling them to be "faithful" and "reconciled" with the Lord. Again, this is the sort of decision which should be openly discussed.

Music

- All Flesh Is Grass (Haugen/GIA)

- Ashes (Conry/New Dawn)

- Come Home Child (Farrel/PMB)

- Draw Near, O Lord (Douglas/ML 9:8)

- Hosea (Weston Priory)

- Lenten Psalm (Keyes/ML 11:6)

- Lord, We Are Sorry (Raffa/ML 8:4)

- O Lord, You Are My Refuge (Dicie/ML 9:3)

- Praise the Lord, My Soul (Jesuits/New Dawn)

- Return All Things (Dicie/ML 9:3)

- This Is Our Acceptable Time (Gannon/PMB)

1st Sunday of Lent

Gn 2:7–9; 3:1–7
Rom 5:12–19
Mt 4:1–11

The Scriptures of the First Sunday of Lent always involve us in the struggle with evil. The story of the primordial Fall told in Genesis embodies all human sinfulness — enslavement to the desire to be the source of our own fulfillment. Jesus' temptations were specifically against his mission as Messiah, and therefore they speak very directly to the whole church community that is the continuation of his life and ministry into the here and now. Each of Satan's suggestions involved a misuse of power to accomplish self-centered ends rather than human liberation.

Deep down, many of us still believe that we are saved by our own efforts and that God's role is to help out as needed. Paul's insight is important to counter this "bootstrap" Pelagianism that can have a strong hold on us. Overcoming evil is fundamentally God's business.

The answer to sin is not trying harder, but surrendering to God's gift. In the Rite of Election the candidates are given the power to overcome evil. Lent is called the Period of Purification and Enlightenment in the *Rite of Christian Initiation of Adults*, and the whole community as well as the elect need to cultivate faith in this gift.

Liturgy Notes

The Sundays in Lent are marked in the sacramentary by the omission of the "Hymn of Praise" and the singing of a "Gospel Acclamation" (other than an "Alleluia"). How else might you highlight the Sundays in Lent through your creative use of the penitential rite and/or Kyrie throughout the six Sundays?

The presence of and prayers with the elect also set this season apart. Their presence enriches the parish and can be used to instruct and remind.

The lenten retreat of purification and enlightenment is a "desert experience" provided by the lectionary itself. Absence of flowers and "holy water" will highlight their beautiful reappearance at the Great Vigil of Easter.

RCIA Thoughts

A parish ritual is appropriately designed to send the catechumens with the blessing of the parish community. (When the bishop or his delegate does not preside over the election, this rite takes place today at the parish Sunday Eucharist.)

The catechumens/elect may reflect on the three questions put to their godparents during the "presentation of the candidates," comparing them to the temptations placed before the Lord on his journey toward his mission. How does it feel to be "chosen" by God, a calling affirmed by the community?

Music

- Beginning Today (Dameans/New Dawn)

- Be Not Afraid (Jesuits/New Dawn)

- Fear Not (Fatten/ML 8:3)

- May We Praise (Jesuits/New Dawn)

- On Eagle's Wings (Joncas/New Dawn)

- O Lord You Know Our Weakness (Weston/New Dawn)

- Praise To The Holiest (Newman/PMB)

2nd Sunday of Lent

> Gen 12:1–4
> 2 Tim 1:8–10
> Mt 17:1–9

A sense of timing and transition pervades the readings and the spirit of this Sunday. Abram, deeply rooted in a land and his kinsfolk, is compelled to go forth from them in faith to be the foundation of God's people and source of blessing for all times and places.

Jesus has received his disciples' profession of faith in his messianic mission and has just begun to reveal to them the implications of that mission—rejection, death, and triumph over death. The transfiguration is not a "light show" or an external display of glory; it is a fundamental affirmation of Jesus being rooted in the tradition of God speaking to humankind.

As God's faithful heard the Lawgiver and the Prophet in the past and were formed by God's word through them, so now God affirms that they must be formed by Jesus' word. Another temptation is presented here in the person of Peter wanting to stay and take possession of the moment. We cannot rest in the word; the word impels us forward.

Liturgy Notes

Today's vision gives us a glimpse of the glory we are preparing to commemorate during the Easter Triduum. Consider using incense today.

The evangelism committee may use the Bible verse, "Lord, it is good for us to be here!" as a reach out to those who feel alienated from the church. Make your community known as a place of welcome!

Publicize retreat centers in your area that your parishioners may go to for some time apart — with the Lord.

RCIA *Thoughts*

God breaks into human history over and over again. He continues to choose to love creation and promise salvation.

God has chosen us, the elect. When did I receive his promise into my life, accepting his gift of faith? How do I bring my own experience of God to others?

Music

- Psalm 33:4–5,18–20,22

- Gather Us In (Haugen/GIA)

- God's Holy Mountain (Westendoff/PMB)

- How Beautiful (Wise/GIA)

- In God Alone (Anderson/ML 8:2)

- Jesus, The New Covenant (Deiss/PMB)

- Lord This Is the People (Burne/ML 8:3)

- Psalm 89 (Barrier/PMB)

- The Voice of the Lord (Blunt/ML 11:3)

- This Alone (Jesuits/New Dawn)

- Transfiguration (Landry/New Dawn)

- Yahweh (Weston Priory)

3rd Sunday of Lent

> Ex 17:3–7
> Rom 5:1–2,5–8
> Jn 4:5–42

Today is the First Scrutiny of the elect, in which they and the whole church are to allow the scriptural word to probe their hearts. The church verbally immerses us in the symbol of water today, and it may be helpful to recall an insight of psychology that water in our unconscious mind symbolizes sexuality. Sex, although much distorted in our strangely repressed and hedonistic society, is essentially an immersion into the life-giving power of God. Jesus, the Living Water, is the love embrace of God that cannot fail to be fruitful, except through our fear and frigidity. Vulnerability is key to fruitful love. The hard-hearted Israelites in the first reading embody the deadening need to control, while the

Samaritan woman is the model of openness in the face of new life, even if the process probes painfully deep into the heart.

Liturgy Notes

The absence of holy water as well as the Rite of Sprinkling will mark a contrast to today's readings. There are proper prefaces related to the Gospels for this and the next four Sundays.

RCIA Thoughts

What are you thirsting for? How has God quenched the ultimate thirst of your life?

If the elect identify their "thirst" these may be incorporated into the litany "prayer" for the "elect" (which may be chanted) while the elect may bow their heads to the Lord.

The Apostles Creed may be presented to the elect this week during a parish celebration of Evening Prayer or a Liturgy of the Word.

Music

- Psalm 95:1–2,6–9
- A Living Hope (Jones/PMB)
- As the Deer (Goglia/ML 10:6)
- Come to the Water (Anderson/ML 8:2)
- Give Us Living Water (Dameans/New Dawn)
- Glory & Praise (Jesuits/New Dawn)
- Lord, to Whom Shall We Go? (Conry/New Dawn)
- O Healing River (Joncas/GIA)
- The Church Is One Foundation (Stone/PMB)
- The Path of Life (Blunt/ML 11:2)
- You Will Draw Water (Conry/New Dawn)

4th Sunday of Lent

1 Sam 16:1,6–7,10–13
Eph 5:8–14
Jn 9:1–41

In the Second Scrutiny, the elect, and the whole community with them, are invited by the readings to explore the stories of both King David and the man born blind. As water was last

week, so light and sight are key this week. Perhaps the most significant statement is the one in the first reading about the difference between the human and divine perspective (v 7). It is a call to rise above the limited and weak vision that so restricts the full capabilities of graced humanity.

It is important to recognize the initiative of God in the Gospel. The blind man did not ask to be enlightened. In fact, he might have been pretty comfortable in his former state—no responsibility, sustenance provided without working for it. The unasked-for gift of sight gave him so much trouble we might wonder if he was tempted to desire to be blind again. To his credit, he measured up to the challenge and grew in the faith that sight symbolized. Note that his cure became light that revealed the inner spirit of others (Pharisees, parents, disciples).

Liturgy Notes

Today's opening prayer recalls the former observance of Laetare Sunday. The light of faith is embraced by the man born blind (a glimmer of Easter — rejoice!).

The memorial acclamation "Lord, by your cross …" seems to echo the words of those who meet Jesus on these lenten Sundays.

RCIA Thoughts

How has the Lord enlightened your life? What areas of your life are journeying toward the light (however painfully)?

Those parts of the elect's lives still needing to be transformed by the light may be incorporated into the purification litany. The "prayer for the elect" may be sung while the elect kneel. The assembly may be invited to raise their hand in blessing toward the elect during the final prayer of exorcism.

If the anointing with the oil of the catechumens will be anticipated prior to Holy Saturday, it may occur this week at a parish Liturgy of the Word or celebration of the Liturgy of the Hours using today's Samuel reading and Psalm.

Music

- Psalm 23:1–6
- Amazing Grace (Traditional)
- Awake, O Sleeper (Dameans/New Dawn)
- Dedication Song (Raffa/ML 8:3)
- Eye Have Not Seen (Haughen/GIA)

- Immortal, Invisible (Smith/PMB)

- Kyrie Eleison (Clark/ Celebration)

- Let Us Walk in the Light (Haughen/GIA)

- Light of the World (Kendzia/New Dawn)

- Little Closer (Sexton/ML 8:7)

- Lord, Your Almighty Word (Marriott/PMB)

- O Radiant Light (Sotrey/PMB)

- Sing Out the Goodness (Dameans/New Dawn)

5th Sunday of Lent

Ez 37:12–14
Rom 8:8–11
Jn 11:1–45

Death and life are themes that play with each other throughout this Gospel. After Jesus announces Lazarus' death and his intention to go to Jerusalem, Thomas says "Let's go die with him." Lazarus dies, but this is not the end. (Note that Jesus had not said in verse 4 that Lazarus would not die but that the sickness would not end in death.)

Finally, the supreme irony is that Jesus' life-giving act is precisely what seals his own death (vv 46–53, not included in the liturgical reading). It is a mystery that God is glorified through death—not death that ends in destruction of life but death that reveals new life. The Third Scrutiny, today, invites the elect and the whole community to face together their own mortality in a positive, grace-filled, and life-giving way.

Liturgy Notes

Today's liturgy marks a shift of focus to death and life, cross and resurrection.

The Eucharistic Prayer for Masses of Reconciliation I may be appropriate today.

RCIA Thoughts

How has your life become "new" since you have embraced Jesus by faith? What are some of those things which you must still put to death that will make your road toward eternal life even clearer?

The Lord's Prayer may be presented to the elect this week at a parish Liturgy of the Word or celebration of the Liturgy of the Hours.

Music

- Psalm 130:1–8

- Awake, 0 Sleeper (Dameans/New Dawn)

- An Everlasting Song (Sessions/ML 11:5)

- I Am the Bread of Life (Toolan/GIA)

- I Am the Resurrection (Dameans/New Dawn)

- I Believe in the Sun (Landry/New Dawn)

- I Have Waited (Gilsdorf/ML 8:5)

- In Him We Live (Landry/New Dawn)

- Keep in Mind (Deiss/PMB)

- Lift Up Your Hearts (Jesuits/New Dawn)

- There's a Wideness in God's Mercy (Faber/PMB)

Passion Sunday

Mt 21:1–11 (Procession)
Is 50:4–7
Phil 2:6–11
Mt 26:14–27:66 (Passion)

Sing "Hosanna!" Shout "Crucify him!" No other liturgical day so vividly reveals the duplicity inherent in our sinful human nature. This is the day when the homily must be short; therefore the community's participation in the symbols must be strong and lively. Let the procession be jubilant (and well prepared) so that all can feel deeply the emotion of the moment. With the proclamation of the readings, the mood abruptly changes, and the Passion should allow the assembly to experience the full weight of what it means for the Savior to die.

Let the liturgy itself speak and little else needs to be done. The call to realize the contradiction within our own sinful but graced humanity fittingly begins Holy Week and sets the stage for liturgically exploring and celebrating the redemptive passage of Christ in the Triduum.

Liturgy Notes

Minimally celebrate the Solemn Entrance as the gathering rite at all liturgies. If weather permits, gather with all neighborhood Christian churches for the liturgy of the palms, and process to your parish for the Eucharist of Passion Sunday. The processional cross may be decorated in red, with palms. Avoid play-acting the passion account. Have readers proclaim sections of the reading with a refrain sung by the assembly after each one.

Eucharistic Prayer II, whose brevity focuses upon the words of institution, may be appropriate.

A silent dismissal, without formal procession, may mark this final lenten Sunday prior to the Triduum.

RCIA Thoughts

All the world loves a parade. A number of people seem to love watching court cases as well.

Candidates for full communion may celebrate the sacramental reconciliation at the parish penance liturgy marking the end of the lenten penitential period on Wednesday night or Thursday morning.

All those who will be baptized and/or confirmed may wish to attend the Chrism Mass usually celebrated this week.

Music for the Palm Liturgy

- Psalm 24
- Psalm 47
- All Glory, Laud and Honour (Neale/PMB)
- Hosanna (Dicie/ML 9:4)
- Hosanna (Weston Priory)
- The King of Glory (Jabasch/PMB)
- Lord of Glory (Jesuits/New Dawn)

Music for the Passion Eucharist

- Psalm 22
- All Hail the Power of Jesus' Name (Perronet/PMB)
- Behold the Wood (Jesuits/New Dawn)
- Crown Him with Many Crowns (Farrell/PMB)
- In Honor of the Holy Cross (Dicie/ML 9:4)

- Jesus, the Lord (Keyes/ML 11:6)
- My Refuge (Vessels/GIA)

"Planning Guide for Lent — Cycle A" originally appeared in MODERN LITURGY magazine (Resource Publications, Inc.).

Planning Guide for Lent — Cycle B

Parish planners must first of all approach Lent with the conviction that a private Lent is impossible. The call that the Christian community hears most clearly during Lent is a communal one, a call to a journey together in faith and penance. Most particularly, it is a call with the catechumens, called the elect. No one attending Sunday liturgy should be able to avoid an encounter with the elect.

The Hebrew Scriptures for the Sundays of Lent in Year B go through the progression of covenants that God made with the chosen people. The Gospel reveals Jesus as the fulfillment of these covenants.

The emphasis is on passage, through water and through desert and wilderness. This is the model for the baptismal passage of the Christian. Our encounters with the elect, as well as with the ritual and symbols of Lent, serve to remind us of our own baptism, while ever emphasizing the communal nature of the lenten adventure.

Distributing the elect among all the Sunday Masses breaks up the carefully maintained catechumenal community and tends to put the elect on display. This is a demonstration rather than a representation of our oneness.

Perhaps it is best to do all the rites at one Mass but reflect on them homiletically at the other Masses. The scrutinies call for Cycle A Gospels on the Third, Fourth, and Fifth Sundays — don't fail to use them. The commentaries given here are for the Cycle B readings; the thematic content of Cycle A for the Sundays of Scrutiny are similar, but richer. The Samaritan woman at the well (Third Sunday, A) presents Jesus as living water, which harmonizes with Jesus' purification of the Temple and the promise of himself as the New Temple (Third Sunday, B).

The faith journey of the man born blind (Fourth Sunday, A) echoes the faith journey of Nicodemus (Fourth Sunday, B), but is graphic and lively in the narrative. The exceptional clarity of the major themes for these readings in Year A are very important for candidates for the scrutinies and also because of their traditional usage at the scrutinies from at least the fourth century.

It is important to note though that Year B presents Gospel stories which are not repeated in Sunday liturgies elsewhere — specifically, Jesus cleansing the Temple and the woman caught in adultery. These powerful stories are important in the Gospel tradition and should not be neglected.

1st Sunday of Lent

> Gn 9:8–15
> Ps 25:4–9
> 1 Pet 3:18–22
> Mk 1:12–15

Lent begins with a passage through water, a reminder of baptism. Christian tradition sees the flood as an image of the "waters of baptism that make an end of sin and a new beginning of goodness." Water, an agent of death in the flood story is also an agent of life in 1 Peter. After his baptism, Jesus seeks the meaning of the water of life by enduring the thirst of the desert, an ancient symbol of the soul thirsting for God.

Besides the symbol of passage through water, Lent begins with the symbol of passage through desert temptation. A marked contrast between the water images in the first two readings and the Gospel story must be felt. The barren worship space provides a yearning, haunting thirst for the new water and the bright colors of Easter.

2nd Sunday of Lent

> Gn 22:1–2,9a,10–13,15–18
> Ps 116:10,15,16–19
> Rom 8:31–34
> Mk 9:2–10

The transfiguration is celebrated along with the difficult story of the sacrifice of Isaac. The transfiguration affirms the divinity of Jesus and offers reassurance to those who live by faith. Abraham as the model of faith demonstrates complete reliance on God. The cross is seen in the epistle reading as a sign of victory and we are reassured of a God who saves us and does not condemn us, all the more poignant because of the Abraham story.

An emphasis on surrendering of whatever stands in the way of our lenten progress will capture well the essence of these readings while avoiding the difficulties presented in any literal understanding of the Abraham and Isaac story.

3rd Sunday of Lent

> Ex 20:1–17
> Ps 19:8–11
> 1 Cor 1:22–25
> Jn 2:13–25

Continuing on our covenant journey we come to the decalogue. The commandments are a minimum requirement of the lenten proclamation in Joel 2:13. Jesus affirms the whole Law while purifying the temple and proclaiming himself the New Temple, the fulfillment of all that has gone on before him. This law is enshrined in Jesus. The request for a "sign" is a literary device, used to develop the theological lesson of the temple clearing. It is not an adverse comment on "the Jews." In this context, the question is that of the Gospel writer.

Human wisdom is left in the dust by "God's folly," and the weakness of God is stronger than any human power. Never can we, in some mad and futile gesture, attempt to substitute some human resource or ability or craving in the place of the living God.

If the readings from Year A are used today, the same lenten message is central. The Samaritan woman at the well is the figure of us all: thirsty and empty, needing less of her own devices and more of the living water.

4th Sunday of Lent

> 2 Chr 36:14–17,19–23
> Ps 137:1–6
> Eph 2:4–10
> Jn 3:14–21

John's Gospel today provides an immensely significant context in which to hear the proclamation of the passion a few short weeks from now at the Good Friday liturgy. John's theological sense of the meaning of the cross is at the center of lenten and paschal spirituality. The agent of death becomes the instrument of healing and new life. The cross is the same kind of experience, though unique.

This is a persistent them in Lent: life discovered in death. It was formerly stressed that Lent was a time of death and Easter a time of life. Stress that Lent is the community's journey of progressive immersion in the mystery of death transformed into life which is celebrated during Easter.

Penitential can mean somber but it is not without joy. Lenten liturgies should be austere while holding tight to the call of joy in this message of death turned inside-out. Always keep in mind the needs of your community. In certain circumstances you might need a more up-beat liturgical experience.

5th Sunday of Lent

> Jer 31:31–34
> Ps 51:1–2, 10–13
> Heb 5:7–9
> Jn 12:20–33

The lenten theme of life from death continues as does the emphasis on God's covenant. Unless the grain of wheat falls to the earth and dies, it remains only a grain of wheat. This points ultimately to Jesus, whose death becomes resurrection and new creation. It is also true of all of us.

The psalm provides an open door to consider personal and corporate sin. It is a response to God who forgives us, places his law in our hearts and declares that he belongs to us as our inescapable God. God's faithfulness is contrasted to our bent toward sin and is announced with a promise that we can trust God to save us.

A special setting for the psalm and silence to ponder the depths of its meaning could prove significant in helping the assembly persevere in the final days of Lent.

"Planning Guide for Lent — Cycle B" originally appeared in MODERN LITURGY magazine (Resource Publications, Inc.).

Planning Guide for Lent — Cycle C

Many of us have memories of Lents gone by that were dreary, seemingly endless times of penance and darkness and death. Lent was a time when we acted as if Jesus were dead and we were rotten horrible people who do nothing but sin. We couldn't even say the A-word (alleluia)!

We are increasingly discovering the power of this season and unlocking more meaning and a deeper reality in our celebration of it. Lent is about transition and movement. It is not about doom and gloom. Lent is not a season of death. We cannot separate the death of Jesus from the resurrection. They are connected. Life is about death and vice versa.

The Scriptures of the lenten liturgy reflect this. Throughout the season we hear stories of transformation. God reaches into the lives of his people and makes them new. The activity of creation is never ending. God's presence transforms those who see it.

Lent shows us a God who is active in history and present in the lives of his people. During Lent we are reminded of the great people who came as prophets and leaders to reveal the truth about life to us. Abraham, Isaiah, Moses, and Jesus recognize, accept, and follow the will of God in their lives. Jesus lives God's will to his death. Jesus shows that in obedience unto death there is life.

By following Jesus we are changed. Lent is a time for changing. God's way demands change. It demands we let go of where we are and what we are in order to be filled with a new, more abundant life.

Lent is a time for reflecting. We take time to evaluate our lives. We look at our shortcomings in the light of Scripture to see what and where we need to change. Lent is a time to call on God to

be with us and help us to make the changes we need to make.

Lent is a time of challenge and hope. The Scriptures we hear demand a response from us. We are challenged by the examples of others. We find hope in the promise and delivery of new life for those who believe in God's presence.

Death and resurrection are daily and seasonal occurrences. We experience the reality of death and life in all we do. We let go of something old and welcome something new. Lent expresses this. God calls us to let go, to live in his presence, to be open to change. By doing these things we allow God to give us new and more abundant lives.

The Lenten Environment

Hospitality

As people are drawn to your celebrations they may have some new and different thoughts inside them. They may come to liturgy more reflective or introspective. As you greet people during Lent be especially respectful of mood and disposition. Don't overpower them. Greet them in perhaps a different way than the rest of the year. Instead of "Hello" maybe "Welcome" or "Peace."

Homilies during Lent should be messages of hope, of death conquered by life, and not vice versa.

Decoration

The length of Lent presents a real challenge to decorators of the worship space to create something visually appealing that people will not grow tired of before Easter arrives. The space should reflect the message of the season: change and transformation.

Images of life springing forth or growth are appropriate. Trees without leaves could throughout Lent grow leaves. Spread them around the sanctuary. You could also use cacti. A desert motif captures lenten symbols. The waters of baptism and entrance during the Vigil will refresh all who wander the desert searching for God.

Don't feel compelled to decorate using lenten liturgical colors. Contrast the traditional violets and purples. Earth tones make excellent contrast. This will enable the vivid liturgical colors to stand out more.

Music

Choose a song that will be your underlying theme during Lent. Let this guide your decoration and hospitality. Community activities could be set up during Lent to further enrich the theme and your experience. *Change Our Hearts* (Cooney/New Dawn) is rich in symbol and easy to learn and use throughout Lent.

Psalmody

- Psalm 90: Be with Me Lord (Haugen/GIA; Joncas/World Library; Willcock/Cooperative; Mattingly/Resource)

- Psalm 129: With the Lord There Is Mercy (Hagen/GIA; Gelineau/GIA)

- With Our God There Is Mercy (Manion/New Dawn)

- Psalm 10: The Lord Is Merciful (Cooney/New Dawn)

Hymns

- The Glory of These Forty Days (Erhalt Uns Herr/Bell)

- Jesus, Remember Me (Taize)

- My Song Is Love Unknown (Love Unknown/Crossman)

Songs

- Change Our Hearts (Cooney/New Dawn)

- Create in Me (Hurd/Oregon)

- As a Doe (Kendzia/New Dawn)

- Just As a Deer (Joncas/New Dawn)

- Now We Remain (Haas/GIA)

Acclamations: During Lent it is appropriate to use a Gospel acclamation other than "Alleluia." Suggestions:

- Speak, Lord (Ault/New Dawn)

- Lenten Gospel Acclamation (Regan/New Dawn; Mattingly/Resource)

Ash Wednesday

Jl 2:12–18
2 Cor 5:20–6:2
Mt 6:1–6,16–18

The reading from Joel proclaims God's call through the prophet that we must change our lives. We must be open to change. In Paul we hear the specific call to reconciliation in Christ and that now is the time to get in on it. Jesus calls us to disciplines of change but warns us against doing them for a human reward rather than the reward of relationship with the Father. A change of behavior will be unrewarding (perhaps deadly) without a change of heart and attitude.

In the response today (Ps 51) we cry out to God "Create in us clean hearts, O God." We acknowledge we need God's help and presence to change our hearts and our lives.

Message

By calling upon God to be with us to change us we acknowledge our need for God, our need to be saved. This acknowledgment is our salvation. For in calling we are received and given love and presence with God. Jesus Christ reaches into our hearts and makes us new. We share in his life, death, and resurrection and even become ambassadors of reconciliation for others. The strength of Jesus enables us to change our lives, our communities, our country, our world. But it all starts with a simple and quiet call for help.

Music

Hymns

- Forty Days and Forty Nights (Heinlein/Smytten)

- Lord, Who Throughout These Forty Days (St. Flavian/Hernamann)

- Just As I Am Without One Plea (Woodswoth/Eliot)

- Today Your Mercy Calls Us (Anthes/Alien)

Songs

- Son of David (Foley/New Dawn)

- God, Make a Heart in Me (Reith/OCP)

- By Name I Have Called You (Landry/ New Dawn)

- Change Our Hearts (Cooney/New Dawn)

- Lenten Psalm (Keyes/Resource)

Anthems

- Ashes (Conry/ New Dawn)

- Create in Me a Clean Heart (Willcock/Oxford)

Drama

The penitential rite is omitted today and replaced by the blessing with ashes. Have a number of people distribute the ashes to the assembly.

You might try something different during the Liturgy of the Word. Have the first reading proclaimed dramatically as a voice. Someone out of sight could proclaim the reading over the sound system. Have the second reading proclaimed from the assembly. A person could stand in a pew and proclaim from right there. This reinforces that the word today is a call from God and the church to change.

1st Sunday of Lent

Dt 26:4–10
Rom 10:8–13
Lk 4:1–13

The wandering Aramean was Jacob, renamed Israel. The people are saying their father was Israel therefore they are Israel, named by God, loved by God, and protected by God. Their expressions of this identity reaffirm and strengthen it.

Paul exhorts the Romans to confess their faith and believe in salvation. It is real because God is present always and rich in mercy toward all.

The psalm (91) is a prayer for the people of Israel, for Jesus, and for us. As we seek to live lives worthy of God we need to really pray this psalm.

Message

Fears and doubts can paralyze us. Today we are called to move through our fears and beyond our doubts. We are called to see, believe in, and confess God's presence, a presence that can transform us as it transformed Jesus. God calls us out of our complacency and comfort into new life as active, contributing members of our world.

Music

Hymns

- Forty Days and Forty Nights (Heinlein/Smytten)

- God Loved the World (Die Helle Sohn Lecht/Crull)

- A Mighty Fortress (Ein Feste Burg/Luther)

- Somebody's Knockin At Your Door (black spiritual)

Songs

- Be Not Afraid (Schutte/New Dawn)

- Hosea (Norbet/Weston)

- New Life (Lawrence/Resource)

- Like the Dawn (Sexton/Resource)

- Change Our Hearts (Cooney/New Dawn)

- We Choose Life (Manion/New Dawn)

- Do Not Fear (Consiglio/New Dawn)

Anthems

- Man Shall Not Live by Bread Alone (Gardner/ Flammer)

Worship Note

The Rite of Election (part of the Catholic Rite of Christian Initiation of Adults) takes place this Sunday. The church ratifies the catechumens' readiness for initiation and they in turn express their will to continue their journey as members of the elect.

2nd Sunday of Lent

Gn 15:5–12,17–18
Phil 3:17–4:1
Lk 9:28–36

God's covenant with Abram radically changes his life, not to mention his descendants'. By trusting in God's faithfulness Abram is transformed. Paul contrasts the transformation awaiting those who follow his example with those whose lives will end in destruction.

Today's Gospel is a story of resurrection. Jesus is the new covenant, the new and most present revelation of God's kingdom. Jesus, the one God desires us to follow, reveals the new and more abundant life available to us when we enter a relationship with God and his people.

In the Psalm today (27) we proclaim our belief in God's love and steadfastness. Steadfastness is a term the people of Israel used to describe God's nature. It works for us too!

Message

The Liturgy of the Word today is strong. We are challenged to live in relationship with God, with all that entails. This means we must act as God acts as Jesus has shown. We must reach beyond ourselves, trusting in God's presence and love, acting for justice and peace. By our actions we proclaim God's kingdom and bring hope to all we meet. By our actions we experience the joy of the resurrection in our lives of service. By our actions, like Jesus and Abraham, we are radically transformed.

Music

Hymns

- 'Tis Good Lord to Be Here (Swabia/Robinson)

- Lord Christ When First Thou Camest (Mit Freuden Zart/Bowie)

- O Jesus Christ May Grateful Hymns (City of God/Webster)

Songs

- Hosea (Norbet/Weston)

- The Steadfast Love (Foley/New Dawn)

- Abba, Father (Gilsdorf/Resource)

- Taste and See (Dean/Oregon)

- Your Love Is Never Ending (Haugen/GIA)

- I, the Lord (Kendzia/New Dawn)

Anthems

- Examine Me, O Lord (Boyce/Novello)

Worship Note

The acclamations and musical setting of the eucharistic prayer called *Mass of Remembrance* from Marty Haugen's collection *Shepherd Me, O God* (GIA) would beautifully express the scriptural message of today's liturgy. It is also very appropriate throughout Lent.

3rd Sunday of Lent

Ex 3:1–8,13–15
1 Cor 10:1–6,10–12
Lk 13:1–9

The reading from Exodus today is an instance of how one life transformed by God is an instrument of great deeds in God's name. God's promise of never-ending presence is revealed in the relationship God starts with Moses and Israel. The call of Moses presents to us a deepening revelation of God. God reveals his name and purpose. Yahweh is liberator of people's lives.

In the time of Jesus, sickness and death were at times seen as caused by sin or faithlessness. In the parable of the fig tree, Jesus implores the people to hear his words that their lives might bear fruit giving them new life, lest they too be cut down by sin and faithlessness.

The psalm today (103) is a statement. God reaches out to us and frees us by his mercy and presence. So we sing, "Bless the Lord, my soul, and forget not his benefits."

Message

God called Moses to be the instrument of his liberation of the people. Jesus urges the people to live lives that will bear fruit, lives that enable others to gain new Life. We must listen and accept our call from God. Through our actions we bear fruit with our lives. We bring others to God by our actions.

Our God can transform lives, but only those who allow God to do so. The choice throughout history has been ours. If there is war and injustice it is not God's fault. We must accept our challenge, hear our call, and work to be signs of the kingdom, of the transforming and liberating presence of God.

Music

Hymns

- The God of Abraham Praise (Leoni/Olivers)

- Forty Days and Forty Nights (Heinlein/Smytten)

- In the Cross of Christ I Glory (Rathbun/Bouring)

- O Cross of Christ (St. Flavian/ Stanbrook)

Songs

- On the Road (Wood/Resource)

- Song of Thanksgiving (Dicie/Resource, Ducote/New Dawn)

- The Lord Is Kind (Triel/Resource)

- Turn to Me (Foley/New Dawn)

- Do Not Fear (Consiglio/New Dawn

- Change Our Hearts (Cooney/New Dawn)

- Servant Song (Cooney/New Dawn)

Anthems

- Praise the Lord, O My Soul (Tomkins/Novello)

4th Sunday of Lent

Jos 5:9a,10–12
2 Cor 5:17–21
Lk 15:1–3,11–32

By following God's prophet Moses, the people were liberated and experienced new life in the promised land. By following God's Holy One, Jesus, the people are liberated and experience new life. Paul tells us that this new life has with it a mission. We must be reconcilers as Jesus Christ is Reconciler.

The parable of the prodigal son is not about the son's leaving and returning as much as it is about the father's (God's) never forgetting. God awaits our return always. We may leave, but God

is steadfast. Without God there is death and wanting. With God there is freedom from death and wanting. There is abundant new life.

We remind ourselves today to be open to change. We must be willing to experience new life. New life takes risks. We sing in Psalm 34, "Taste and see the goodness of the Lord."

Message

This Sunday, more than the others of Lent thus far, we are challenged to risk, to change, to be open to the liberating and transforming presence of God in our lives. We are called to live as Jesus did, to be reconcilers. We must be signs of wholeness and peace and justice. The transformation God offers is available and present. We must decide for ourselves. God will not force us to be aware or to accept. Taste and see.

Music

Hymns

- Our Father, We Have Wandered (Passion Choral/Nichols)

- There's a Wideness in God's Mercy (In Babilone/Fisher)

- God So Loved the World That He Gave (Die Helle Sohn Leucht/Crull)

- Amazing Grace (Amazing Grace/Newton)

Songs

- My Son Has Gone Away (Dufford/New Dawn)

- Prodigal Son (Culbreth/Resource)

- Taste and See (Joncas/New Dawn)

- Hosea (Norbet/Weston)

- Here I Am, Lord (Schutte/New Dawn)

- We Remember (Haugen/GIA)

Anthems

- O Taste And See (Ralph Vaughan Williams/Oxford)

5th Sunday of Lent

Is 43:16–21
Phil 3:8–14
Jn 8:1–11

The prophet reminds us that as God has led the people from oppression and bondage before, He does so again and again. God is present and active in creation with the gifts of wholeness, justice, and peace.

Paul proclaims that in Christ, the Presence of God's kingdom, there is wholeness, justice, and peace. Paul speaks of the journey we all make, striving to live as Jesus did, as examples and bearers of the new life of God's kingdom.

Jesus liberates the woman from the sin that held her captive. He liberates the hearts of the crowd held captive by their blindness and fears. Whatever blocks the way of God's mercy and forgiveness can be overcome and cleared away by Jesus, God's son and our signpost for the journey.

Message

The message really never changes. We may use different words or images to relay it to each other, but it is generally the same. God says, "I love you. I want to give you life. My prophets and my son have shown you how to respond and attain this love and life. Come back. Let me love you."

Our challenge is to reach back to the outstretched hand of our God. Reach out to the oppressed, the poor, the homeless, the imprisoned, the lonely. Break the chains of hunger and death that block the way to life. If and when we do, God will transform us while we transform our world.

Music

Hymns

- Forgive Our Sins (Detriot/Herklots)
- God So Loved The World (Die Helle Sohn Leucht/Crull)
- What Wondrous Love Is This (Wondrous Love/Traditional)
- Where Charity and Love Prevail (Christian Love/Westendorf)

Songs

- Lenten Psalm (Keyes/Resource)
- Only This I Want (Schutte/New Dawn)
- Remember Your Love (Ault/New Dawn)
- This Is Your People (Keyes/Resource)
- Change Our Hearts (Cooney/New Dawn)
- Bread of Life (Cooney/ New Dawn)
- Shepherd Me, O God (Haugen/GIA)

Anthems

- Be Not Afraid (Bach/Peters)

Lenten Catechesis

Many people intensify their search and deepen their commitment to journey with God during Lent. Lent is a time of promises and vows to "give something up" to sacrifice. It is important that we see this not so much as penance for leading rotten, sinful lives but as actions of agape. We give something up or do something extra in order to better live out our call to love one another, to more closely experience God's presence as we journey.

"Planning Guide for Lent — Cycle C" originally appeared in MODERN LITURGY magazine (Resource Publications, Inc.).

Planning Guide For Passion Sunday — Cycle A

Mt 21:1–11
Is 50:4–7
Phil 2:6–11
Mt 26:14–27:66

Sing "Hosanna!" Shout "Crucify him!" No other liturgical day so vividly reveals the duplicity inherent in our sinful human nature. This is the day when the homily must be short; therefore the community's participation in the symbols must be strong and lively. Let the procession be jubilant (and well prepared) so that all can feel deeply the emotion of the moment. With the proclamation of the readings, the mood abruptly changes, and the Passion should allow the assembly to experience the full weight of their power to do away with the Savior in their own world. Let the liturgy itself speak and little else needs to be done. The call to realize the contradiction within our own sinful but graced humanity fittingly begins Holy Week and sets the stage for liturgically exploring and celebrating the redemptive passage of Christ in the Triduum.

Liturgy Notes

Minimally celebrate the "Solemn Entrance" as the gathering rite at all liturgies. If weather permits, gather with all neighborhood Christian churches for the liturgy of the palms, and process to your parish for the Eucharist of Passion Sunday. The processional cross may be decorated in red, with palms. Avoid play-acting the passion account. Have readers proclaim sections of the reading with a refrain sung by the assembly after each one. Eucharistic Prayer II, whose brevity focuses upon the Words of Institution, may be appropriate. A silent dismissal, without formal procession, may mark this final Lenten Sunday prior to the Triduum.

RCIA Thoughts

All the world loves a parade. A number of people seem to love watching court cases as well. What was your experience of the palm procession and the passion proclamation? Candidates for full communion may celebrate the sacramental reconciliation at the parish Penance liturgy marking the end of the Lenten Penitential Period on Wednesday night or Thursday morning. All those who will be baptized and/or confirmed may wish to attend the Chrism Mass usually celebrated this week.

Music for the Palm Liturgy

- Psalm 24
- Psalm 47
- All Glory, Laud and Honour (Neale/PMB)
- Hosanna (Dicie/ML 9:4)
- Hosanna (Weston Priory)
- The King of Glory (Jabasch/PMB)
- Lord of Glory (Jesuits/New Dawn)

Music for the Passion Eucharist

- Psalm 22: All Hail the Power of Jesus' Name (Perronet/PMB)
- Behold the Wood (Jesuits/New Dawn)
- Crown Him with Many Crowns (Farrell/PMB)

- In Honor of the Holy Cross
  (Dicie/ML 9:4)

- Jesus, the Lord (Keyes/ML 11:6)

- My Refuge (Vessels/GIA)

"Planning Guide for Passion Sunday — Cycle A"
originally appeared in MODERN LITURGY magazine
(Resource Publications, Inc.).

Planning Guide For Passion Sunday — Cycle B

Mk 11:1–10 or Jn 12:12–16
Is 50:4–7
Ps 22:8–9,17–18,19–20,23–24
Phil 2:6–11
Mk 14:1–15:47 or Mk 15:1–39

In fifth-century Spain and Gaul this Sunday was the occasion for the catechumenal rite of ephphatha, with the reading of John 12:1–25, the anointing at Bethany and the triumphal entry into Jerusalem (*The Liturgy and Time* [Liturgical Press, 1986], 70). Some scholars see the origin of the procession with palms in a popular response to the second half of this Gospel, of which only verses 12–16 are given as an alternate to Mark.

John 12:12–13 is illustrated and commented on from the perspective of an artist in Ron Brown's article "Liturgical Ikebana," ML 14:8. The absence of the usual intervening readings between the Gospels of the three cycles has enabled the lectionary to lay them out "synoptically." Homilists should certainly avail themselves to this convenient aid to comparing and contrasting the different treatments of the same topic.

The first half of the reading from the Hebrew Scriptures radiates sheer joy in the prophetic ministry. Paul demonstrates that Jesus similarly delighted in doing God's will, a thought which may, perhaps, make it less distressing to listen to the Passion narrative.

Liturgy Notes

Today, the last Sunday in Lent, draws our attention toward the events of the final week of our Lord's earthly life. (This day also begins a time called Holy Week, which consists of the end of Lent and the Three Days of Triduum.) If you use the term "Holy Week," be sure that it includes Easter Sunday night. Remember that the Triduum does not end at the Easter Vigil but includes Vespers of Easter Sunday.

Let the gathering rites (some sort of procession with palms) be fun and celebrated at as many services as possible. The more enjoyable this part of the liturgy, the more apparent the shift in recalling the Lord's passion, beginning with the opening prayer of the day.

Avoid acting out the passion account. Instead, have a group of good readers proclaim sections of the text, dividing these by acclamation or song, e.g., "Adoramus Te" by Marty Haugen (GIA).

Publicize your schedule for the Triduum as well as any event you may celebrate to close the lenten season (ideally, the parish penance liturgy).

RCIA Thoughts

Be sure catechumens get to experience the procession with all its excitement. Use the processional Gospel from John: What is the hope expressed in the passage? How is this hope similar to your own?

How is this hope fulfilled in the processional Gospel? In the readings from the Eucharist?

Remind catechumens that Lent ends and the Triduum begins with its special schedule. Emphasize its centrality to our entire life and our "high holy days." The principal liturgies of the three days and the principal hours of morning, evening, and night prayer are central to parish celebration. How will they arrange their schedules to enter into the tomb and rise anew?

Music

Hymns

- All Glory, Laud and Honor
  (St. Theodolph/Neale)

- O Sacred Head (Herzlich Tut Mich
  Verlangen/Gerhardt)

- At the Name of Jesus (King's
  Weston/Noel)

- Ah, Holy Jesus (Herzliebster Jesu/Bridges)

Songs

- My God, My God (Haugen/GIA)

- Let All Who Fear the Lord
  (Foley/New Dawn)

- May We Praise You (Foley/New Dawn)

- Suffering Servant Song
  (Smith/New Dawn)

Anthem

- Behold the Lamb of God (Handel)

*"Planning Guide for Passion Sunday — Cycle B"
originally appeared in MODERN LITURGY magazine
(Resource Publications, Inc.).*

Planning Guide For Passion Sunday — Cycle C

Luke 19:28–40
Is 50:4–7
Phil 2:6–11
Lk 22:14–23:56

Properly celebrated, the liturgy of Passion/Palm Sunday should have the effect of walking along in a mood of joyous abandon — and suddenly having the ground give way under your feet. We are the same people who shout "Blessed be he who comes as king" one moment and "Crucify him, crucify him" the next. We are the disciples who confidently obey the Master's instructions to secure a beast of burden for him one day and a week later find our hopes shattered in the same Master's violent execution as a criminal between two thieves.

In this very human tug-of-war between good and evil within our hearts and this confusion of shattered hopes and unfulfilled expectations, we hear Paul introducing the hymn of Jesus' lordship: "Your attitude must be Christ's." The celebration of liturgy expresses and brings about our identity with Christ and confronts us with the price of self-emptying that he paid for fidelity to God's goodness, lifts us up out of the limitations of our own human weakness and begins to heal our dividedness.

Today's liturgy begins a process of reflection on the mystery of our union with Christ in death and resurrection — a process to be completed in celebration of the Paschal Triduum. Thus praise of Christ's lordship, which is the joy and the duty of the Christian community, is not an easy or automatic activity — not if it is to be genuine. To praise we have to allow God to challenge us with the hard demand of love — self-emptying and vulnerability — not just as individuals but as community. The Servant Song of Isaiah must be ours as well as Christ's. Otherwise, as is too often the case, our lips may say "Glory" but our hearts continue to find ways of saying "Crucify."

RCIA Thoughts

- The elect and the candidates for full communion at the Great Vigil of Easter should be encouraged to rest, pray, fast, etc., as they prepare for the Easter sacraments.

- Are you ready to "put on Christ" (that is, the Suffering Servant)?

- What response would you have given to the unrepentant thief? Also, what is your reaction "after seeing what has taken place" (cf. Lk 23:47)?

- What was your experience (memories) as you participated in the palm procession?

- How is your life still divided like the crowd, that is, often crying "hosanna" and "crucify him" simultaneously?

- Prayers: "The Sorrowful Mysteries of the Rosary"; "Holy, holy, holy Lord …"; Memorial Acclamations

- Sacramental Reconciliation should be celebrated by the candidates early in the week during the parish penance liturgy.

- Symbols: palm, cross, crucifix

- Prayer over Catechumens: Book of Occasional Services, p. 118, no. 3.

Music for the Palm Procession

- All Glory, Laud and Honor (Neale/PMB)
- Hosanna (Dicie/ML 9:4)
- Hosanna (Weston Priory)
- Hosanna (Prezio/K&R)

Music for the Passion Eucharist

- Psalm 22:8-9,17–24
- All Our Joy (Dameans/New Dawn)
- Father, Forgive Them (Murphy/ML 11:6)
- Holy Cross (Douglas/ME 9:8)
- In Honor of the Holy Cross (Dicie/ML 9:4)
- Into Your Hands (Boecker/ML 8:8)
- Into Your Hands, Lord (Goglia/ML 10:7)
- Jesus, the Lord (Jesuits/New Dawn)
- Lift High the Cross (Kitchin/PMB)
- Lord, Let Me Walk (Miffleton/PMB)
- My God, My God (Haas/Cooperative Music)
- My Refuge (Vessels/GIA)
- O Cross of Christ (Stranbrook/PMB)
- O Sacred Head (Baker/PMB)
- When I Behold the Wondrous Cross (Watts/PMB)
- When We Think How Jesus Suffered (Jabusch/PMB)

"Planning Guide for Passion Sunday — Cycle C"
originally appeared in MODERN LITURGY magazine
(Resource Publications, Inc.).

Part 3

Stories and Dramas

Dying to Live: A Lenten Drama

Kathleen T. Choi

This drama was written for lectionary cycle B, but it can work for cycle A if the ending reference to the Gospel reading is changed. Act One is performed on the First Sunday of Lent and the next act is performed on the Fifth Sunday of Lent.

Act One (1st Sunday of Lent)

Priest *(after Gospel)*: We, like Christ, are often tested. Let's take some time to think about how Satan tests, or tempts, us. How can we use this season of Lent to become better at resisting him? What is there in our spiritual diet or exercise that needs improving? *(Takes seat.)*

Satan *(enters)*: You, come here.

Woman: Who me?

Satan: Yes, you. Come here a minute.

Woman: No! There's a Mass going on!

Satan: Don't worry; they're all meditating. See? Come here and explain this diet and exercise business.

Woman *(rises and approaches)*: What's to explain? It's Lent. We're trying to get in better spiritual shape so we can resist Satan when he — oh, that's you. I recognize you. You're Satan!

Satan: Quiet, you're disturbing the meditation.

Woman: I'm getting out of here! It's not safe to talk to you. *(Hurries back toward seat.)*

Satan: Come back here. What are you so scared of? I'm not going to hurt you. Tell me what's going on.

Woman *(slowly returning)*: Well, Father suggested we approach spiritual fitness like physical fitness. See, here's the explanation sheet.

Satan: Let me see that. "Diet-Suggestion #1: Fast." There's nothing sinful about eating.

Woman: No, but fasting is a form of self-discipline. If we give our bodies whatever they want, whenever they want it, pretty soon our bodies starting bossing us around. Fasting helps remind us who's in charge. And, of course, the money we save helps others.

Satan: Appetite is your body's way of telling you what it needs. It's not healthy to ignore those signals.

Woman: Not all appetites are healthy. What about drug addicts, alcoholics, and junk food junkies?

Satan: Oh sure, there are always extremes, but we're talking about ordinary people. Look at these people. They need three square meals. They won't give them up.

Woman: Some will. Sometimes we have to die a little to live. Besides, there are other ways to fast. Here's one: "Abstain from TV one night a week."

Satan: So now TV is a sin?!

Woman: TV can lead to sin. Some women resent their husbands for not being as romantic as their favorite soap opera stars. Some husbands watch so much football that they never play with their own children. Some kids fight over what program to watch. In some families you'd think TV was a god, the way no one can talk during certain programs. That's sure not healthy.

Satan: Sure it is. Escape is very healthy. Everyone needs a little fantasy in their lives.

Woman: A little, maybe, but the average American doesn't watch "a little." Besides, I don't think Jesus would approve of the values most TV shows push.

Satan: Like what?

Woman: All those ads trying to convince you that a VCR, two cars, and a trash compactor are what make life worth living.

Satan: A wise man once said, "I've been rich, and I've been poor, and rich is better." There's nothing wrong with being comfortable. Besides, aren't you the lady I see at every dress sale?

Woman: Yes, clothes are a weakness of mine. But that just proves my point. I start thinking I always have to be in the latest style. Lent helps me rethink my priorities.

Satan: Calm down. I was just kidding about the clothes. I think you look great, and, besides, a woman in your position needs to make a good impression.

Woman: Isn't doing a good job the most important thing?

Satan: To get ahead in this world, you've got to play all the angles. With your looks and brains you could go places, if you played your cards right.

Woman: You really think so?

Satan: I know so. I can show you some ways to really be someone important, someone who matters.

Woman: Wait a minute! You've tried that line on me before! I want to be successful, but it's not the most important thing in my life. And I'm sure as

heck not going to take advice from you on how to get ahead!

Satan: Why? Because Jesus called me the Father of Lies? I'll tell you the same thing I told him. This life is all there is, so you'd better grab whatever pleasure you can. But did he listen? Oh no, his Father was going to take care of him. Well, look where he ended up (*gestures to cross*). Is that what you want?

Woman: But that wasn't the end. He came back. The Father did help him, and he'll help me, too.

Satan: You believe that now. Life is going good for you. What are you going to do if things get a little tougher?

Woman: That's why I need to exercise. If I learn to work with God on the little things, like keeping my temper, or not bragging, then I can handle the tougher tests when they come along.

Satan: Even the big things? Unemployment? Sickness?

Woman: If I keep exercising, even those. You're not going to get me, Satan.

Satan: Right now all I see you exercising is your mouth. Who are you kidding? If it were that easy to diet and exercise, no one would be overweight. You'll quit, just like everyone does.

Woman: Maybe alone I would, but my Christian family will support me. We're in this together.

Satan: Them? Without even straining my eyes, I see a man who cheats his employer, a woman who gossips about her neighbors, teenagers who are experimenting with sex, and kids who lie to their parents. Some army of saints.

Woman: Yes, we sin, but part of exercising is getting up and trying again.

Satan: Dream on. While you're making yourself miserable giving up *Miami Vice* for Stations of the Cross, they'll be going on as always. Come Easter, they'll be the same selfish, flabby souls they are now. That's human nature, and no clever lenten program will change it.

Woman: Lent won't change us. God will. And you're wrong! If we let Him, God will make us all more spiritually fit by Easter. I'll bet you anything that before Lent is over, there will be people from this congregation ready to testify as to how God helped them beat you, Satan.

Satan: Don't you know what happens to people who bet with me? I always win.

Woman: You do not. Jesus beat you, and he'll help us beat you too. You come back here at the end of Lent, and you'll see.

Satan: I'll take your bet, and I'll be back. In fact, I'll be right behind you every minute of this Lent. You can count on it. *(Exits.)*

Woman *(to congregation)*: I was right, wasn't I? We are going to work together, aren't we? We will win, won't we? Won't we? *(Exits.)*

Act Two (5th Sunday of Lent)

Priest *(after Gospel, John 12:20–33)*: This Gospel speaks of hard things: hating our lives, dying. This Lent, we've been trying to grow stronger in these difficult areas. Are we succeeding? We know who wants us to fail: Satan. We know who tries to make us fail: Satan. Is he winning? *(Takes seat.)*

Satan *(enters)*: Did I hear someone call my name? Well, well, here we all are again. So, where's my friend?

Woman *(rises from pew)*: I'm right here, Satan, and I'm not your friend.

Satan: Okay, okay, I didn't come to argue. In fact, I'll make it easy for you. You failed, right? You made a lot of great resolutions, but human nature was too strong for you. Hey, don't feel bad. It happens to everybody.

Woman *(approaches Satan)*: But I didn't fail. I haven't been perfect, but I kept my lenten covenant most of the time. It wasn't easy. In fact, it felt like dying sometimes, but I did it.

Satan: It felt like dying, huh? You'll have to die for real soon enough. Why hurry the process?

Woman: But I didn't just die. I also experienced new life. I felt the power of Christ grow in me. When I fasted, prayed, and did acts of charity, I did it with Christ. I know him better now than I did a month ago, and I feel more alive than I did a month ago.

Satan: Please, spare me the sermon. So maybe with you I went too far. Scared the hell out of you, did I? But one lady in a congregation this size is not exactly an overwhelming victory.

Woman: That's what I thought you'd say. Wait there. I want to show you something. *(Gets sack and tablecloth.)* Give me a hand with this. Come on, haven't you ever set a table before?

Satan: What's all this?

Woman: These are our Rice Bowl envelopes. That's the church's effort to fight world hunger. I'm not the only one who made sacrifices this Lent.

Satan: Big deal. A guy throws a buck in an envelope before Mass. These guys can afford it. I'm not impressed.

Woman: But it isn't just a buck. And on the backs of the envelopes they wrote what sacrifices they made. Here, let me read you one. This person fasted every Friday, attended daily Mass, and invited a friend to church.

Satan: Some old lady with nothing better to do, I'll bet.

Woman: The prayers of those so-called "old ladies" have defeated you more than once, Satan. But I'm sure I can find a young person's envelope. Here's one. This boy contributed one tenth of his allowance and went to confession. Do you realize how hard it is for a 14-year-old boy to be seen at church on a Saturday afternoon? That's dying to self.

Satan: I notice you're doing all the picking. Let me see some of those. Hah, right away I find a blank one.

Woman: How much is in it?

Satan: $7.79. Wow!

Woman: From?

Satan: Mrs. Andrade's seventh grade home room.

Woman: Seventh graders, huh? Not bad. Read another.

Satan *(muttering):* Abstain, novena, rosary — this is ridiculous. I've obviously got a stacked deck. Give me some more.

Woman: I've got a better idea. Ask them, yeah, those same people you were calling names a month ago. I'll do it for you. If you fasted during Lent, would you please stand? Thank you, you may be seated. Well?

Satan: Well, what? They skipped some meals. Dieters do it all the time. They don't claim to be spiritual champions.

Woman: Christian fasts are for the purpose of penance, self-discipline, prayer, and charity. And I didn't say we were champions yet. I said we were training, and the Lord has done great things for us. Listen to this testimony from *(volunteer testifies).*

Woman: I told you there would be people in this congregation ready to testify as to how the Lord has helped them.

Satan: One religious fanatic.

Woman: One?! Okay, folks, how many of you said extra prayers this Lent? Please stand. Gee, Satan, looks like we've got a church full of religious fanatics. Thanks, folks, you can sit down. Hey, Satan, where are you going? Don't you want to hear how many Bible verses we studied? How many shut-ins we visited? I want to tell you about the man who — where are you going?

Satan: I got things to do. I can't hang around here all day. *(Exits.)*

Woman: What did Jesus say in the Gospel today? "Now will this world's prince be driven out, and I, once I am lifted up from earth, will draw all people to myself." Lifting Christ up sounds like the best exercise of all. *(Exits.)*

"Dying to Live" originally appeared in MODERN LITURGY magazine (Resource Publications, Inc.).

The Laborers in the Vineyard

Michael E. Moynahan, SJ

Narrator: The reign of God is like the case of the owner of an estate who went out at dawn to hire workers for his vineyard.

Direction: *The mime opens up with a man ("A") and a woman ("B") standing back to back down stage left. The man faces left and the woman faces right. When the narrator says that the owner went out at dawn they rotate clockwise so that "A" addresses/engages the first worker. "C", the first worker comes from stage right out of the congregation. If you have difficulty visualizing the movement involved diagram it before attempting the drama.*

N: After reaching an agreement with them for the usual daily wage, he sent them out to his vineyard.

D: *A and B rotate clockwise back to their original positions. C goes down stage right. The workers will eventually form a bowling pin configuration. C assumes the "head" pin position. Once in position, C mimes picking grapes. There are four hand gestures from the vine to an imaginary bag on his left side. These gestures are 1st up right, 2nd down right, 3rd down left, and 4th up left. C freezes at the conclusion of these.*

N: The owner came out about midmorning and saw other people standing around the marketplace without work, so he said to them, "You too go along to my vineyard and I will pay you whatever is fair." At this they went away.

D: *Workers D and E come in down stage left. After the owner's speech, he motions for them to go work with C in the vineyard. As they cross over right, A and B rotate counter clockwise back to their original positions. When*

D and E are in position behind C they go through the fourfold "picking" motions again. Then they freeze.

N: He came out again around noon and mid-afternoon and did the same.

D: *As A and B rotate clockwise, F and G come from the congregation to the right of A and H comes from the congregation to the left of A. A motions them to join C, D and E. They cross down stage right and fall in behind D and E. A and B rotate counterclockwise back to their original positions. C, D, E, F, G and H repeat the fourfold "picking" motions. Then they freeze.*

N: Finally, going out in the late afternoon he found still others standing around. To these people he said, "Why have you been standing here idle all day?" "No one has hired us," they told him. Then he said, "You go to the vineyard too."

D: *As A and B rotate clockwise, I, J, K, and L move across down stage right to positions on either side and in front of C. All the workers start the fourfold "picking" motion. C, D, E, F, G, and H freeze, however, after the first gesture. They look to the right and the left. They notice these latecomers in front of them. They all motion with their right hands for I, J, K, and L to move to the rear. A and B have rotated counterclockwise back to their original positions. When the order has been established, all the workers do the fourfold "picking" motion.*

N: When evening came the owner of the vineyard said to his foreman, "Call the workers and give them their pay, but begin with the last group and end with the first."

D: *A and B turn counterclockwise. The woman now pays the workers. C begins to move toward B. B holds up her hand and motions him back to his place. The same thing happens with each row until B finally motions I, J, K and L to come forward.*

N: When those hired late in the afternoon came up they received a full day's pay...

D: *B embraces I, J, K and L. They return to their places. B then calls/motions F, G and H to come. As they do, B embraces each of them. They return to their places. B then calls/motions D and E to come. As they do, B embraces each of them. They return to their places.*

N: And when the first group appeared, they supposed they would get more; yet they received the same daily wage. They complained to the owner about this. "This last group did only an hour's work but you have put them on the same basis as those of us who have worked a full day in the scorching heat." "My friend," the owner replied, "I do you no injustice." You agreed on the usual wage, did you not? Take your pay and go home. I intend to pay these workers who were hired last the same pay as you. I am free to do as I please with my money, am I Not? Or are you envious because I am generous?"

D: *C comes expecting much more than the others. He gets the same embrace from B. He circles around B stunned, then comes and confronts her to the right of B. Finally C wanders back to his position and A and B rotate clockwise back to their original positions.*

N: And I, J, K and L lift up their hands joyfully in response to the Narrator's proclamation. The others do not and look disappointed, angry or confused.

Finis

"The Laborers in the Vineyard" originally appeared in MODERN LITURGY magazine (Resource Publications, Inc.).

The Parable of the Ten Maidens

Michael E. Moynahan, SJ

Narrator: Then the kingdom of heaven shall be compared to ten maidens who took their lamps and went to meet the bridegroom.

Direction: *All five players stand sideways with left side to the congregation. Stick mask is in the left hand and down. Foolish mask is concealed in right hand at their sides.*

N: Five of them were wise.

D: *Players turn left toward congregation, raise mask, take step forward, then step back, turn to side, and finally turn fully away from congregation with their backs to them.*

N: And five of them were foolish.

D: *Players put on foolish masks and pivot right towards congregation.*

N: For when the foolish took their lamps, they took no oil with them;

D: *The players pivot left so their backs are to congregation. They remove foolish masks. They turn to the side as the wise maidens.*

N: But the wise took flasks of oil with their lamps.

D: *Players turn left toward congregation, raise masks, take step forward.*

N: As the bridegroom was delayed, they all slumbered and slept.

D: *Players turn back to side position, lower masks, then bow heads.*

N: But at midnight there was a cry, "Behold, the bridegroom! Come out to meet him."

D: *Players' heads come up sharply.*

N: Then all those maidens rose and trimmed their lamps.

D: *Players turn so backs are fully to congregation and put on foolish masks.*

N: And the foolish said to the wise, "Give us some of your oil, for our lamps are going out."

D: *Players pivot right on heels towards congregation, then pivot left on heels so their backs are to the congregation again. They take off the foolish masks.*

N: But the wise replied, "Perhaps there will not be enough for us and for you; go rather to the dealers and buy for yourselves.

D: *Players turn to side position. They turn left towards congregation raising the wise mask. They take a step and lean towards the congregation.*

N: And while they went to buy, the bridegroom came, and those who were ready went in with him to the wedding feast;

D: *Players take three steps forward.*

N: And the door was shut.

D: *Players turn right fully so backs are to the congregation. They put on foolish masks.*

N: Afterwards, the other maidens came along also, saying "Lord, lord, open to us."

D: *Players pivot right on their heels. They face the congregation.*

N: But he replied, "Truly, I say to you, *I do not know you.*"

D: *Players take three steps backwards on the emphasized words, then bring forward foot back to other foot on final word.*

N: Watch therefore, for you know neither the day nor the hour.

D: *Players slowly take the foolish masks off and gradually bring them down to their sides. They look out at the congregation. After some moments of pause, all the players turn their backs to the congregation, pause, and go to their places.*

"The Parable of the Ten Maidens" originally appeared in MODERN LITURGY magazine (Resource Publications, Inc.).

The Parable of the Good Samaritan

Michael E. Moynahan, SJ

(Note: The following mime is done prior to the oral proclamation of Luke 10:25–37.)

At the beginning of this mime five characters come into the playing space. They each have a large paper bag mask with faces appropriate to their characters painted on the front of the bags. There are holes for eyes and mouth as well.

The Robber goes to an "up stage right" position and turns his/her back to congregation. The Priest, Levite and Samaritan go to a "down stage left" position and turn their backs to the congregation. The Victim goes to "center stage" position, takes bag off of head and lies down and goes to sleep.

First Scene

If possible, have the sound effect of an alarm clock going off. The Victim wakes up and stretches, gets up, cleans him/herself, dresses and then puts his/her mask (paper bag) over his/her head. The Victim goes out an imaginary door and begins to move "up stage right."

Second Scene

As the victim turns to move "up stage right" the Robber turns (with mask on). The Robber's mask has holes in it from wear and tear. The Robber moves on a diagonal line "down center" to meet and confront the Victim.

The Victim is surprised. The Robber grabs the Victim and begins violently ripping the Victim's mask off. The Victim is helpless, frightened and confused. The Robber throws the pieces of the ripped mask on the ground and leaves "down stage left."

Third Scene

The Victim is bewildered. The Victim feels naked. The Victim's hands keep trying to cover his/her face. The Victim tries frantically to get the pieces of the mask back together. No piece will stay on his/her face. S/he grows increasingly desperate. Finally, s/he collapses in frustration and exhaustion on the floor.

Fourth Scene

The Priest turns around. We see a male face drawn on the bag he/she wears. The Priest begins moving on a diagonal line "up center." When s/he sees the Victim s/he is horrified. S/he looks up at the congregation then down to the Victim. S/he then hurriedly rushes off on a continued diagonal "up stage right."

Fifth Scene

Next the Levite turns around. We see a female face drawn on the bag he/she wears. The Levite begins moving on a diagonal line "up center." When s/he sees the Victim s/he looks up at the congregation, down to the Victim, then kneels down to take a closer look.

The Victim begins to quicken slightly. The Levite looks at all the pieces of the Victim's mask torn apart and thrown all over. The Victim begins stretching out a hand toward the Levite for help. The Levite grows frightened. The Levite gets up quickly and uses his/her hands to ward off the begging hand of the Victim. The Levite turns head away and continues off "stage right." The Victim's hand, which had been suspended in the air, falls with a loud "thump" to the ground.

Sixth Scene

The Good Samaritan turns and reveals his/her mask to the congregation. It is a mask that has been torn apart and put back together with the help of masking tape. It is important that this is visually graspable by the congregation.

The Samaritan begins moving "up center" and sees the Victim. The Samaritan looks up at the congregation and then quickly back down to the Victim. The Samaritan goes and kneels down by the Victim. The Samaritan slowly and carefully gathers the fragments of the Victim's mask.

Next, the Samaritan slowly takes off his/her mask and places it on the floor next to the Victim. The Samaritan puts the fragments of the Victim's mask in his/her own. Then the Samaritan gently picks the Victim up in his/her arms and comforts him/her. This is all on the floor.

After some time, the Samaritan slowly helps the victim to his/her feet, picks up the Samaritan's mask, and with the mask(s) in one hand and the Victim supported with the other, begins moving "down stage right."

After a few steps, the Samaritan and Victim turn their backs to the congregation along with the Robber, the Priest and the Levite. They freeze for a few moments and then go to their places.

After some moments of silent reflection, the passage from the Gospel of Luke (10:25–37) is proclaimed.

Finis

"The Parable of the Good Samaritan" originally appeared in MODERN LITURGY magazine (Resource Publications, Inc.).

The Breakdown

James L. Henderschedt

It was a dumb thing to do, Charlie realized, after kicking the tire of his disabled automobile for the second time. The pain that radiated up his leg after the first kick should have been warning enough. But no, he was so frustrated and angry that he wound up and gave the tire a second kick.

Charlie limped to the front of the car and stuck his head under the hood, trying to make sense out of the jumble of hoses and wires.

"Modern contraptions," he muttered as his fingers probed around the maze of automotive technology. "You pay a fortune for these darned things, and they still aren't reliable."

He restrained the urge to give the tire another kick. He said to himself, There was a time I could repair my own car, but now I can't even find the dipstick.

It was then that he heard footsteps. He looked around the side of the car and saw a man walking toward him. He didn't remember passing anyone along the way. It had been a very deserted stretch of road.

It was difficult for Charlie to tell the stranger's age. He wasn't young, that was for sure. But he wasn't old. His well-trimmed beard was streaked with gray, and his skin was weathered from exposure to the sun, wind, and rain. But he had an ageless quality about him. The backpack strapped to his shoulders looked very heavy, yet he walked with ease, as though he was totally oblivious to its weight.

"Hi," the stranger called out. "Having trouble?"

"No, I'm frying eggs on my engine," Charlie mumbled. Then, so that he could be heard, he spoke up, "Of course I'm having trouble. Why else would I be standing by the side of the road with my head stuck under the hood of my car? Whenever you see anyone like this, it's a sure bet that there's trouble.

"My, aren't you a bit testy? I was just trying to be neighborly. If you want me to get lost, just say the word and I'll continue on my way."

Now Charlie felt sorry for being so rude. "No, don't go. Please forgive me. It's just that I don't know what to do. Here I am, stranded in the middle of God knows where with a very expensive piece of junk that won't work."

"Mind if I have a look?" the stranger asked, unstrapping his sack and lowering it to the ground.

"Be my guest. Maybe you can make some sense out of the mess under there."

The newcomer stepped to the front of the car and surveyed the engine compartment. "Hmmm," he muttered as he stroked his beard. "Yep. Oh, yes. Ah, ha."

Charlie became excited as he listened to the man, and he watched carefully as the man took his inventory. "Do you think you know what's wrong?"

"Hardly," came the answer. "Actually, this is the first time I've looked beneath the hood of a car."

"What!" screamed Charlie. "Then what in the…?" Charlie checked himself. "Are you trying to tell me you don't know anything about cars?"

"That's right," the man said. "I've never owned a car in my life. In fact, I've never driven one either."

"Then why are you studying under the engine?"

"Oh, just curious. I've heard so much about them. I thought this would be as good a time as any to see one for myself."

"Great, just great. It's not bad enough being stranded, now I have to put up with...oh, never mind. Get out of the way, and let me see if I can find anything."

Charlie all but pushed the stranger aside and resumed his blind search for the problem.

"I think I know what's wrong," said a sheepish voice behind Charlie.

Charlie raised his head too quickly and banged it on the hood. "Ow! What are you talking about? You don't know the first thing about cars."

"Yes, but I do know that little wire there," he pointed to it, "looks like it ought to be connected to something—maybe that doodad just below it?"

Charlie looked. Sure enough, a tiny wire was dangling uselessly from its connector. "Naw, it can't be something as simple as that."

"Won't hurt to try."

"I guess not." Charlie connected the wire, got in the car, turned the ignition, and the car roared to life.

The stranger stood there with a wide grin on his face. Charlie looked appropriately humble. He got out of the car and went up to the stranger and offered his hand. "I guess I owe you an apology. The least I can do is offer to take you as far as I can."

"There's no apology needed, and it's mighty kind of you to do so."

The stranger started to lift his backpack into the car, but Charlie ran around him. "Here, let me get it for you."

"Don't bother. You won't be able to lift it."

"Nonsense," Charlie said as he grabbed the straps with both his hands. When he tried to lift it, he went down on his knees.

"Didn't I say you wouldn't be able to lift it?" The stranger smiled and took the straps from Charlie, who was still on his knees, then hefted the backpack with what seemed to be little effort. They got into the car and started down the road.

"Where are you going?" Charlie asked.

"Wherever the road takes me," answered the stranger.

"Are you homeless?"

"I guess you might say that."

"Gee, that's too bad. How long have you been without a home?"

"Just about as long as I can remember."

"You're all alone then?"

"I am now. I used to travel around with some friends, but they're all gone now."

"It must be tough being lonely."

"I'm alone, but I didn't say anything about being lonely."

"Yeah, I guess you're right."

They rode in silence for a while. Then the stranger turned and said, "Look, Charlie, I think we have to talk."

The car swerved to the right as Charlie applied the brakes. The tires squealed in protest at the abrupt stop.

"You called me Charlie. How did you know my name? I never told you it. Who are you anyway?"

"It doesn't matter who I am. But what I have to say to you does. You're a great guy, Charlie, with a lovely wife and fine kids. You and they do not deserve what you are going to do to them and yourself."

"What do you mean?"

"Well, there's that little indiscretion with Millie at the office, for one thing."

"That's over."

"Yes, but only because Millie put a stop to it. And there is that shady deal you are on your way now to finalize."

"My business needs the money. Besides, who'll know? Everybody does it."

"You'll know, Charlie, and you are the one you must face every morning when you look in the mirror. It's not worth it. The other things you do that sap your dignity aren't worth it, either. It's beneath you. You're better than all that. Why, Charlie, you are my Father's child, created in his image, just a little less than the angels themselves. And what you are doing isn't worth it."

Charlie sat staring out the windshield, his hands tightly gripping the wheel. "I know," he whispered, "I know. I guess it took someone else to hold up the mirror so I could see what I am really like. But what can I do?"

"Let go of all of that. Become what God has made you. You can do it. Just walk away from that stuff. You'll be surprised how good things can be."

"You're right. I will. In fact, I'll begin by turning around and going home. To hell with the deal. I can make it without it."

"That's the way, Charlie. I know you can do it."

"But, if I turn around now, I'll have to leave you off."

"That's fine. This is as far as I am going, anyway. Just let me get my backpack."

He stepped out of the car, opened the back door and lifted the pack onto his shoulders. His knees buckled slightly under the weight.

"That's a mighty heavy backpack," Charlie observed. "I couldn't budge it."

"You can't carry what is in this pack. Only I can. In fact, talking with you has made it a little heavier."

"What's in it?"

"What's in my backpack? Sins, Charlie. I carry the sins of my brothers and sisters in my backpack."

He closed the door, and Charlie made a U-turn and drove away with a wave to the stranger. Charlie watched him in his rearview mirror until he could see him no more.

Prayer

Lord, I confess that all too often I use "I'm just human" as an excuse. Help me to realize what that really means: that I am made in the image of the Creator, that I am God's child, and that my sins have been forgiven, and I am redeemed by grace. To be human cannot become an excuse for a sinful nature but an affirmation of who and whose I am. I am sorry for the burden of my sins that you had to carry. Amen.

"The Breakdown" originally appeared in The Dream Catcher *(Resource Publications, Inc., 1996).*

Part 4

Reconciliation

The Revised Rite of Christian Initiation Of Adults — A Commentary

James L. Empereur, SJ

The *Rite of Christian Initiation of Adults* represents the best in contemporary theological reflection and pastoral experience. Hence, in considering the rite, it is imperative that mere rubrical concerns not be allowed to obscure or abort the intent of the Vatican Council which authorized the revision or the work of those who fashioned the rite. It represents the work of many international scholars in the areas of catechists, ecumenism, and liturgy as well as the experience of many years of pastoral practice both in East and West, and it can only be understood in terms of its fundamental pastoral intent and theological presuppositions.

In commenting on this new rite, we must bear in mind that in it we are touching the very depth of the church's birth and formation. The catechumenal process is not the private concern of a few but is rather synonymous with the church's very life, with the emergence of a mature belief in a new Christian, and hence with the renewal of the Body of Christ in the world today.

A Process

The *Ordo Initiationis Christianae Adultorum* has six chapters:

1. The Rite of the Catechumenate received in stages.

2. The Simple Rite of Adult Initiation.

3. Short Rite in case of danger or death.

4. Norms for preparing adults for Confirmation and Eucharist who were baptized in infancy but uncatechized.

5. Rite of initiation for children of catechetical age.

6. Various texts for use in the celebration of adult initiation.

All the commentators point out that it is the first method — the adult catechumenate done in stages — which is of primary importance. The other forms are to be used in situations peculiar to individuals or countries, and to consider them as normative (e.g., to use the simple rite as a matter of course) would be to contradict the spirit of the reform. Therefore, it is primarily with the first chapter of the new rite that we will be concerned here with brief, concluding looks at the theologically derivative but pastorally significant fourth and fifth chapters.

A Process. The first essential aspect of the new rite is that it treats Christian initiation as a process which occurs over time. Indeed, the ordinary initiation of an adult will take place over two or three years. The precise length of time will be determined by the progress of the candidate, since what we are dealing with is the maturation of a life of faith, not the most efficient induction of a volunteer or draftee into an organization.

Stages. The new rite divides this process into four distinct stages:

- First is the *pre-catechumenate*. This is the period of evangelization and is quite flexible both in structure and in length. It is the time when the individual hears the Good News and through informal exchanges with believers begins to respond.

- Second comes the *catechumenate* proper. When an individual expresses a desire to become a member of the church, s/he enters this state. It is a special state in the church, a special order analogous to the presbyterial order. During this period, there are more organized catechetical instructions and formative exercises in prayer and Christian charity. It is usually several years in length and has its own specific activities, its own proper liturgies, its particular interpersonal relationships. In short, it has a unique and quite specific place in the dynamics of church life.

- The third stage is the *enlightenment* stage, a period of intense paschal preparation. This time is coterminous with Lent, and is described in the documents as a time of "purification and illumination." It is like a long retreat.

- The final stage is the *mystagogia*, or the time of the first sacramental experiences of the newly initiated. It coincides with the paschal season and is characterized by the kind of catechesis which proceeds by means of the experience of sacramental celebrations.

First, one is called an inquirer or sympathizer; then in the first stage, a precatechumen; in the second stage, a catechumen; candidates or elect in the third stage; and neophytes in the last stage.

Of course, the foregoing is but a bare bones description of a rich maturation process for becoming a Christian and hardly begins to touch the depth of personal conversion and growth which occurs.

Community. Initiation, then, is a gradual, step-by-step movement wherein the catechumen matures in faith, and the Christian community — and here is the difficult part — progressively receives this person in a warm and loving way. But this means, as liturgical scholar Andre Aubry has put it so well, "There can be no catechumenate without a community." For it is the *community* which is renewed by the catechumenate process because it is the community which is challenged to conversion and given new life by the faith commitment of the new believer.

What this rite brings out so forcefully is that baptism can only really occur in a community which is ready to transcend itself. The catechumenate is a mutual task on the part of the catechumen and the community. Only a community which is ready to look at itself in terms of the still unexplored and unaccepted implications of its own faith will qualify to be the soil in which the faith-life of a new Christian can take root and grow.

Ministries. To say that a community is essential to the process of Christian initiation is another way of saying that a variety of ministries are involved. After all, how can we ask so much of the catechumens unless the Episcopal conferences work out a method of reception, unless the local church finds the means to bring about the necessary evangelization, and unless the laity, the catechists, the sponsors and priests do provide the atmosphere, and the nourishment, and the challenge needed to assure the growth of this new faith life?

Time. In terms of organizing the initiation process, it cannot be a question of fitting a person into some predetermined juridical stages or schedule. Rather, the organization of the catechumenate awaits the movement of the individual inquirer. Indeed, the whole process will only succeed if it is the result of the progress of the candidate and if the commitment of the welcoming community respects the unique qualities — in terms of time and depth — of the faith life of the new believer.

The decision for moving from stage to stage then, will depend first on the rhythm of the candidate and, increasingly, on the discernment of the community. Ordinarily, it will be the candidate who will initiate the time of the catechumenate. But the length of time of the catechumenate and the decision for election (the start of the third stage) will require community involvement. Only the precise time for the election presents some structural constraints, since it should ordinarily coincide with the beginning of Lent.

Catechesis. It is important to keep before our minds that the catechumenate is not a school. It is, as the rite is called, an initiation. It can never be reduced to a series of classes, or to the learning of a body of knowledge, since the experiential component is so important. After all, no one is baptized because he or she knows doctrine, laws, and rituals. To become a Christian liturgically, one must be motivated by God's initiative in one's life.

Catechesis, therefore, must be understood more as reflection on and articulation of experience, rather than merely assimilating information (although it does include the latter). And it is extremely important not to view the four stages of the catechumenate as only juridical grades or periods. They refer, rather, to levels of faith. Such differentiation is necessary to avoid the kind of educational errors we have made in the past regarding the introduction of the person into the Catholic community. Pre-catechumenal catechesis, for example, cannot have the same sophistication in liturgy, relationships, and doctrines which would characterize the time of the neophyte.

Liturgical Stages

Liturgically, the new rite is concerned primarily with the first three stages of the initiation process. Each of the stages has its own proper liturgies, and each concludes with a "threshold" rite which completes one stage and begins the next. They act as "hinges" between distinct periods.

Stages. Liturgically, that is ritually, the first period is very sparse until the actual rite of becoming a catechumenate (the "threshold" liturgy between the first and second stages). This first stage is one of dialogue, of discovery, of spontaneous association with Christians.

The second period, that of the catechumenate proper, is more highly liturgical in character. It is filled with celebrations of the Liturgy of the Word, with minor exorcisms and blessings. These are to help the catechumen to form his/her life in preparation for the Eucharist and Christian living. The exorcisms highlight the fact that this preparation involves struggle and separations, and the blessings indicate that there is also peace and thanksgiving. This second stage ends with the rite of inscription of names, which ritualizes the decision to become a candidate for baptism, and hence initiates the third stage, that of the enlightenment: the intense preparation for the sacraments of initiation.

The third period, the final lenten preparation, is even more liturgically rich. It is the time of the election, the scrutinies, the presentations, and the anointings. It concludes with the Easter Vigil and the reception of the initiation sacraments of baptism, confirmation, and the Eucharist.

The fourth and final period has no special liturgical rite. It is a time when the convert, the neophyte, with the help of the community and his/her sponsor, is to discover more deeply the meaning and experience of the Eucharist and eventually the sacrament of reconciliation. It is a time when the newly initiated is to exercise his/her baptismal priesthood.

Public Celebrations. Ordinarily, these liturgical rites should take place in the liturgical assembly. Entry into the catechumenate will normally take place in the church building. Other places are acceptable, especially if the church building would make it difficult to achieve an atmosphere of friendliness, acceptance, and freedom. Such places might be meeting rooms in catechetical centers, living rooms in homes, and any other suitable place. Flexibility is the note here.

Adaptation. That one is not to follow the various rituals in the new rite according to some kind of computer-like regularity or impersonal a priori is clear from the option that the rite gives to move the presentation of the Creed and the Our Father to earlier stages. These particular rites can well be used during the celebrations of the Word or at the beginning or end of catechetical meetings. The point is that they are to be adapted to the faith of the one involved.

Having made these general observations, let us now examine each of the stages of initiation liturgically in some detail.

Pre-Catechumenate. The first stage, that of the pre-catechumenate, because it is so liturgically parsimonious, may give some the impression that this time can be dispensed with. But such would be a great mistake. It should never be omitted because it is the time of initial conversion and it is here that the community must be assured of the candidate's sincerity, freedom and stability. There should be no hesitation in postponing the rite of becoming a catechumen until this rooting in faith has become manifest. This first evangelization must be characterized by attraction to the Gospel, by separation from sin, and by a sense of what it means to be church.

Catechumenate. The rite of entrance into the catechumenate, the second stage, introduces the person into an order in the church. S/he is now a Christian even though baptism with water is still to come. This is the first ritualized action of a long sacramental process which comes about in stages. But the catechumen already possesses certain rights in the community: the Liturgy of the Word, exorcisms, blessings, sacramentals, Christian marriage and burial. S/he is a genuine Christian.

What is presupposed in all this is a church of entrance, some kind of apparatus whereby the faithful, the catechists, and priests can accompany the catechumens along the lengthy way of their initiation. This is necessary if this period is to be the decisive moment for the growth of the church.

What especially characterizes this period is called catechesis. As was noted, catechesis is not instruction, doctrinal impregnation, or moral and sacramental information. It is experience. It is an experience of the local church. Hence, the catechumenate cannot be modeled on a school; it is not to be seen as comparable to the former convert classes or present adult education classes. It resembles more closely the novitiate training period of religious orders. It is a time when the sponsors, godparents, and the community can give the candidates a new outlook, a different perspective, encouragement in the Christian life, and inspiration to be Christian witnesses. It is not a time primarily for the passing on of objective knowledge. What this rite is all about is the expression in peak liturgical moments of the various steps by which the initiate is progressively passing into the church.

Before the candidate can move into the third stage, the election lenten period, considerable discernment on his/her part as well as on the part of the community will be necessary. Have his/her attitudes and behavior changed? What is the degree of doctrinal understanding that s/he possesses? In general, what is the direction of the initiate's life? It is not to be expected that there will be hoards of people who, each Lent, will be inscribed into this high degree of the catechumenate, the order of the elect, the enlightened.

Enlightenment. This third stage is relatively short since it is the length of the lenten period. The election, or perhaps we should use the words option or choice, begins this period of retreat. It is the stage in which the whole community should take part with particular intensity. The main catechesis is now over and the purpose of the scrutinies is to prepare the conscience of the elect for the celebrations of Holy Week. In that sense, they are not only for the candidates but for the whole community as it prepares to celebrate the sacrament of reconciliation at the end of Lent. The presentations of the Creed and Our Father show that faith is received through the church. They are also one way in which the community recalls the great deeds of God, the events of salvation history, as it attempts to renew itself.

No community should attempt to take upon itself the task of accompanying these elect through this important stage of their catechumenate unless it is also committed to renew its own commitment as well. The lenten period, which has lost so much of its significance today because fasting and abstinence are no longer the central occupations, can gain a deeper meaning when it becomes the time for the local church to revisit the sources of its faith by reliving its own initiation along with that of the catechumens

Ordinarily, the First Sunday of Lent will be reserved for the election, the Third, Fourth, and Fifth Sundays for the three scrutinies, the intervening weeks for the presentations. Like the two presentations, the three scrutinies are not to be seen as rites of passage. They are, rather, the means in the catechetical process for the initiate to be instructed little by little in the mystery of sin.

Normally, more than one scrutiny will be celebrated, but again, this is according to circumstances and persons. It is good to note that the scrutinies are done in the form of intercessions rather than adjurations. The ancient formulas of adjuration run the risk of appearing as magical and suggesting the physical presence of Satan.

Because the community must be in involved in this process, both the baptized and the not yet baptized must be converted during the lenten period. Both must enter into the paschal reconciliation process. That is what Christian initiation and Lent are all about. Thus it might be helpful that when the catechumens are going through the scrutinies and are being prepared for the sacrament, the rest of the parish be engaged in some kind of penitential rites which will prepare them for the sacrament of reconciliation during Holy Week.

This stage comes to an end on Holy Saturday. The three sacraments of initiation, baptism, confirmation, and Eucharist, are received during the Easter Vigil, even if the bishop cannot be present. Their common reception indicates the unity of the paschal mystery. These sacraments bring to awareness the fact that baptism is more about newness than purification and that the Eucharist is the high point of the exercise of the priesthood that the neophytes now articulate.

The most important innovation of this rite is the introduction of confirmation between baptism and Eucharist. The rule of the Latin Church that reserves confirmation to the bishop is now extended to the presbyter who baptizes in these situations. The theology expressed in this change is not shared by all, although there is near consensus among liturgists and sacramental theologians.

What is being emphasized is that confirmation is closely bound to baptism and that its meaning must be sought in terms of baptism, that is, as the completion of the birth in new life which baptism is. It is not a step in the growth of the baptized's life which occurs at some later time, unrelated to rebirth in Christ. If for some reason confirmation is to be delayed, it should be conferred on Pentecost.

Mystagogia. The final mystagogical stage which is celebrated during the Easter season brings this lengthy initiation process to a conclusion. Again, the catechesis during this time is not that of didacticism but of sacramental experience. This will be possible only if the neophytes feel part of the community because of personal contact and deepened relationships. The rite suggests that for those Sunday liturgies where the neophytes are present, the lectionary for Year A should be used because those readings speak more of the meaning of community and Eucharist. The real catechist during this period is the Sunday assembly itself.

It is not easy to differentiate the prebaptismal catechesis from the postbaptismal one. But one can say that the catechesis preceding the Easter celebration will concentrate on conversion, sin, a sense of community and how to live the Christian life according to the Christian ethic. Those following the sacraments of initiation will be of a more theological nature in that they are reflections on an experience just had. In this case, it is first necessary to have the experience before trying to possess it systematically. One cannot speak of love to an unloved or unloving person.

The Non-Catechized and Children

I believe there is one ritual in this new document which can be immensely important for the present time in the strengthening of the Christian church. That is the rite of dealing with those who have been baptized as infants but who have never been catechized. It may well be that until the time comes when we are no longer under the tyranny of indiscriminate baptism, this will prove to be the beneficial way of dealing with Catholics. They, like those becoming Christians, are asked to go through a preparatory period. In their case however, it is not to prepare them for baptism but rather to actualize this baptism. And so the *Ordo* provides for a reception into the community rather than entrance into the catechumenate.

It is also possible to make use of those rites of the catechumenate which are not intrinsically tied to baptism, for instance, the rites of presentation: the recital of the Creed and the Lord's prayer. One might also add the rite of presentation of the Gospels. In place of the scrutinies, one would use penitential celebrations.

Another important ritual which this *Ordo* contains is that which concerns children of school age. It may be that it will be this rite of catechumenate which will become the transitional one to an adult catechumenate It is the adult rite adapted to children between seven and twelve. It attempts to be suitable for their age and psychology. It differs from the adult catechumenate in two ways. First it stresses the importance of the community, but one which is composed of both peers and adults, and second it has less celebrations than the adult rite, three or four in number, with one or two scrutinies.

Some Conclusions

It seems necessary to stress again:

1. The catechumenate is not a marginal institution, not a romantic dream of some early church liturgical scholars, but is part of the expansion process of the church. The catechumenate will only be an enormous failure unless it is intimately connected with a preceding evangelization period and a subsequent sacramental life. The catechumenate must be something organized on the diocesan level so that it can be closely connected with core faith communities, various catechetical centers and with communities where the liturgical and sacramental life is emphasized.

2. It is necessary to redefine what we mean by catechesis. It is not the same as the old days. The paradigm of the catechetical process is not conceptual instruction with increasing degrees of theological content and more sophisticated pedagogical devices. Rather, it is a process of growth which consists of gateways, steps, and movements. Each of these has its corresponding liturgical level.

3. The task it to find room in the church for those who belong to the order of catechumens. The catechumenate is not just a transitory experience for a few adult converts of something which is to be

utilized in mission countries. It is a permanent feature of the church and the whole church must nourish itself from it because it is the instrument of the church's continuing rebirth. It is the method for the church to be ever youthful.

(In developing this article, I wish to acknowledge my debt to the following article: "Pastoral Dimensions of the Rite of Adult Initiation," by Andre Aubry, *Ephemerides Liturgicae*, Vol. 88; "The Norm of Baptism" by Aidan Kavanagh, *Worship*, Vol. 48; "Christian Initiation: The State of the Question," by Ralph Keifer, *Worship*, Vol. 48; and, of course, the introduction to the *Rite of Christian Initiation of Adults*.)

"The Revised Rite of Christian Initiation of Adults — A Commentary" originally appeared in MODERN LITURGY magazine (Resource Publications, Inc.).

Anointing with the Oil of Catechumens

Rita Ferrone

The *Rite of Christian Initiation of Adults* realistically acknowledges that the path of conversion can be tortuous and difficult at times and that catechumens need God's help and strength to persevere in it. The ancient metaphor of Christian conversion as an athletic contest finds unique expression in one of the rites that can be celebrated several times during the initiation process: anointing with the oil of catechumens.

Unlike the oil of the sick, which is for healing, or the oil of chrism, which consecrates a person to a particular mission (as when a king is anointed), the oil of catechumens is the oil of athletes.

In the fourth century, this anointing was performed immediately before the great moment of truth in the baptismal ceremony itself, when the elect would make their profession of faith. It was preparation for a kind of spiritual wrestling match against evil in which the elect would finally win the victory.

In the gymnasium, muscles are massaged with oil to make them relaxed and supple; wrestlers anoint their bodies so that they will slide out of their opponents' grasp. Catechumens today are anointed so that "undeterred by the bonds of the past and overcoming the opposition of the devil, they will forthrightly take the step of professing their faith and will hold fast to it unfalteringly throughout their lives" (99).

When to Celebrate Anointing

In the dioceses of the United States, the bishops have decided that this anointing may not be celebrated either at the Easter Vigil itself or in the preparation rites on Holy Saturday (33.7). Rather, it is to be used exclusively as a "rite of passage" (33.6) during the catechumenate period and the period of purification and enlightenment (33.7). It may be celebrated several times during the course of the initiation process (100), "wherever this seems beneficial or desirable" (98).

Some good occasions to make a "rite of passage" might be signaled by actual changes in the catechumen's life or by his or her involvement in some aspect of the church's mission (75.4). Other occasions might be suggested by the rhythms of the process itself, such as a summer break or the commencement of Lent (if the catechumen is not to be elected that year).

The anointing takes place in a celebration of the Word (see ML 33:8). The celebration ordinarily would include at least the catechumenate group if not a larger representation of the parish. In case of special need, a catechumen may be anointed privately (100) but such occasions would be very rare.

Presiders, Catechists, Sponsors

The presider for the rite is a priest or deacon. Because of its history of close association with the sacrament of baptism and the ministry of the bishop, anointing is always ministered by the ordained, even when several ministers are needed (103). Lay catechists can and should play a significant role in the celebration, possibly through ministries of the Word, or by presenting the catechumens or calling them forward by name with their sponsors, or bearing the oil for anointing, or some other visible involvement. Sponsors join in prayer and support of their catechumens as they are anointed, often by the simple gesture of placing their hands on the catechumens' shoulders.

The Baptized Candidates

The already baptized should not be anointed with the oil of catechumens (see *National Statutes*, 31). Only those who are preparing to cross the fundamental threshold of baptism are envisioned as the subjects of this anointing. Nevertheless, including an additional prayer of blessing or exorcism in the same celebration, addressed to the needs of the candidates, is certainly an adaptation worth considering.

The Oil

The oil with which the catechumens are anointed is blessed by the bishop at the Chrism Mass, but for pastoral reasons fresh oil can be blessed by a priest in the celebration of anointing at the parish (see 101 and 102B). Olive oil is normally used and should only be lightly scented so as not to be confused with the more lavish fragrances associated with the festive oil of chrism. If the blessing of oil is chosen, the prayer of exorcism of the catechumens is omitted.

The oil should be displayed in a beautiful container, such as are used in your ambry at church — preferably a glass carafe that allows its contents to be seen. This graceful vessel should be of an appropriate size for your assembly and worship space and should be set in a visually prominent place of its own during the whole of the service. When the time comes to anoint, enough oil should be poured into a shallow bowl so that the presider can use liberal amounts of it when anointing.

Exorcism or Blessing?

Is it preferable to bless the oil on the spot or to pray an exorcism over the catechumens and use oil blessed by the bishop? The prayer for the blessing of the oil presents the oil as a sign of God's power and so performs an explanatory function. This could be an enriching option, perhaps for the catechumens' first experience of anointing. In general, however, I would tend to prefer option A (one of any of the exorcism prayers found in RCIA 94, followed by anointing with oil already blessed) because I think it is more engaging for the catechumens. The exorcism prayers are rich in scriptural imagery (see ML 22:10), involve a change in posture (kneeling), and focus on the catechumens rather than the oil. Using oil that is blessed by the bishop is a good reminder of the interdependence of all ministries in the church.

In either instance, the text spoken with the anointing that follows the prayer remains the same and underscores the profound meaning of this gesture. I find it helpful to repeat the text to each catechumen, though if there are many catechumens, it could be said once for all.

Both the exorcism prayer and the prayer for blessing the oil are fairly long. To heighten their intensity, they may be sung or interspersed with sung acclamations by the assembly. Another adaptation which will increase the assembly's sense of participation in the prayer is to have them extend their hands when the presider extends his.

Anointing

According to the rite, the catechumens may be anointed "on the breast or on both hands or, if this seems desirable, even on other parts of the body" (103). It is unlikely that a total body anointing such as was practiced in the ancient church can be considered feasible today — especially when such an anointing is separated from its original context in the bathing ritual of baptism — but anointing of the breast (at the collarbone) is easily accomplished if the catechumens are instructed to wear open-necked clothing to the rite.

I would recommend anointing the breast and both hands, so as to involve more of the body and enhance the symbolism of strengthening. (The forehead should not be anointed because the head is reserved for consecratory anointing.) To insure that an adequate amount of oil is used, the presider should anoint with four fingers rather than the thumb. Large, generous, unhurried gestures — rather than little dabs — are called for here.

Concluding the Celebration

After the anointing, a blessing of the catechumens may be added, but my sense is that few words are needed at this point. It would be better to conclude with a blessing and dismissal for all present and a closing song.

"Anointing with the Oil of Catechumens" originally appeared in MODERN LITURGY magazine (Resource Publications, Inc.).

Scrutinies

Catherine H. Krier

A source of great renewal for parish life today is the *Rite of Christian Initiation of Adults*. The various rites of passage within the liturgical year are well defined within the document. However, I have presumed to adapt the scrutinies. Over eight years of experience with the catechumens I have had only one candidate who did not come out of another Christian tradition. Most of them were already disciples of the Lord to some degree. I have found the following process to be much more beneficial for both the candidates and the assembly.

First Scrutiny: 3rd Sunday of Lent

After the final general intercession:

Will the sponsors of those being initiated into our community at the Easter Vigil please come forward. In the fall you began to sponsor a candidate in the ways of Christ.

At this time we would like you to renew your promise to this candidate, and to what that commitment entails. In the name of this community, I ask you then.

Do you promise to be a friend and companion to your candidate?

Will you continue to pray for this person?

Will you be an example of Christian living?

I now invite all of the assembly to extend your hand toward these sponsors as we ask the Lord's blessing upon them. What is asked of them can only be accomplished with God's grace.

Let us pray.

Lord, giver of life, we ask your blessing upon these chosen people. You have called them to serve those who will commit themselves to You in a newer and deeper way at the Easter vigil. Rid these sponsors of any hindrances toward their own holiness. Help them to live in Your presence now and for all eternity. We ask this in Jesus' name.

Amen.

Second Scrutiny: 4th Sunday of Lent

After the final general intercession:

At our Easter vigil we will celebrate the entrance of some of our adults into full membership through the sacraments of Baptism, Eucharist and Confirmation.

These men and women have been prayerfully and wholeheartedly involved in their preparation for initiation into our community for a year. This has required dedication, sacrifice and commitment. Do you, as members of (*Name*) parish, have any questions that you would like to ask them at this time? (*Allow time for questions.*)

I now invite the assembly to extend a hand toward these elect as we invoke God's blessing.

Let us pray.

Lord of unending grace, we implore You to generously bestow your blessings upon these elect as they draw nearer and nearer to You. May these be holy days of anticipation as they look forward with us to the day when they will be in full communion with us. We ask this blessing through Christ our Lord.

Amen.

Third Scrutiny: 5th Sunday of Lent

After the final general intercession:

At our Easter Vigil we will celebrate the sacraments of initiation with our elect. As a preliminary preparation for this celebration we have been introducing them to you. Last Sunday you were given an opportunity to question them. Now it is their turn to question you. Please respond to their questions if you like. We don't want to leave their inquiries "up in the air." *(Allow time for each candidate to speak.)*

Thank you for your participation in this scrutiny. Let us ask God's blessing upon this assembly. Heavenly Lord, You have called these Christians to commit themselves more deeply to You and this community. We ask You to strengthen the faith of this assembly gathered here in prayer. Help us to be present to these new members; help us to be authentic witnesses to Christian values. We ask this through Christ your Son and our Brother.

Amen.

"Scrutinies" originally appeared in MODERN LITURGY magazine (Resource Publications, Inc.).

Themes and Symbols of Reconciliation

Sarah O'Malley, OSB, and Robert Eimer, OMI

Introduction

Using the following skeletal ideas, we invite the pastor, the liturgist or liturgy committee, the retreat master, youth minister or religion teacher to create his or her own communal reconciliation. We suggest the theme and symbol and occasionally a Scripture text, but the rest is left to the creativity of the reader.

Most of the themes and their symbols were possible reconciliation services of the future, services we ourselves one day wanted to construct. It is left up to your imagination to take the themes and construct a communal reconciliation that animates the theme in every way, including a symbolic gesture by the penitent.

I. Theme: Renewing the Covenant With God

Symbol: Marriage Vows

The Bible is a love story of God's covenant or marriage with his people. From the creation story on down through the ages, God chose a people as his own. In the story of the Israelites, idolatry was seen as adultery (e.g., Hosea) or the breaking of the marriage bond with God. In the New Testament, through Jesus Christ, the covenant is extended beyond the Jewish people to all people. A Christian's sinfulness is also seen as a form of idolatry and infidelity to the covenant — a choosing of someone or something over God Himself. In this reconciliation service, the marriage vows (or a modification of them) could be used to renew the covenant between the congregation and God. The priest or a leader could represent God in renewing His love and faithfulness to the people; the congregation could then renew their vows to God. The renewal of vows could come after the absolution.

II. Theme: Heal Our Blindness

Symbol: Loaf of Bread

This reconciliation service builds on the Gospel of Luke — the story of Emmaus (Lk 24:13–50). The disciples were blinded to the meaning of Scripture and its promise as well as to the true identity of the stranger. In John's Gospel, Jesus often refers to sin as blindness. Because of our rationalizations, our refusal to look at the needs of others (note the meaning of the parable of the Good Samaritan), we also sin. Like the disciples of Emmaus, we close eyes and ears to the meaning of Scripture and the promises that Jesus attaches to the Eucharist.

The symbol for this service could be small loaves of bread to be taken home to share with the family, or people could be invited to a post-service gathering of bread, cheese and beverage. The bread must be broken and shared to emphasize that, in breaking, Christ continues to be present in the Eucharist and in our neighbors.

III. Theme: Judge Not, For We Too Have Sinned

Symbol: Sand

This reconciliation service builds on John's story of the woman caught in adultery. Instead of condemning the woman as the Law and the Pharisees were prone to do, Jesus in some way mirrors back to the Pharisees their own sinfulness. According to some commentators, Jesus was doing more than doodling in the sand; he was actually revealing the hidden sins of the accusers. We do not come to this service to point fingers at others but rather to take a look at our own sinfulness. Jesus reveals his compassion for all people regardless of how serious their sins might be.

The symbol for this service is sand. A large shallow box filled with sand could be placed in a prominent place in church. As a gesture indicating their own sinfulness, the penitents would be requested to draw a line in the sand prior to their confession of sins.

IV. Theme: Jesus Gives New Life And New Freedom

Symbol: Resurrection Plant
Or Seed Taped to Cloth

This reconciliation service revolves around John's account of the resurrection of Lazarus. Jesus came not just to give new life to Lazarus but also to remove the burial wrapping which impeded his freedom of movement. Likewise in the sacrament of reconciliation Jesus comes not only to give us God's grace of new life but also to help free us from the compulsions of sin, the fetters of sin.

Here there could be two possible symbols, a seed taped to a small piece of cloth. The seed would symbolize new life; the burial cloth, new freedom. The resurrection plant would be an optional symbol for this service. When placed in water, this seemingly dead plant comes to life. Individual sampling of this plant could be given as a take-home to each penitent so that they could experience the wonder of new life. If the plant is used as symbol, the homilist should emphasize that the sacrament of reconciliation was often referred to as a second baptism by the early church fathers.

V. Theme: You Are the Salt of the Earth

Symbol: Salt

The success of this theme depends heavily on the way the homilist handles the topic of salt. Because of medical warnings, salt today has some negative connotations. In Jesus' time, salt was a precious preservative and the principal way of flavoring food.

Jesus called on the Christian to preserve the human values of the Gospel in the midst of a sinful world. He also asks us to give flavor and zest to life by living out the hope-filled message of the Gospel. In the pre-Vatican II ritual of baptism, salt was used to represent Jesus' call to become salt for the world. A small amount of salt can be put in a cellophane container and blessed before giving it to each penitent to remind him/her of his/her call and mission.

VI. Theme: We Are Restored To New Life in the Second Adam (Jesus) and the Second Eve (Mary)

Symbol: Apple

This reconciliation service would be a good one for Advent. The theme is that humankind finds a new beginning in the Second Adam and Eve. The service centers on a French folktale which, for theological reasons, has been modified. The story unfolds this way: "Note revealed in the Scripture is the visit at Bethlehem to the Christchild and Mary by a very ancient couple. Their only gift to the Christ child is an apple. The story reveals that the ancient couple is Adam and Eve coming to the Savior for forgiveness for their sin in the Garden of Eden. As they give the gift, they are blessed by becoming young and vital once more."

The apple is the basis symbol in this service. Each penitent receives an apple as they enter church. They will return the apple to attending ministers before the absolution as a sign that their sins have been forgiven and they have been renewed in Christ, the second Adam.

VII. Theme: Advent And a Call to Conversion

Symbol: Washing Hands

The theme for this service must include the Gospel story of John the Baptist calling us to repentance. John's mission is to call a people to conversion so that they might be ready to receive salvation from Jesus the Messiah. John's baptism is a baptism of repentance. Water thus becomes the dominant symbol for this reconciliation service.

As at the end of the offering of gifts at Mass and as a symbol of cleansing, the priest washes his hands in preparation for the coming of the Savior in the form of bread and wine. So, too, the penitents are invited to do the same symbolic gesture in preparation for the absolution and coming of Christ the Savior. Several servers may be necessary to allow this washing to happen smoothly.

VIII. Theme: He Was Put to Death For Our Sins

Symbol: Hammer

The theme for this reconciliation service reiterates the ageless truth that sin is not just a private act. Every sin affects other people. In that sense, Jesus not only dies because of the sins of the Romans or the Jews but also because of the sins of humankind. A wooden cross is placed in a prominent position in the sanctuary. The penitents are invited to take a hammer and pound the cross as a sign of their participation in the crucifixion of Jesus. The hammer thus becomes the dominant symbol of the penitent's guilt and sinfulness. Obviously, this theme would be most appropriate for the lenten season but could be used for other times as well.

IX. Theme: Christ Helps Us With Our Shadow Self

Symbol: Masks

In the West, we speak of the seven capital sins; in the East they refer to the nine basic compulsions, our shadow side. (Refer to the Sufi Indian Enneagram concept.) In Western spirituality, we are seen to have a basic dominant weakness. In Eastern thought, we are seen as having a shadow side of our personality which needs first to be acknowledged, then dealt with and finally healed.

This reconciliation service could center on the seven capital sins or the nine compulsions of the Sufi wisdom. The purpose of the service is to unmask our dominant sin or compulsion and ask Christ to draw us toward healing and wholeness. The basic symbol for this service is the various masks by which we cover up our sins or weakness. This idea could well serve for All Saints Day, using Halloween masks and/or mime to illustrate sins or compulsions.

X. Theme: Jesus, Light of Forgiveness, Removes the Darkness of Our Sins

Symbol: Candle

John's Gospel especially makes Jesus the Light of the World. Jesus is not only the Light revealing the identity of the Father, but he is also the Light in direct opposition to the darkness of sin. In this reconciliation service, Jesus comes to reveal the compassion of the Father and also to reveal our own sinfulness and to be a healing Light for our darkness.

The basic symbol for this service is the lighted candle. The Easter candle could hold a place of prominence in the sanctuary. If possible, the church atmosphere should exemplify the dark-light contrast.

XI. Theme: Letting Go Of Our Sinfulness

Symbols: Nickel

The theme of this reconciliation service would center on the idea of letting go of things which attract us, feed our selfishness and prevent our openness to God and to others. A nickel is given to each penitent as he or she enters the church. The coin represents not just our poverty (sin is often very shallow and superficial) but also the pleasures and talents God has given us for our use. When we grasp these things for our own selfish pleasures (contrary to the will of God), we often misuse God's gift of life, the body and mind. he give us the material things for our growth and development. The homilist can emphasize the above ideas and the coin can be returned or let loose in a symbolic gesture of the penitent's willingness to let go. The assigned penance could focus on using one's talents or material gifts to enrich the lives of others.

XII. Theme: More Than Crocodile Tears

Symbol: Oil

True conversion is more than hypocritical and shallow tears in the eyes; it involves tears in the heart. Likewise, true conversion in the heart leads to action and service to our neighbor.

In the Gospel story of Luke 7:36–50, a sinful woman finds Jesus eating in the house of a Pharisee. She not only had tears of repentance but washed Jesus' feet with those tears and then anointed them with precious oil. Her conversion led her to offer Jesus a service of hospitality that had been omitted by a self-righteous host. She overcame human respect in order to offer Jesus a gesture of respect and love.

The story of Luke's would be an interesting one to mine. The homily could point out the contrast between the pride of Simon and the humility of the sinful woman. The examination of conscience could focus on our own areas of insecurity. The anointing of the penitents' hands after the absolution could be connected with some common penance involving service to his/her neighbor.

XIII. Theme: Die to Self and Be Saved

Symbol: Ashes

The theme of this reconciliation service is that new life can come from death. The ashes not only represent death to our own selfish and sinful actions and desires, but they also represent the potential of new life. The legend of the Phoenix Bird can easily illustrate the theme. The Phoenix in burning itself to ashes gives birth to a new life. This is a symbol of the paschal mystery, the mystery of death and resurrection in Jesus. The relationship of this service to Ash Wednesday is obvious. If possible, a fire could be started at the beginning of the service so that ashes could be available for signing each penitent during the service.

"Themes and Symbols of Reconciliation" originally appeared in MODERN LITURGY magazine (Resource Publications, Inc.).

How To Plan Communal Reconciliation Form II

William Cieslak, OFMCAP

Below is an outline for planning communal reconciliation services with individual confession and absolution.

General Principles

1. *Good liturgy is for the assembly, not vice versa.* Liturgy must be shaped to the assembly's form and style. Prepackaged liturgies seldom work. Preplanned "penance services" should stimulate creativity, not cut it off.

2. *Good liturgy needs to be well planned.* Good intentions do not in themselves plan good liturgies; cooperative hard work does. Understanding the assembly and the rite are a must.

3. *Good liturgy needs to be performed well.* The best laid plans have crumbled under the weight of unprepared ministers. Not only must *each* minister be prepared, but *all* must learn to work *together*.

Planning

1. The *liturgical assembly* is the focus of the liturgical planning. You must have some idea as to who will participate in this rite, when they will participate, and under what circumstances. The number of people expected determines the space needed and, to some extent, the kind and amount of music used. The time of day suggests whether people will be exhausted from a full day's work, ready to celebrate, or reluctant to give up too much of a free day to church matters. After all, the purpose of the rite is to enable the assembly to worship.

2. Consider the *structure* of the rite. Communal reconciliation services seek to enable the community gathered and the individuals who make it up to: a) express sorrow for sinfulness and b) experience the reconciling power of the Lord in their midst.

There are special "moments" in this rite:

- the experience of being called and gathered by the Lord.

- the experience of hearing the good news of the Lord: how God loves us so deeply in Christ and wants us to be one with Godself.

- the recognition of the power of sin in our lives both as a group and as individuals.

- the specific recognition of what in my life keeps me from living the Gospel as I know I ought.

- the confession of sinfulness in the light of God's grace and God's call to conversion.

- the experience of being reconciled by the Lord through the ministry of the priest and through the prayerful support of the assembly.

- joyful thanksgiving to the Lord and a desire to live the Gospel life.

These moments are experienced through a structured rite that contains songs, readings, prayers, silence and ritual gestures

Entrance Rites

- Opening Song

- Greeting

- Prayer: called and gathered in the Lord

Celebration of the Word of God

- Reading: hearing good news

- Response (psalm/song): God's love for us

- Reading (optional): our awareness of sin

- Gospel-Homily: our awareness of sin

- Examination of Conscience: call to conversion

Rite of Reconciliation

- General Confession (prayer or litany and Lord's Prayer): expression of sorrow

- Individual Confession and Reconciliation: personal encounter, communion

- Communal Praise: thanksgiving (song, prayer, gesture)

Closing Rites

- Blessing and Dismissal: sending into the world

3. Keep in mind the *liturgical season*. Lenten communal reconciliation services should have the lenten flavor of penance, conversion, renewal of the baptismal life; Advent services should prepare for the coming of the Lord, etc.

4. *Readings* ought to reflect both the structure of the rite and the liturgical season. The selections taken as a whole should include a focus on a) God's love and mercy in Christ, and b) call to conversion from our sinfulness. Both elements are important; both must be kept in balance.

5. *Music* ought to reflect the liturgical season and the devotional needs of the assembly as well as fit properly into the structure. Opening songs set the mood; a song after the reading should respond to the reading both in text and feel; songs or taped (recorded) music during the individual confessions should focus more on God's love and mercy and on our willingness to convert rather than on our sinfulness; songs after reconciliation should express our communal heartfelt praise and thanksgiving, etc. Music should be pitched for the assembly.

6. *Prayers* ought to express the heart of the assembly. They should be composed of short sentences rich in imagery rather than filled with theological language.

7. *Gestures* ought to be planned. Common gestures are often overlooked: kneeling, bowing, standing and sitting, signs of the cross. Gestures call the body into prayer and attention. They need to be varied and appropriate to the assembly: they should "fit" this group at this time.

8. *Environment* should fit the occasion. The temperature of the church should be right for prayer: not too hot, nor too cold. Lighting should be appropriate (softer lighting usually works well). Candles in the sanctuary (but not focusing attention on the altar table) give the sense that something important is about to happen. Seasonal foci might be appropriate: baptismal font or cross or empty paschal candle stand for Lent; Advent wreath or paschal candle for Advent. Color and vestments are important: purple for Lent, perhaps blue for Advent, albs and stoles that match for priest confessors, hangings, etc.

The word of God is the focus for the rite; it is that word that calls us to reconciliation, that word in our hearts that changes us and allows us to confess. Perhaps the Scriptures should have a visible focus.

Plan and mark, if necessary, the places

where individual reconciliation will take place. Confessors can stand at the stations. (Anonymity can be respected by the use of visiting priests.) Movement of people toward the front or sanctuary area is better than movement toward the back corners (reconciliation is not like standing in the corner!). Spacing between stations is necessary and can be facilitated by background music that covers up individual voices.

9. Use *effective symbols*. Symbols that work for the assembly are: incense rising at moments of communal prayer, confession, thanksgiving (a high ceiling is a must!); candles being lighted by those who have just confessed bathing the room in Christ's light; hands being anointed with oil as part of the absolution or as part of a communal reconciliation gesture after individual reconciliation; hands laying on each other's shoulders as this sign; the sharing of the sign of peace. Some have used masks effectively prior to reconciliation showing sin as masking our true identities in the Lord. Sacred movement or dance might work in some assemblies. However, symbols ought not be multiplied carelessly: less is better. Simplicity in sign and gesture is powerful.

10. The *right length* of the service is what the assembly expects. If people expect to be in church for an hour, an hour is the right length. Services extended beyond what the assembly expects will be unpopular and less effective. Longer services are a sacrifice, but they're not necessarily more redeeming!

Performance

1. The *assembly* and the special ministers alike need to know what they are to do and how they are to do it. No one wants to be made a fool of. Normal movements need not be rehearsed; special moves need to be practiced. Special requests made of the assembly need to be explained before the service. One caution: the more the rite seems unknown to the assembly, the less they will be able to give themselves over to prayer.

2. *Special ministers* need to look like they know what they are doing and sound like they mean what they are saying.

3. *Presider and musicians* together set the pace of the service. Presiders who speak when they should be quiet call attention to themselves; presiders who say more than they should do the same. Some musical selections lead to quiet meditation; some to immediate response. Some music arises out of the depths of the praying heart, some out of joyful good news. Both the way the music is accompanied and the musical selections themselves must fit the context in which they are used and contribute to the flow of the service. Seconds of silence make all the difference here: music that begins too quickly cheapens what has taken place; music that begins late calls attention to lack of preparation and understanding and drags the service.

4. *Readers* should treat the readings as gentle rain and allow quiet time after them for the words to nourish the soul. Note that "gentle" rain says something about the pace of the reading as well.

5. *Useless vocal directives* call people out of prayer and interrupt the service. "The responsorial psalm is on page ten," and "please stand," are two such directives. If possible, use the hand to gesture rather than the voice; use a program to give directives.

6. All in the sanctuary must look like they are paying attention at all times. Musicians who talk to each other while the homily is being given call attention to themselves; priest confessors who look out at the congregation compete with the presider for the attention of the assembly. Good liturgy is the activity of the entire assembly, each person supporting each other in gesture and attention.

7. Mistakes will happen; so will the unexpected. Good liturgy builds on good manners. It gives a voice to God's word and a soul for God's Spirit. Mistakes are not sinful. If God can forgive sin, great as that is, we ought to be able to overlook each other's mistakes.

"How to Plan Communal Reconciliation Form II" originally appeared in MODERN LITURGY magazine (Resource Publications, Inc.).

Communal Reconciliation Service: Invitation to New Life

Sarah O'Malley, OSB, and Robert Eimer, OMI

Dominant Symbol: Sacramental symbols, especially water, oil, stole. "I came that they might have Life and have it to the full." (Jn 10:10) (The lights in the church are lowered. The priest celebrants enter directly from the sacristy and go to their seats. The congregation remains seated also. Then after a few moments of silence, the lector announces the theme.)

I. Introduction

A. The Theme: "Among all the channels of grace, there are seven special channels designated by the church, called the sacraments. Today we want to highlight three sacraments — Baptism, Confirmation, and Reconciliation. These sacraments invite us to New Life."

B. Entrance Procession: In a semi-darkened church, background music begins. Then three lay ministers dressed in choir robes lead three other lay ministers, dressed similarly. Down the right aisle, one candle bearer leads a minister bearing a bowl of water as a symbol of Baptism. Down the left aisle, another candle bearer leads a minister bearing a flask of oil, the symbol of Confirmation. Down the center aisle another candle bearer leads a minister bearing a stole, the symbol of Reconciliation. The candle bearers place their candles on stands near the symbols and the other ministers place the symbols in their proper positions in the sanctuary. The symbols are displayed in the following fashion from left to right:

- Baptism — bowl of water
- Confirmation — jar of oil
- Matrimony — wedding candle
- Holy Eucharist — loaf of bread and grapes
- Holy Orders — chalice
- Anointing of Sick — sick call set
- Reconciliation — stole

C. Opening Prayer: (Priest stands and asks congregation to do likewise.)

> "Lord you came to give life, life in its fullness. It was from the cross that the life of the Spirit and all sacramental life follows. Lord, through your cross, may you heal, forgive, and bring New Life. We ask this through Christ, our Savior. Amen."

D. The priest will incense the symbols displayed before the altar, and then be seated.

II. Liturgy of the Word

(Congregation sits.)

A. Romans 6:1–4: (We are called to die to sin with Christ so as to rise with Him to New Life.)

B. Response: Remember your love and your faithfulness, O Lord, remember your people, and have mercy on us, Lord. ("Remember Your Love" by Ducote, Daigle)

C. John 19:33–35: (Stand) (Soldiers pierced Jesus' side as He was dying on the cross. From his side came forth water and blood, the symbols of Baptism and Eucharist.)

D. Homily Hints: It would be good to explain briefly the symbol-displays of the seven sacraments.

- The cross is the source of all sacramental life.

- By Baptism and Confirmation especially, we are all called to be disciples of Christ. By our sinfulness we fail to follow Jesus in his Way of the Cross and in turn become anti-life.

- Through the Sacrament of Reconciliation, we can heal the cancer that is sin and restore the brokenness of our relationship to Christ and to our brothers and sisters.

- Although Baptism is initiation into the "Christ-Life," Reconciliation has often been called a "Second Baptism."

- Through the Sacrament of Reconciliation, we renew the call to our discipleship initiated in Baptism and accept our adult commitment of Confirmation.

E. Song: "Turn to Me" by John Foley, SJ

III. Examination of Conscience

(Remain seated.)

Leader:
For the times I have wandered away from my Father's House like the Prodigal Son … (*pause*)

All:
Lord, help me say "Yes" to New Life

Leader:
For the times I have been ashamed to call myself a Christian … (*pause*)

All:
Lord, help me say "Yes" to New Life

Leader:
For the times I never got involved with the church and its mission … (*pause*)

All:
Lord, help me say "Yes" to New Life

Leader:
For the times I have neglected the Sacrament of Reconciliation and its call for forgiveness … (*pause*)

All:
Lord, help me say "Yes" to New Life

Leader:
For the times I've failed to live out my vocational commitment, whether as a religious, married, or single person … (*pause*)

All:
Lord, help me say "Yes" to New Life

Leader:
For the times out of selfishness or hardness of heart I have not admitted my sinfulness … (*pause*)

All:
Lord, help me say "Yes" to New Life

Leader:
For the times I have squandered the Father's Gifts, whether of time, talents or material possessions … (*pause*)

All:
Lord, help me say "Yes" to New Life

Leader:
For the times I have separated myself from the members of God's Family, through hatred, pride, stubbornness, slander … (*pause*)

All:
Lord, help me say "Yes" to New Life

Leader:
For the times I have been slow to say "I'm sorry," or seek forgiveness of others and of God … (*pause*)

All:
Lord, help me say "Yes" to New Life

Leader:
For the times I've failed my faith community by not joining in Sunday worship when I might easily have done so … (*pause*)

All:
Lord, help me say "Yes" to New Life

IV. Sign of Sorrow

As an act of sorrow, the priest and people kneel and recite together the confiteor.

V. Receiving of the Symbol And Absolution

Ask congregation to sit until ushers direct them, pew by pew, to approach the altar. The people are asked to come up and follow the ushers' directions as they form two lines in the center aisle. Near the front pew of the center aisle, two lay ministers hold bowls of water. First, each penitent takes holy water and makes the sign of the cross as a symbol of the cleansing water of Baptism. Secondly, the penitent approaches the priest to receive the blessing of oil on his/her forehead. During the absolution the priest places the stole on his/her shoulder as a symbol of forgiveness of sins. (When using the non-sacramental penitential celebration, the priest places the stole on the penitent's shoulder and anoints with oil while asking the question, "Will you answer the call to New Life?" to which the person responds, "Yes." The penitent then returns to his/her pew.)

VI. Common Penance

People stand and sing the "Our Father."

VII. Sign of Peace: "Peace Prayer" by John Foley, SJ

Suggestions

1. Instead of the elaborate decor as described in Suggestion #2, a less elaborate decor could be used. With the cross always as the source of the sacramental signs, three sacraments (Baptism, Confirmation and Reconciliation) could be highlighted instead of all seven.

2. Liturgical Setting: Darkened church, spotlight on large wooden cross in center of sanctuary. Rainbow colors of cloth emanate from the cross. At the end of each piece of cloth, one of the sacramental symbols is placed. Since three sacraments are being highlighted, these three symbols are strategically placed in the sanctuary arrangement.

3. Other suggested songs for this service:
   - "If God Is For us" by John Foley, SJ
   - "You Are Near" by Dan Schutte, SJ
   - "I Long for You" by Balhoff, Ducot, Daigle
   - "Light of the World" by Tom Kendzia
   - "Redeemer Lord" by John Foley, SJ

"Communal Reconciliation Service : Invitation To New Life" from Come Let Us Celebrate! Creative Celebrations of Reconciliation *(Resource Publications, Inc., 1986).*

Converting the Liturgist

Nick Wagner

Editors' Note: Lent is a time of conversion and serious pondering of our personal faults. This article by MODERN LITURGY editor Nick Wagner has been included to assist the liturgist in the process of personal reflection.

Someone once said a liturgist is a person sent by God so that those who have never had the privilege to suffer for their faith will not be denied the opportunity of doing so.

As we survey the landscape of pastoral ministry today, it seems no one is more intent on bringing about conversion than is the liturgist. The question is: conversion to what?

When I am with a pack of fellow liturgists, I am often reminded of a charismatic-fundamentalist crowd I was involved with as a teenager. "Are you saved?" was the question first asked of and often repeated by me. There were many others like it, all of which had very precise answers.

My liturgical colleagues remind me of that other charismatic crowd because we tend to have the same glint in our eye and the same tone in our voice. "Do you know what the GIRM says about that?" said with an imperious lift of the left eyebrow effectively cows most profaners into submission.

This attitude, of course, endears us liturgists to no one. In fact, a study titled "New Parish Ministers: Laity and Religious on Parish Staffs" (National Pastoral Life Center, 1992) showed that while most pastoral workers reported a high degree of job satisfaction and collegiality among their co-workers, liturgists felt little satisfaction and felt isolated. The fact is, a liturgist can be a pain in the neck.

How then to convert this unruly brute into a compatible, smooth-functioning team member?

The first step is to understand that the liturgist is not always a liturgist. What most parishes have is a liturgy planner whose "real" job is something other than liturgy. The liturgy planner in your parish might be the pastor, the DRE, the musician, or a volunteer. Even if you have an actual person called "liturgist," chances are his or her formal education is in some field other than liturgy.

While many of these people are fine liturgists who bring a great deal of talent to their communities, a fair number are also what I call the Frank Burns of liturgy. Frank Burns, you will remember, was the bumbling doctor from *M.A.S.H.* He knew just enough to be dangerous. His biggest fear was someone would discover just how little he actually knew about his profession. His fear made him defensive, arrogant, and inflexible. He was not really a bad person. He was just in the wrong job.

The first step in converting your liturgist is to determine if he or she really knows liturgy. Does your liturgist know the rubrics, the history, the deep structure, the ebb and flow, the *story* of the liturgy inside and out? Or is your liturgist simply blowing incense?

The key to making that determination is flexibility. A general rule of thumb is, the more a person knows about a subject, the more relaxed and flexible he or she is within that subject.

It's like cooking. A good cook knows when to stretch the rules, deviate from the recipe, and substitute ingredients without spoiling the sauce. A bad cook either disregards the cookbook altogether because it is too complicated, or the bad cook follows the recipe so strictly that the food turns out with a bland sameness which numbs the diners into lethargy. (See the Mexican film *Like Water for Chocolate* for a classic illustration of the good cook/bad cook distinction.)

Your goal is to increase the flexibility of your liturgist. You can increase your liturgist's flexibility by increasing his or her knowledge. This may seem paradoxical, but you can increase your liturgist's knowledge by acting as though he or she really does have an expert background.

Most disagreements with the liturgist come down to a parishioner or staff member wanting to do something out of the ordinary and the liturgist putting his or her foot down because the request is not liturgically correct. A second source of disagreement is the flip side; the liturgist does something out of the ordinary which rankles the staff or the parishioners.

In either case, two questions need to be asked.

First, is the "something out of the ordinary" good liturgical practice? Second, is the "something out of the ordinary" good pastoral practice? A great number of disputes could be reconciled if pastoral teams would ask these two questions. In fact, these words are often used but the real questions are different.

Often, liturgical innovations are argued for or against based on whether *I* like it, *you* like it, or *the people* like it. These are the wrong arguments. There is no resolution to such arguments. Supporters can always be found for either side, and the argument degenerates into how many people each side can line up either for or against. Moreover, any change from the status quo is going to displease somebody. Therefore, the questions have to remain, is this good liturgically, and is this good pastorally?

You will probably imagine my left eyebrow arching when I tell you that what is good liturgically is almost always good pastorally. I know that is not the lived experience of many of you, so let me explain. Because we know him, we know that what Frank Burns says is good medicine is not always good for your body. Just so, what the person who is under-trained as a liturgist says is good liturgy is not always good liturgy. So how do you know what is really good liturgically? Here's the paradox. Ask the liturgist!

Remember, we are presuming your liturgist is inflexible (why else would you be reading this?) and that inflexibility stems from a lack of knowledge. If you ask your liturgist to help you locate resources on confirmation, he or she will have to come up with some. If you ask your liturgist to explain particular paragraphs in the introduction to the Rite of Penance, he or she will have to read it. If you ask your liturgist to give a presentation on the various ritual options in the Rite of Baptism to the parents in the baptismal preparation group, he or she will have to become familiar with those options. The strategy here is to increase the knowledge your liturgist has by asking him or her to do some study and some teaching in order to help you out in your own ministry. A high-school teacher once told me you never really learn a subject until you have to teach it.

By using this strategy, you are treating the liturgist as an expert. The liturgist, knowing you perceive him or her as an expert, is more likely to trust you. He or she will also learn more about liturgy and grow in self-confidence about that knowledge.

A second strategy is to pick your battles. Sometimes disagreements can degenerate into each side ticking off a list of demands. If you have such a list, look through it to see what is *most* important to accomplish this year. What can wait until next year? What can wait until you either get a new liturgist or you move on to another parish? Focus on your most important objectives. To be successful, you should not have more than three in a given year. Having only one is ideal.

My intent here is not to say the liturgist is always right and is always more expert in liturgy than any other member of the pastoral team. I am saying that is likely to be his or her perception, however. If your goal is to convert the liturgist, you will not succeed by challenging that perception. No one likes to be told they are not who they think they are. You will more likely succeed by helping the liturgist grow into his or her self-perception.

That doesn't mean you can't disagree or challenge. It does mean being tactful about the way you go about it. "I don't think you know what you're talking about" won't get you nearly as far as "Can you help me understand why the church teaches that?"

And be patient. True conversion takes time. I've considered myself a converted liturgist for many years now, and I still find myself pompously quoting the GIRM on occasion. But I hardly ever arch my left eyebrow anymore.

"Converting the Liturgist" originally appeared in MODERN LITURGY magazine (Resource Publications, Inc.).

Examination of Conscience

Denise Anderson

The following examination of conscience can be used in any penitential service and might be especially appropriate for a lenten communal reconciliation. It is part of a lenten communal reconciliation service used by parishes in the Dioceses of Belleville, Ill. Several musical settings of the response are included.

fter the homily, the priest is seated and some silence follows. Then the priest stands and begins the examination of conscience with the following. The assembly can remain seated during the examination of conscience.

Let us think now on those things which have caused disharmony in our lives, estrangement with our God and separation from one another.

After some silence, the priest, another reader or group of readers can continue with the examination of conscience.

Loving God, we are people seeking forgiveness and consolation in your care. We pray that your light might illumine that which is dark in us, so that we might see you more fully. May we hear your call of conversion in our lives and through us, may your love flourish more abundantly.

R. Come, Let us set things right.

The cantor either leads this invocation in song and the assembly answers back or the reader reads and gestures for the assembly to answer back in spoken voice.

The ashes of Lent remind us that only in you, O God, do we have life. Forgive us for when we have not respected that life, when we have harmed ourselves or disrespected the freedom and uniqueness of another person. Help us to see that you have given the gift of salvation to all of us; that it is each of us together that forms one church in which we see the fullness of your glory. We ask your help in respecting and greeting the Lord in each of us.

R. Come, Let us set things right.

As we reflect on your life, O Lord, during these forty days of prayer, we see that your ministry must not have been easy. We see that people doubted you, ridiculed you, turned you in and turned you away. But like the prophet Isaiah, you declared that you were anointed to bring glad tidings to the poor, to proclaim liberty, healing and freedom. Though those around you were sometimes with you and sometimes against you, your love remained constant. Forgive us, Lord, for when we have not made the most of an opportunity to share your love; when we have let feelings and circumstances stand in our way; when we have thought that it was better to be right than to help your light shine.

R. Come, Let us set things right.

We are so human in our sin. We hurt those we love the most, we get trapped in small lies, we profess to commitments of care, discipline and time, only to find our resolve easily broken. Thank you, Lord, for these human failings that remind us that we depend on you and that though our sin is always with us, your grace abides more fully. May we forgive one another again and again for past and current disappointments, betrayals and broken promises. May we support one another as we struggle to become your holy people.

R. Come, Let us set things right.

No matter what the sin, O Lord, your forgiving love and compassionate mercy are waiting to heal, if we are open to admitting our faults and renewing what is in need of repair: our relationship with you, with those around us in work and home, and with family members and those memories that have haunted us with anxiety, anger and resentment. Though we cannot change the past, forgiveness can change the future. Help us to forgive when we do not see your way or wisdom; help us to love when we see no reason except your command to do so. Come with your spirit, Lord, and help us set things right.

R. Come, Let us set things right.

"Examination of Conscience" originally appeared in MODERN LITURGY magazine (Resource Publications, Inc.).

Reconciliation Means Change

Sr. Mary Charles Bryce, OSB

At one point in Kurt Vonnegut's novel *Slaughterhouse Five*, the hero imaginatively experiences a World War II movie in reverse. Accordingly, every destructive act of war becomes a healing act.

The German MiGs "sucked bullets and shell fragments from some of the planes and crewmen" of both American and English bombers and the latter flew backwards to their respective bases. From flaming German cities, English bombers sucked up bombs and snuffed out flames by a "miraculous magnetism." The bombs were carefully re-located on the shelves inside the planes and flown in reverse formation back to England where they were unloaded and returned by rail to factories. There they were dismantled and the minerals carefully put aside. In turn, those minerals were shipped to remote areas where specialists, whose business it had been to extract them, now put them back "into the ground, to hide them cleverly so they would never hurt anybody ever again."

It was wishful, hopeful fantasy diverting the concentration of plans, persons, money and materials from the military industrial complex into efforts to heal and reconcile people and cities.

The shortcoming in Vonnegut's fantasy is that there is one missing element of that healing. *Not* just that it was an imaginative and unreal thing, but to presume that in restoring things to "exactly the way they were" (which, of course, is an impossibility), in turning the hands of the clock back to a given time, things go on just as though nothing had happened.

One element in real healing is change. A scar may remain but healthy tissue grows together and the body soon functions normally again. In fact scar tissue sometimes has more strength than the original. Growth is descriptive of change in other areas, too. One "grows" intellectually; one "grows" in maturity; one "grows" physically. As we grow, we change.

Sinners Converted, Reconciled, Changed

An annual theme for Lent could be "The Church forgiving and forgiven." One reason it can be, and is, a forgiving church is because it is a church of sinners, a sin-full church. And the sinner in each of us is called to be sympathetic, to extend a reconciling hand and an open, forgiving heart to the other.

One Christian thinker (Bernard Cooke) has commented that "sanctity which is the mark of the Church is not a matter of superiority over sinners; it is rather a question of extending that merciful concern for humankind which Christ has, though he himself never sinned."

In the profound reality of his becoming (human), Christ found identification with us who are sinners, and this mission he transmits to us. In the midst of sinful humankind we must testify that sin is incompatible with all that God wants for us but proclaim at the same time that this loving God understands our condition and deals with us in mercy and forgiveness.

There is no joy for us in our sinful state. As all things are brought to perfection, sin will someday be destroyed and we will stand eye to eye with God wholly loved and wholly known. Meanwhile, there is much beauty in who we are because we are God's own.

We remember with incredible awe that annual reminder in the Easter vigil — *O felix culpa*, "O happy fault that brought us so great a Redeemer. That is to say, the sinfulness of man is more than matched by the redeeming power of divine love" (Cooke).

We are sinners. The church has always taught this with straightforward honesty. *But* we are redeemed sinners, dependent always upon the continuing redemptive power of Christ. Christians can never rest content with a sin-filled environment for in Christ they (we) are called to participate in the redemption which overcomes sin. It is, in God's grace, that admission of our "sinfulness that will preserve us from complacency and keep us in contact with our fellow human beings" (Cooke).

The communal nature of sinfulness demands consideration here. "Sin itself is so far-reaching in its social consequences that no one is ever free from its effects" (Kieran Conley). The line between my sin and your sin, between my guilt and your guilt, is not readily discernible. Our togetherness in the church and in the world is far too radical for us to be neatly packaged off from each other and from the consequences of our sinfulness. *There is no such thing as private sin.*

In light of this, the new rite of penance is remarkably better suited to the concept of reconciliation than that of previous practice. The sacrament of reconciliation is the act of a gathered people and the new rite admits the communal nature of and responsibility for both sin and forgiveness. It projects quite simply an element of *honesty* and *openness*, a simplicity and forthrightness that calls upon all of us to acknowledge our unity in faith, in confidence (hope), in love — and in sin. Not to be overcome by the latter, however, for even more important than humankind's sin is God's love.

As people loved just as we are, it's reasonable to expect that we would be loving and accepting of others. However, we often fail to be what we ought to be. But that "ought" disappears into thin air when one stands before the sinless person. How can he, who is the sinless Lord of us all, be so understanding and generous?

I have no answer for that except to point out in history and Scripture that his love has never known any bounds, whether for the unfaithful Israelites or the repentant Peter. His ways far outclass our ways. The best place to learn not only what sin is but what forgiveness is, is in the Bible. Matthew's Gospel account records an explanation

in a specific eating context. As Jesus sat at the table many tax collectors and sinners came and sat down with him and his followers. When the Pharisees saw that, they questioned his disciples: "Why does your teacher eat with tax collectors and sinners?

But when he heard it, he said, "People who are in good health do not need a doctor; sick people do. Go and learn what this means, 'I desire mercy and not sacrifice.' For I came to call, not the self righteous, but sinners" (Mt 9:11–13).

Sometimes penance is referred to as the "sacrament of conversion" as well as the sacrament of reconciliation. Not only is that an appropriate description but one of long standing. Michael Prieur described conversion as the "biblical breath of reconciliation" and insisted that "there is no more necessary, constant or fundamental aspect of this sacrament than that of deep, unremitting and ever growing biblical conversion."

The Old Testament expressed that idea in phrases such as "turning back," "retracing one's steps," "incline the ear of your heart" (Ps 95) or "circumcise your heart" (Dt 10:16). The most basic meaning is "a change of heart," which one Irish metaphor describes as "bending the knees of your heart." Often associated with the Greek term *metanoia*, it carries with it the implications of profound change. According to Prieur, Jesus "emphasized that conversion meant a deep change in our priorities. We had to change, become like little children and not only accept God as our Father, but actually live with that radical acceptance manifest in our lives."

There are times when we all feel that conversion and change isn't happening. We find ourselves wrestling with the same weakness, seemingly endlessly. Getting unstuck, and beginning to heal, as did the imaginative writer in the opening paragraph of this article, seems beyond us.

Progress is not easily charted or measured. We don't make a good yardstick for ourselves. Besides, change comes gradually, with effort and not in isolation.

The Christian community and the Holy Spirit enable and assist us in the process of *metanoia*.

One can hardly think of approaching the sacrament of penance without the intention to change. That is what we used to speak of as "firm purpose of amendment." In some way, the penitent manifests an intention to convert by acknowledging sinfulness and being accepted back into that community, especially into the eucharistic community.

Both the Eucharist and penance are rightly called sacraments of reconciliation. Sharing the bread of the Eucharist symbolizes reconciliation already experienced in our own lives as well as that reconciliation we shall celebrate together at the eternal banquet table. Forgiveness in penance is a necessary dimension of our existence in time as we journey toward ultimate reconciliation. The intimate connection between the two is "absolutely necessary and *conversion* is the leitmotif of this whole sacramental dynamism" (Prieur).

There appears to be, then, at least three integral aspects of change in the sacrament of reconciliation. They may be distinguished as *change of attitude, change of intention* and *conversion.*

Actually, they are integrally linked but for the sake of review I separate them here. The first might be described as interiorization. One interiorizes the experience and grows through it to a new attitude, a deepened appreciation of one's neighbor and of God.

A decided intention to turn from sin and instead to adhere more courageously to love is the second. In a given instance that might become a resolve to avoid a particular situation and the like.

The third may be called a state of on-going conversion and re-conversion to Christ. This refers to the day-by-day growing and struggling which Paul termed "running a race." "Conversion is a never-ending process of growth in the Christian way" and Christians need to manifest it both personally and sacramentally in their lives (Prieur).

One glaring inadequacy about change as described in all three is the implication that it is self-induced. Not so. The change wrought in us by God in Christ through the Spirit may not be easily discernible but it is nonetheless real, moving us to a deeper faith and love and hope in the risen Lord. Christ, the great reconciler, is the initiator of whatever change occurs. Because he dwells in his church and is active in the sacrament, not only does he "actualize his own work of reconciliation, making it present here and now, but he actualizes the repentance of the sinner" (Crichton).

Arnold Come summed up Christ's reconciling mission in one paragraph when he wrote: "Jesus' life initiated a process of divine activity in history that led to the perfect reconciliation of the whole of God's creation. In his life and death and resurrection the perfect reconciliation was realized. He suffered alienation and betrayal by his friends, conviction of crime and execution by

the government. In his faithful life, his dedicated death, in his victorious resurrection, the perfect reign of God became a reality in human history. The reconciliation of the world to God became an operative reality in human history through the humanity of Jesus."

It is Paul who points this out most clearly. He is the only New Testament author who specifically uses the term "reconciliation." He clearly delineated Christ's role as reconciler. "Therefore, if any one is in Christ he is a new creation; the old has passed away, behold, the new has come. All this is from God, who through Christ reconciled us to himself and gave us the ministry of reconciliation; that is, God was in Christ reconciling the world to himself, not counting their trespasses against them, and entrusting to us the message of reconciliation" (2 Cor 5:17–19).

The healing power of Christ is the central point of the rite. It is he who forgives and re-unites us with our alienated neighbors. United with our brothers, sisters, neighbors we are, by that fact, united with him. Christ it is who transforms (changes) us ever more profoundly in, through and with him, implanting in us a "new heart" and fulfilling in a unique way Jeremias' prophecy, "I will forgive their iniquity and I will remember their sin no more … I will be their God and they shall be my people" (Jer 31:33–34). Peter reminds us that the prophecy is fulfilled and we are the chosen race, a royal priesthood, a holy nation, a people he claims for his own to proclaim the glorious works of the One who called (us).

He has *changed* us, according to Peter, for once we were no people, "but now are God's people; once there was no mercy for you, but now you have found mercy" (1 Pet 2:9–10). That is no literary fantasy. It is a reality beyond our farthest imaginings.

"Reconciliation Means Change" originally appeared in MODERN LITURGY magazine (Resource Publications, Inc.).

Appendix

Lenten Music

Lenten Music

Penitential Rite

- Hold Us in Your Mercy (Penitential Litany) (Cooney/Daigle/OCP)
- Gather Your People/Lord Have Mercy (Hurd/OCP)
- Litany of Deliverance (Cooney/OCP)

Lenten Gospel Acclamations

- Praise to You Lord Jesus Christ (O'Conner/OCP)
- Lenten Gospel Acclamation (Anstey/OCP)
- Lenten Acclamation (Haugen/GIA)

  Thy Word (Grant/Smith/CCLI)

Psalmody

Psalm 51

- Be Merciful, O Lord (Janco/GIA)
- Be Merciful, O Lord (Haugen/GIA)
- Be Merciful, O Lord (Schiavone/OCP)
- Be Merciful, O Lord/I Will Rise and Go to my Father (Smith/GIA)
- Be Merciful O Lord (Cotter/GIA)
- Create in Me (Haas/GIA)
- Create in Me (Hurd/OCP)
- Create Me Again (Cooney/GIA)
- Creator, Reshape My Heart (O'Brien/GIA)
- Have Mercy, Lord (Gelineau/GIA)

- Have Mercy On Us, Lord/Salmo Penitencial (Castillo/OCP)
- Psalm 51 (Isele/GIA)

Psalm 91

- Be With Me (Hurd/OCP)
- Be With Me, Lord (Joncas/OCP)
- Be With Me, Lord (Haugen/GIA)
- Into Your Hands (Brown/OCP)

Psalm 130

- Out of the Depths (Chepponis/GIA)
- Out of the Depths (Soper/OCP)
- With the Lord (Joncas/New Dawn/OCP)

Psalm 25

- Hold Me in Life (Huijbers/OCP)
- Remember Your Mercies (Cooney/OCP)
- Remember Your Mercy, Lord (Inwood/OCP)
- Remember Your Love (Balhoff, Ducote, Daigle/GIA)
- Psalm 25: Remember Your Mercies (Haas/GIA)
- Return, Renew and Remember (Smith/RPI)
- Remember (Cooney/GIA)

Psalm 33

- Lord, Be With Us (Walker/OCP)

- Lord, Let Your Mercy Be Upon Us (Smiths/RPI)

- O God of Love (Soper/OCP)

- The Lord Fills the Earth with His Love (Inwood/OCP)

Other Psalms

- I Will Walk in the Presence of God (Cooney/GIA)

- The Name of God (refrain III) (Haas/GIA)

- Psalm 137: Let My Tongue Be Silent (Johengen/GIA)

- More Than Gold (Booth/OCP)

- Lord You Have the Words (Haas/GIA)

- Bonum Est Confidere (Berthier/GIA)

- My God, My God (Consiglio/OCP)

- Psalm 22: My God, My God (Haugen/GIA)

Music for the Rite of Christian Initiation of Adults

- Dismissal Rite/Let Your Will Be Done (Kendzia/OCP)

- Drawn to the Water (Smiths/RPI)

- Music for RCIA Scrutinies (Smith/OCP)

- Renewal of Baptismal Promises/Si, Si, Creemos (Schiavone/OCP)

- Signing of the Sense (DeBruyn/OCP)

- Who Calls You By Name (vols 1 & 2) (Haas/GIA)

- Who Do You Say That I Am (Smiths/RPI)

See also *Pastoral Music* (Dec 1988/Jan 1989), the journal of the National Association of Pastoral Musicians, for a resource listing of music for the RCIA.

Choral Music

- Wondrous Love (arr. Nowak/GIA)

- Wondrous Love (Goemanne/GIA)

- Keep Me Faithfully in Thy Paths (Handel, ed. Proulx/GIA)

Song Suggestions

- Adoramus Te Christe (Haugen/GIA)

- All Glory Laud and Honor (Various)

- All That Is Hidden (Farrell/OCP)

- All You Who Are Thirsty (Connolly/GIA)

- As For Me and My House (Cooney/GIA)

- As Grains of Wheat (Rosania/OCP)

- As We Remember (Cooney/New Dawn/OCP)

- Ashes (Conry/OCP)

- The Aye Carol (Bell/GIA)

- Because We Are God's Chosen Ones (Smith/RPI)

- Before the Fruit Is Ripened by the Sun (Troeger/Doran/GIA)

- Benedictus Qui Venit (Bertier/GIA)

- Change Our Hearts (Cooney/OCP)

- Come and Fill This Temple (Freisen/CCLI)

- Come Now and Praise the Humble Saint (Williams/GIA)

- Deep Within (Haas/GIA)

- Drawn to the Water (Smith/RPI)

- Dust and Ashes (Haas/Wren/GIA)

- Earthen Vessels (Foley/OCP)

- Gather Us In (Haugen/GIA)

- God Has Chosen Me (Farrell

- God It Was (Bell/GIA)

- God of Abraham (Farrell/OCP)

- God of Adam, God of Joseph (Kaan/GIA)

- God of Our Journeys (Haugen/GIA)

- Grant to Us, O Lord (Deiss/WLP)

- Hold Us in Your Mercy (Conry/OCP)

- Hosea (Norbet/OCP)

- Hosanna to the Son of David (Schutte/OCP)

- I Say "Yes," Lord/Digo "Si," Senor (Pena/GIA)

- If I Forget You (Cooney/GIA)

- In My Very Being (Smiths/RPI)
- In This House (Hill/Evensong)
- Jerusalem My Destiny (Cooney/GIA)
- Jesus Remember Me (Berthier/GIA)
- Jesus Walked This Lonesome Valley (Bell/GIA)
- Joseph, Be Our Guide and Pattern (Newton-White/GIA)
- Just a Closer Walk (Traditional)
- Keep in Mind (Deiss/WLP)
- Lenten Proclamation (Chepponis/GIA)
- Lift High the Cross (Nicholson/Hope Publishing)
- Live the Promise (Cooney/GIA)
- Lord, Who Throughout These Forty Days (Hernamen/GIA)
- Love Consecrates the Humblest Act (Traditional)
- Love One Another (Chepponis/GIA)
- Love the Lord Your God/Ama Tu Senor al Valverde (Freisen/OCP)
- Make Us a Eucharistic People (Smiths/RPI)
- Now (Cooney/GIA)
- O Healing River (arr. Joncas/GIA)
- People of Passion (Smiths/RPI)
- Priestly People (Deiss/WLP)
- Promise (Hillebrand/OCP)
- Rain Down (Cortez/OCP)
- Remember Your Love (Dameans/New Dawn/OCP)
- Return to God (Haugen/GIA)
- Ride On, King Jesus (Rivers/CCLI)
- Ride On Jesus (Haugen/GIA)
- Seek the Lord (O'Connor/OCP)
- Song of All Seed (Huijbers/OCP)
- Still Must We Walk (Conry/OCP)
- Take Up Your Cross — Traditional
- There Is a Longing (Quigley/OCP)

- There Is a River (Manion/New Dawn/OCP)
- There's a Wideness in God's Mercy (Faber/OCP)
- This Is Our Accepted Time (Traditional)
- Tree of Life (Haugen/GIA)
- Turn of a Heart (Manion/New Dawn/OCP)
- Up from the Waters (Haugen/GIA)
- We Are God's Work of Art/Somos la Creacion de Dios (Haugen/GIA)
- We Remember (Haugen/GIA)
- What Wondrous Love Is This? (Hymn)
- When the Lord of Glory Comes (Moore/Smith/GIA)
- Yes, I Shall Arise (Deiss/WLP)
- You Are Mine (Haas/GIA)

Key

RPI	Resource Publications, Inc.
OCP	Oregon Catholic Press
WLP	World Library Publications
GIA	GIA Publications, Inc.
CCLI	Christian Copyright Licensing International